Mobilizing

India

★

DUKE
UNIVERSITY
PRESS
DURHAM
AND
LONDON
2006

MOBILIZING INDIA

Women,

Music,

and

Migration

between

India

and

Trinidad

*

TEJASWINI

NIRANJANA

© 2006 Duke University Press
All rights reserved
Printed in the United States of
America on acid-free paper ∞
Designed by Amy Ruth Buchanan
Typeset in Quadraat by Tseng
Information Systems, Inc.
Library of Congress Cataloging-in-
Publication Data appear on the last
printed page of this book.

CONTENTS

★ Acknowledgments ★ vii

Note on Usage ★ xi

Introduction ★ 1

1 "The Indian in Me": Studying the Subaltern Diaspora ★ 17

2 "Left to the Imagination": Indian Nationalism and Female Sexuality ★ 55

3 "Take a Little Chutney, Add a Touch of Kaiso": The Body in the Voice ★ 85

4 Jumping out of Time: The "Indian" in Calypso ★ 125

5 "Suku Suku What Shall I Do?": Hindi Cinema and the Politics of Music ★ 169

Afterword: A Semi-Lime ★ 191

Notes ★ 223

Bibliography ★ 253

Index ★ 267

ACKNOWLEDGMENTS

★ A book that has been so long in the making accumulates debts without number.

My initial visit to the Caribbean was made possible by the Homi Bhabha Fellowships Council. A crucial follow-up visit was enabled by grants from the Indian Council for Social Science Research and the University of Hyderabad faculty travel fund. The Sephis Programme for South–South Research provided generous support for the research and travel, and I am especially grateful to Ulbe Bosma and Ingrid Goedhart for their warm and friendly assistance. Additional library work in the United States was supported by fellowships from the Chicago Humanities Institute at the University of Chicago and the International Institute at the University of Michigan. The final manuscript emerged out of a writing grant from the Prince Claus Fund, where Geerte Wachter and Els van der Plaas offered timely support. The music collaboration project I embarked on in 2004 also benefited from the fund's innovative grant-making policies. Rohini Nilekani of the Aarghyam Trust, Bangalore, provided additional financial assistance for the music project. The research and writing of the book would not have been possible without reprieves from my teaching and administrative duties, first at the Department of English, University of Hyderabad, and then at the Centre for the Study of Culture and Society, Bangalore. A semester at Yonsei University, Seoul, also gave me much needed time for revisions.

Arguments from the book have been presented in many places: Bangalore, Beijing, Cape Town, Chennai, Chicago, Durban, Hong Kong, Hyderabad, Kingston, Kochi, Mumbai, New Delhi, New York, Palo Alto, Rio de Janeiro, Santa Cruz, Seoul, Shimoga, and Taipei. I have only myself to blame if I have not made full use of my interlocutors' suggestions.

I express my deep appreciation to Arjun Appadurai, Homi Bhabha, James Clifford, Nicholas Dirks, and Mahmood Mamdani for their intellectual and institutional support, and to Stephen Chan, Akhil Gupta, Miriam Hansen, Kim Hyun Mee, Sheldon Pollock, Arvind Rajagopal, J. S. Sadananda, PUKAR, and SARAI for hosting presentations of material from my ongoing research.

I am indebted to Brinsley Samaroo for discussions about Trinidad politics and refreshing drives through the countryside; Rawwida Baksh-Soodeen, Kusha Haraksingh, Merle Hodge, Kenneth Parmasad, Rhoda Reddock, and Cathy Shepherd for their stimulating conversations and keen interest in my work; to Gordon Rohlehr for helping me understand the timespace of calypso; to Hubert Devonish and Patricia Mohammed for sending me off to Trinidad in search of chutney winers; and to those Trinidadians who consented to be interviewed and whose words enrich my analyses.

My thanks to the library staff of the West Indiana collection at the University of the West Indies, St. Augustine, and to the staff at the Caribbean Association for Feminist Research and Action, Tunapuna, for their prompt and efficient assistance.

For offering their friendship and making me feel at home in the Caribbean, and for endless hours of fascinating discussion, my inadequate thanks to Sheila Rampersad, whose own work on race and gender in Trinidad has been inspiring; to Christopher Cozier, whose artistic practice has illuminated for me the trajectory of Caribbean nationalisms; to Sheila Samiel, who apart from great conversation provided Jamaican Blue Mountain coffee in Port of Spain; to Kirk Meighoo, who was a rich source of ideas, jokes, and contacts in my early forays; to Vasanti Boochoon, whose quiet presence and warm hospitality I turned to time and again; to Carolyn Cooper, whose work on sexuality and Jamaican music has been pioneering; and especially to Annie Paul, for all the innumerable occasions on which she has been indispensable.

My gratitude to those who read drafts of the manuscript and provided affectionate but trenchant criticism: Uma Maheshwari Bhrugubanda, Nadi Edwards, Naresh Fernandes, Mary John, Ritty Lukose, Ding Naifei, Seemanthini Niranjana, Rekha Pappu, and S. V. Srinivas, and to the Anveshi Research Centre for Women's Studies—in particular, Susie Tharu—for space to try out my initial ideas.

Thanks to Anita Sharma for the translations of chutney songs, to P. Radhika for painstakingly transcribing my interviews, to H. M. Ali for valuable technical assistance, and to Malathi de Alwis and Indira Chowdhury for helping me obtain rare material. Warm thanks to Ashok Dhareshwar for pit stops, and for his interest in all kinds of music.

Surabhi Sharma was willing to be drawn into my enthusiasm and script a film from my Caribbean dreams. The Caribbean posse—George Jose, Suresh Rajamani, R. V. Ramani—gamely wandered around Jamaica and Trinidad with me. Carla Foderingham and Romita Bocas of the Tourism and Industrial Development Corporation provided invaluable assistance with the film production in Trinidad, as did Sonjah and Jalani Niaah in Jamaica.

My thanks to the Copyright Organisation of Trinidad and Tobago for help with copyright issues.

Remo Fernandes's enthusiasm for the Caribbean set me off on a new track. I record here my continuing appreciation for his brilliant music and his brave negotiation of a difficult journey.

Warm thanks to Rikki Jai for his sparkling performative presence in my project; to Drupatee Ramgoonai for the gracious interviews; to Ataklan for taking us through Laventille and introducing us to rapso; to Denise Belfon for showing us how to wine; and to Mungal Patasar for his many insights into Trinidadian music. I am also indebted to Rishi Gayadeen and Kapil Gayadeen of the Gayatones and to Kenny Phillips and Kasey Phillips of KMP Music Lab for helping me understand the setting of contemporary music production in Trinidad. Grateful thanks to Christopher Laird and the folks at Gayelle TV for their interest in our film.

For their continued and unqualified support of my work and the forging of our common interest in retheorizing the Third World, my gratitude to Vivek Dhareshwar, David Scott, Mary John, and Satish Deshpande; I give thanks to David in particular for his provocations and all the liming opportunities over the years.

Ashish Rajadhyaksha compelled me to finish the writing, tolerating my obsessions with grace and good humor and commenting on multiple drafts of the manuscript. Traveling with him to Trinidad has given me fresh insights into Caribbean cultural practice. From sorting out my software problems to turning music producer on the last journey, he has contributed to this book in ways that words can scarcely acknowledge.

Thanks to Ken Wissoker at Duke for his sound advice, and to the two anonymous readers of the manuscript for their perceptive suggestions.

Tejaswini Niranjana
Bangalore, 2005

NOTE ON USAGE

★ People of Indian origin in Trinidad are usually called East Indian or Indo-Trinidadian. When I refer to the indentured laborers who were brought to Trinidad from the Indian subcontinent in the nineteenth century, I use the term *Indian*. Today this term is reserved for those who are citizens of the nation-state called India. When I refer to ethnic Indians in contemporary Trinidad, I use East Indian or Indo-Trinidadian. On occasion I also use the term *Trinidad Indians* as contrasted with India Indians.

INTRODUCTION

★ [Edouard] Glissant said to me: "I have never met you in Barbados, and you have never met me in Martinique. Why?" And I replied, "Because those journeys were not on our agenda."
—George Lamming (*Conversations*)

This book is a strange beast. It straddles the imaginative geography of three vast regions— South Asia, Africa, the Americas—but is not ethnography, travelogue, or sociology. The attempt has been to bring together questions relevant, however differently, to two specific contexts: Trinidad and India. The hope is that, while the comparisons might produce new shadows, new regions will simultaneously be cast into relief.

The central focus of the book is the "woman question" as it emerges through the mobilization of "Indianness" and other related notions of region, ethnic group, or race and the intertwining of gender issues with the formation and assertion of different kinds of identities in Trinidad and India. What might it mean to intellectually traverse these spaces, and what might it mean to ask questions that have some resonance in each of them? One of the main tasks of this research project has been to conceptualize frameworks in which comparative discussions across the South can be undertaken.

Key critical terms in relation to the cultural turn in the social sciences have included, among others, "colonialism," "nation," "modernity," "citizenship," "identity," and "subjectivity." Such terms are often explicated in the bounded context of nation-states in the South or with reference to Western European societies. Indeed, an important feature of twentieth-century scholarship could well be the nation-centrism of the analyses of intellectual formations of the period. My project proceeds on the assumption that South–South comparative work problematizes the standard use of these terms and adds new dimensions to their usage even in specific national contexts.

The project draws on materials obtained from Southern libraries and archives located in the Caribbean, South Africa, and India. The fieldwork and interviews on which the book draws were conducted from 1994 to 2004. A series of fortuitous fellowships allowed me, a scholar living and working in India, to make periodic research visits to Trinidad. Without this kind of admittedly rare assistance, a researcher living in the Third World is unlikely to be able to carry out research in other Southern societies, since most available grants are for visiting First World universities. The presumption, to put it baldly, is that people in the global South do not have much to learn from each other, while they have everything to gain from going to Cambridge or Princeton. But having crossed the innumerable hurdles posed by consular authorities suspicious of anyone from a "poor" country like India trying to visit another where the economic opportunities are allegedly better, once having actually entered other Southern spaces, it is not as though the Third World scholar finds easy admittance into their institutions or their communities, carrying as she or he does the burden of ethnic origin (in my case, Indian), a burden that is as likely to provide one with unwanted allies as to confront one with unexpected hostility in the fraught racial situations in Trinidad, for example.[1]

My work, however, is haunted by the figure of the traveler as well as of the ethnographer. As the Trinidadian calypsonian Mighty Dougla (Cletus Ali) put it in a different context, "I am neither one nor the other/Six of one, half a dozen of the other," the scholar living in the South who cannot afford the leisure and expense of tourism or anthropology. This has contributed, for instance, to my peculiar relationship to Trinidad, which combines familiarity and opacity at the same time and mixes seeming recognition with utter incomprehension. Annual visits over several years puts one in a position where the streets and shops, the maxi-cab rides and the shortcuts, acquire an eerie intimacy; they provide the illusion of "knowing" where one is. But the geographical familiarity does not substitute for the constant stumbling in conversation, the mutual lack of intelligibility in a host of social situations.

How do I conceptualize my relationship to a place that has become an intimate part of my subjective past while remaining, at the same time, outside any assertion of my cultural authority? Where Trinidad is concerned, the nature of my research there as well as the rejection of a particular subject position—that of the anthropologist—does not allow me the privilege of deploying an "ethnographic authority." My writing about India, by contrast, manifests a confidence, a *cultural authority* (as distinct from that produced by the ethnographer's gaze) brought to bear on the intricacies of contemporary political-cultural maneuvers. In writing about Trinidad, I often find myself caught between the disavowal of ethnographic authority and the impossibility of claiming cultural authority. My difficult task in this book, then, has been to address as substantially as possible the ambiguity of my position as a scholar from and in India face to face with other "Indians" whose histories and futures may have little relation to my own but whose claim to India and Indianness may well change the way in which Indians in India understand questions of cultural identity.

A word about the book's structure of address: I have often been asked whether this is a book "about Trinidad," and if it is, whether it was written for readers in South Asia or for Caribbeanists. For reasons that have to do with the location of the researcher and the concerns coming out of that history, I cannot claim that I am writing for a universal readership or for a specialist, Caribbean-focused audience. I do have in mind fellow South Asians when I frame the questions that animate the book: questions about nationalism, the colonial past, cultural identity in the former colonies. Hence, the position from which I speak is obviously not an unmarked one. My attempt is to render strange an all too familiar set of preoccupations—about nationalism, Hindus and Muslims, caste and culture, femininity and the public sphere—by locating them in a geographically distant place where they have taken on altogether different significations even while they continue to call themselves "Indian." One can only hope that the strategy of entering the debate at a tangent will yield insights not only for those interested, and invested, in either South Asia or the Caribbean, but also for anyone engaging with contemporary postcolonial situations.

To sketch quickly the immediate historical-political context of the contemporary critique of "nation" in the case of India, one might recall that for radical politics in the 1970s and '80s, especially those of the Marxist-Leninist groups and the women's movement, the nation-state was a significant addressee. While the critique of the nation was central to radical politics, it was in many ways still part of the political and cultural logic of the national-modern. The secularism and modernity of the politics depended, as we can now see, on the disavowal of caste, community, ethnicity, and regional and linguistic difference. Indeed, the energy and reach of feminism or the Marxist-Leninist movement seemed to be made possible by these very disavowals. In the 1990s, however, political events such as the anti-Mandal (anti-affirmative action) agitation,[2] the rise of the Bharatiya Janata Party, the formation of successful "regional" parties, and so on, combined with the drive to privatize and liberalize the Indian economy, disrupted the narratives of the national-modern, a disruption within which the work of many critical scholars is situated today. For someone like me, affiliated with the critique of the languages of dominance in her society, a rethinking—and redeployment in a different context—of the concept of "Third World" may suggest yet another entry point into the problematization of the universal-modern. My own stakes in this redeployment will be discussed in what follows.

I shall begin by glancing at my own profession, teaching, and my own former discipline, English studies, which for some time has been subjected to various strands of political questioning. Looking back on what has come to be called the critique of English studies in India, we have come to recognize certain impasses—in particular, around the problem of relevance. The post-Independence generation of English teachers (R. B. Patankar, Ayyappa Panikkar, and U. R. Ananthamurthy, to name just a few figures who were teaching in the 1970s) seemed to resolve the question of the relevance of its profession by doing business as usual in the classroom, teaching English literature but engaging actively in the intellectual life of the community in Marathi, Malayalam, and Kannada, respectively. By the 1980s, however, a few teachers—in Hyderabad, Delhi, and Calcutta, for example—were beginning to raise different sorts of questions in the English classroom, largely due to their involvement in feminism. And by the 1990s, the sharpening of conflicts around issues of nation, community, and caste, as well as gender, appeared to bring the dissatisfaction and unease of both students and teachers more directly into the classroom, leading to a sustained questioning of received curricula, pedagogical practices, and research emphases.

Putting it somewhat schematically, we might say that two kinds of work have begun to receive increased attention within English departments: (1) research that seeks to examine Indian languages, literatures, and cultural practices, to investigate different kinds of writing (such as writing by women or *dalits*, a political identity claimed by former untouchables and other lower castes), or to enlarge the discipline by studying hitherto devalued cultural forms such as popular cinema or children's literature; and (2) research into "commonwealth" or even Third World cultures and literatures. Although the first kind of agenda does seem to require major reorientations in terms of methodologies and politics, the Indian student or teacher is, when all is said and done, not particularly handicapped in the study of what is in some sense "ours." (Given the burden of nationalism—clearly visible in their curricula—that the post-Independence social sciences carry in India, and given the necessarily belated relay of this burden to English studies, the most predictable response I used to get when I said I taught Caribbean and African texts is, "But why not *Indian* texts?") The second sort of agenda, that of teaching "Third World literature," is handicapped from the start. Scarce institutional resources can barely be stretched to acquire conventional materials required by the discipline, let alone diverted to the purchase of little-known texts from non-metropolitan places. The teacher's woes are magnified in those of the researcher, whose access to primary and secondary material is severely limited. Since both teaching and research in the area continue in spite of these problems, I would like to argue here for a reexamination of the implicit premises with which we in India set out to teach and study other Third World contexts and suggest that the times call for a critical fashioning of new research agendas that might rethink the assumptions, even as they emphasize the importance, of comparative work.

Indians, Indians Everywhere

One of the signs of our times is the spectacular international visibility of the "Indian"—from beauty queens to software professionals, technologists, scientists, artists, economists, filmmakers, historians, and literary theorists. As a self-congratulatory cultural nationalism overcomes us, we seldom stop to think about the formation of this "Indian" and his or her deployment by the political economy of global capitalism—an economy that, we do not need to emphasize, is also an economy of academe and the production of knowledge. At mid-century, in the age of Nehruvian socialism and the Nonaligned Movement, and in the aftermath of the worldwide anti-imperialist struggle, Indians claimed solidarity with other formerly colonized peoples and extended support of various kinds to nations less privileged than we were. At the end of the millennium, however, the Indian is not simply another postcolonial but one who would claim to have attained exceptionality or special status, an achievement that increasingly sets him off from inhabitants of other post-colonies. Earlier axes of identification are transformed and old solidarities disavowed as the middle-class Indian, even as she vociferously asserts her cultural difference, becomes a crucial relay in the circuits of multinational capital. Although a good deal of recent critical scholarship has focused on the formation of the Indian citizen-subject and analyzed the exclusions (of caste, community, and gender, for instance) that underwrite it, the subtle changes occurring in the composition of the "Indian" in transnational spaces have yet to be seriously investigated.

I mention this as one of the concerns arising from my visits to the Caribbean, where I encountered in Jamaica and Trinidad a variety of perceptions regarding Indians—perceptions that often were actively fostered, especially by newly immigrant Indian groups; international organizations such as the Vishwa Hindu Parishad (part of the right-wing Sangh Parivar "family" that includes the Bharatiya Janata Party); and even the Indian nation-state through its overseas High Commissions. Safe in an Indian university, one can simply read the West Indian text as one among other literary artifacts, but the Indian researcher traveling in the Caribbean or in Africa might well be called on to make explicit her motivations for undertaking comparative research. This demand may be related to the deployment of the notion of "culture" by Indians from India as well as people of Indian origin in the West Indies, their invocation of an ancient past and a glorious civilization as proof of racial superiority. As a Guyanese friend put it, "Indians always say culture is what *they* have and the black people don't." The situation is further complicated when we have Indians from India studying "East Indian West Indians." The cultural forms of these diasporic communities are often imaged by Indians as fragmented, deficient, or derivative. As I discuss in chapter 1, "The Indian in Me," there is a complex politics to the invocation of Indianness in the Caribbean, the details of which often elude the visiting Indian researcher, partly because of his or her own unexamined notions of what "Indian culture" means.

Teaching the Caribbean

Another profound disorientation I experienced in the Caribbean was that of being in a west that was not the West. Earlier visits outside India had always been to First World spaces, and however different each might have been from the other, they were, for me, collectively that which was not Indian, not Third World. The encounter with the Caribbean forced me to begin asking questions about sameness and difference, whether in the realm of the political (with regard to notions of nation and region), the economic (questions of "dependency" and "development"), or the cultural (the tradition-versus-modernity debate), that were different from those I was accustomed to asking—for example, in relation to India and the West. Moreover, the encounter had a crucial impact on the questions I addressed in the classroom, the teaching strategies I adopted, and the texts that I taught.[3]

Some years ago, I wrote a paper, based on a course I had taught in 1989 on Africa and the Caribbean, in which I attempted to explore the implications of teaching non-Western literary texts in Indian Departments of English.[4] For me as well as my students, it had been a first-time exposure to these texts, contexts, and histories. Given the dearth of material in our largely Eurocentric libraries, the task of teaching the course was a difficult one, and the engagement with the texts had to be carefully negotiated and renegotiated at every step.

Clearly, our concern was not just one about "content," using new texts in place of the old. I had suggested in the paper that this kind of easy substitution does not question the need for a canon of great texts, a need that brings with it the imperative to teach the canon in particular ways. My argument was that the demand to be included or accommodated within the existing paradigm did not pose a threat to the paradigm itself, "since it never questions the criteria which determine exclusion in the first place."[5] Instead, I had proposed that we examine *how* we teach and read and analyze the expectations we bring to our reading of African and Caribbean texts. I had emphasized the importance of teaching nonmetropolitan texts while, at the same time, resisting "their incorporation into the canon" by not employing "customary ways of reading."[6]

My contention then was that the nonmetropolitan texts posed a radical challenge to the discipline and to conventional literary critical approaches, not because of any intrinsic quality they possessed, but because—embedded as they were in histories similar in some ways to ours in India—our questions or interests coincided, or came into a conjuncture, with these Caribbean and African works. The risk, of course, was that in stressing similarities we might ignore real differences between specific societies in the South. All the same, our engagement with these texts "forced our attention away from the aesthetic to the political dimension, . . . making us seek assonance and dissonance not in poetic form but in the realm of culture, politics and history."[7] What we managed to accomplish to a certain extent was "to place the text more firmly amidst material and social practices instead of in a purely literary tradition."[8]

Looking back at these concerns, it seems to me that the emphasis was still on the *literary text*, with not enough attention being paid either to the discursive networks from which it had emerged or to other kinds of cultural artifacts. Perhaps this was a problem, simply, of inadequate information. Perhaps it was also the formulation of the question itself—as one of text plus context—that was coming in the way, for in this formulation the text ultimately can be detached from the context, which is imaged as simply surrounding it. The question of how to decide the demarcations of a text's boundaries (or of what constituted a "text" in the first place) was not addressed, except in passing. Consequently, one ended up displaying as texts in the classroom precisely those sorts of pieces—a Walcott play, an early Brathwaite poem, a Lamming novel—that the discipline of English studies would have no difficulty accepting, omitting entirely, for example, the popular music of the Caribbean, an understanding of which is so central to any attempt to study West Indian cultural politics.[9]

It seems to me now that the problem was related to our Third Worldist attempt to discover cultural artifacts of "our own," which were, to use Kwame Anthony Appiah's words, deserving of dignity. In addition, concepts like the "political" and the "aesthetic" appear in hindsight to have been invoked as though their meanings were "given," and the distinction between them was too quickly posed, although at the time the terms did perhaps serve as a kind of shorthand for entire methodologies. In 1990, the need for disciplinary transformation was certainly being expressed in different quarters, but for me, at least, the larger significance of this proposed transformation was as yet not adequately thought through. It was only after the dramatic national events of late 1990 (I refer in particular to the anti-Mandal agitation of upper-caste youth seeking to deny job reservations for the lower castes) that the question of what it meant to challenge "English" in India could be asked in a different register and the whole terrain on which the dominant "aesthetic" was constructed could be investigated from a different critical perspective. "Mandal" as an event drew the attention of many middle-class, left-oriented secular Indians to the "invisibilizing" of caste in the composition of the citizen-subject. In literary studies, dominated by a modernism congruent in many ways with the secularism of the post-Independence era, it became possible, sometimes by consolidating earlier dalit and feminist initiatives, to directly confront the exclusions that helped create the realm of the aesthetic. Investigating the historical formation of the aesthetic realm, it seems to me, can have important implications for comparative Third World cultural studies in terms of what we set out to compare and how we go about our task.

Although the literary or cultural comparativist often has no formal training in the discipline of anthropology, its modes of argument and its habits of thought are bound to infect any enterprise like the comparativist's, which purports to study cultural formations other than the one inhabited by the investigator. Predictably, the question of anthropology would never come up when Indian students, for example, study British or American literature.[10] The frameworks and locations that endorse the production of "modern" knowledge ensure that the question only applies to the study of non-Western, or "Southern," cultures.[11] Since the project of classical anthropology is to produce a self-understanding of the West through a study of "other" cultures, the anthropological investigator tends to assume the centrality of Western civilization. Given this location provided by the discipline for the investigator, how can the Third World "anthropologist" begin to question this centrality?

When such an anthropologist—and clearly I use this description to name a set of subject positions, no matter what the disciplinary training of the investigator—ventures into another Third World space, the normalization of her or his location, and thereby his or her subject position, is opened to questioning, and the possibility for a critique of the dominant episteme, I would argue, begins to emerge. For the Third World intellectual—in particular, for the Indian intellectual, often by definition upper-class and upper-caste—such a critique would necessarily involve an unlearning of her privilege, which is different from the unlearning that takes place in a "national" context, as well as a recognition of her complicity with the institutions and disciplinary frameworks of metropolitan knowledge production.

By now, of course, it is fairly well established that the modern academic disciplines, including anthropology, were born simultaneously with a new phase in European expansion, underwriting as well as underwritten by the project of colonial governance.[12] Whether scholars in the colonial period helped produce stereotypes about the colonized or detailed information about customs and practices, in either case they were constructing a world variously described as non-modern, traditional or primitive, a world thereby rendered amenable to domination by a more "advanced" civilization. It is the scholar's professed expertise (what James Clifford has so aptly called "ethnographic authority"), certified by metropolitan academic institutions, that continues to endorse the "truth" and factuality of this knowledge.[13]

The ethnographer functions like a *translator*. Indeed, the project of anthropology has been seen as that of translating one culture into terms intelligible to another.[14] What has also come to be addressed within the discipline, in a way that is instructive for scholars in any field, is the question of how relations of power, such as those under colonial or neocolonial domination, determine the direction and nature of translation, often simplifying, as Talal Asad has pointed out, toward the stronger language or culture.[15] This also raises once again the question of audience and of the ethnographer's subject position. What might be the possible differences between metropolitan and Third World representations of Third World contexts?

Bases of Comparative Research

Hitherto, the often undeclared bases of comparative study have been a humanism and a universalism that presumed a common human nature: In spite of their superficial differences, all people in the world were thought ultimately to be the same or in the process of becoming like one another. This was, however, an argument made from above, as it were. The "liberal" Western ethnographer, for instance, could claim the common humanity of investigator and objects of study, even if it was, on the part of these "objects," a humanity that was to be uncovered through the labor of the ethnographer's translation of their words and deeds into his or her Euro-American language. What could then be compared was the non-Western context with the anthropologist's Western one. Implicit in this kind of comparison, despite the protestations of commonality, is what Achille Mbembe, writing about the African context, has called "the perspective of a failed universality":

> The common unit, the ultimate foundation, *even the intrinsic finality of the comparative project is Western modernity*, understood either as the standard against which one measures other societies, or as the final destination toward which they are to move. And each time "African" is introduced into the operation, the comparative act is reduced to an arithmetic relation of "superiority" and "inferiority." Hierarchical figures slip in between these three chimeras of similitude, resemblance, and similarity, establishing orders of value defined in an arbitrary manner, the function of which is to legitimate discrimination and, too often, violence.[16] (my emphasis)

As I have argued in my work on the politics of translation, the very premise of a universal history on which, in comparative study, the unity of human consciousness is predicated allows, as for example in the Hegelian model of world history, the formation of an inner hierarchy that situates Third World cultures below the Euro-American.[17]

So even when Third World intellectuals themselves undertake comparative work, their task becomes one of comparing *their* cultural products with metropolitan ones: Kalidasa becomes the Shakespeare of India; Tutuola becomes the African Fielding. This is part of the urge to find something in our colonized cultures that, as Appiah puts it, "lives up to" the label (whether it is that of philosophy or literature), to find something that is ours that "*deserves* the dignity."[18] The fact, says Appiah, taking the case of Africa, is that "intellectuals educated in the shadow of the West" are bound "to adopt an essentially comparative perspective."[19] The inherent asymmetry of the comparativist project framed in these terms would be, or so it seems to me, at least displaced (since it cannot simply be done away with) when two different Third World contexts are being compared or studied together by one whose subject positions and location are in the Third World.

Outside Metropolitan Circuits?

Although it is now acknowledged that the space from which one is speaking—its histories, its questions—crucially configure the perspective of the investigator, the implications of such a configuration for comparative research in the Third World have not yet been mapped out. If ethnographic work, always comparativist by definition, has hitherto been embedded both literally and figuratively in structures of dominance, we might speculate as to what might happen when the founding impulse is no longer one of greater and more efficient control. If one is not representing, or producing, knowledge to govern and regulate, what could be the alternative impulses?

If one of those impulses is the conscious formulation of the political project of dismantling Eurocentrism, where would one look for resources (besides, of course, in one's own local context, which for various reasons may not be adequate) but in other Third World spaces? The project cannot be an isolated one, located only in a single post-colony. While I would certainly not want to deny that colonial and postcolonial trajectories of various regions have been different from each other, arguments for exceptionality in the contemporary context can only weaken the possibilities for the emergence of urgently needed new solidarities. The silence about our common histories mirrors the silence about the possibility of a shared future. There is perhaps, then, some purchase to be gained by positing shared histories at a certain level, since the colonies as well as the disciplinary networks in which they are produced and held have been part of the global enterprise of colonialism and neocolonialism. What the "gain" might be only the outcome of comparative projects may be able to suggest. Only by risking the formulation of problems in which more than one nationality has similar stakes can we push for a reconfiguration of our research agendas.

Just as work on culture in India needs to take into consideration Orientalist structures of representation,[20] one should undertake similar ground-clearing tasks for other Third World contexts with which one is attempting to engage. As I discovered during my sojourn in the West Indies, my awareness of the ways in which "India" had been produced—in colonialist discourse, for example—did not provide a guarantee that I could perceive related structures of representation in regard to the Caribbean. Third World intellectuals who are beginning to think about Third World spaces other than their own need to address the question of how these different regions have been discursively constructed as objects of knowledge, to examine closely the technologies and theories that have enabled their emergence, and to understand the extent to which our readings of each other in the present is informed by those discursive grids.[21]

Alternative Frames

If the disciplines have so far been caught up in these paradigms of domination, what kind of representations of the Third World might be produced when this agenda is disrupted? What happens, we may ask, when a West Indian reads the Nigerian Chinua Achebe? When a South Asian reads the West Indian Kamau Brathwaite? When Lucky Dube in South Africa sings Jamaican-style reggae? What will be the significance of these new representations? What sorts of cultural transformations do they signal? Would they function differently from metropolitan cultural products in Third World circuits? What new critical spaces might they help open up in the new locations where they begin to circulate?

More questions: Why should we speak to each other across the South? Why should we engage in comparative research across Third World locations? Perhaps the "ends" of the new comparative work are oblique. At best, this kind of work will contribute to the development of *alternative frames of reference*, so that Western modernity is no longer seen as the sole point of legitimization or comparison. Let me emphasize that my intention is not to suggest that we can eliminate First World knowledge structures or produce subjectivities that are entirely unmediated by the "West." My argument is simply that the "norming" of the comparative axis needs to be questioned. In much of our critical work, as well as our popular cultural conceptions, the two poles that make themselves manifest are "India" and "the West." To recognize that there exist outside our everyday sphere geographical and political spaces other than the West, spaces that have always intersected with our history but by the very logic of colonialism cannot be acknowledged in their mutual imbrication with our past, is a first step toward rewriting our histories as well as envisioning, and enlarging, our futures—together and anew.[22]

Critical engagements with other Third World spaces might help inaugurate for and in the South a new internationalism, different—in its motivations, its desires, its imagined futures—from the aggressive globalization set in motion by the First World. Woven into this chapter is an argument about perspective and intellectual and political location. In the Third World, how do we read one another so that we do not appear simply as footnotes to Western history?[23] How do we learn to question the epistemological structures through which knowledges about Third World peoples are produced? I quote here the West Indian scholar and activist Walter Rodney:

> When an African abuses an Indian he repeats all that the white men said about Indian indentured "coolies"; and in turn the Indian has borrowed from the whites the stereotype of the "lazy nigger" ' to apply to the African beside him. It is as though no black man can see another black man except by looking through a white person. It is time we started seeing through our own eyes.[24]

What kind of critical awareness ought we to bring to our teaching and writing so we avoid reproducing the stereotypes about black/brown/yellow people that exist in what V. Y. Mudimbe calls the "colonial library"?[25] How do we learn to ask questions that resonate with the actual concerns of people in other Third World places? What sort of library or archive do we need to construct? What new kinds of literacy do we need to acquire? How can we learn to overcome our multiple amnesias?

I have expressed some anxiety about the emergence of the new cosmopolitan Indian who might actively seek identification with the First World rather than the Third World. I have also tried to suggest why this identification might be problematic by focusing on the common problems faced by comparativists in the South, pointing implicitly to the dangers of Indian researchers' replicating in relation to other Third World contexts the very maneuvers and representational modes that had negated and de-historicized their own spaces. In so doing, my intention was not to argue for a simple return to the international politics of the Nehru era but to urge a rethinking of present possibilities by pointing to forms of solidarity obscured by the growth of the globalized economy.

With the new globalization, the paths to the First World will be defined more clearly than ever before, rendered easier to traverse. Other locations on the map will appear all the more blurred, all the more difficult to reach. Now more than ever a critical perspective on our contemporary political-cultural identities requires that we place those other journeys on our agenda.

My own journey to the Caribbean also took me out of literature and into popular music as I struggled to understand the kinds of spaces in which cultural practice acquired significance. The book begins with this introduction, which explores some of the larger theoretical issues confronting the project, and makes a case for comparative studies involving more than one Southern location. Chapter 1, "The Indian in Me," reflects on the situation of the researcher from India who wants to study the cultural politics of Indian diasporic communities, focusing specifically on what the novelist Samuel Selvon called the "East Indian Trinidadian Westindian." This chapter thus introduces the chief protagonists of the book, "Indians" in the Caribbean. Chapter 2, "Left to the Imagination," discusses the nationalist campaign against indentureship in India—a campaign in which the question of the indentured woman's sexuality occupied a crucial place—against the background of labor migration to Trinidad and other locations in the colonies. Chapters 3 and 4 deal with Trinidad's most central cultural form: popular music. "Take a Little Chutney, Add a Little Kaiso" (chapter 3) explores the phenomenon of "Indian soca" and discusses the 1990s controversy over this new musical genre while tracing the histories of performance and musical traditions that feed into it. "Jumping out of Time" (chapter 4) analyses the Afro-Trinidadian calypso's constructions of East Indian men and women over the best part of the twentieth century, relating those constructions to the larger politics of culture in Trinidad. Chapters 3–5 are accompanied by selections from songs available on the website http://mobilizing-india.cscsarchive.org. It is recommended that the reader listen to the chutney-soca songs and the calypsos while going through these chapters. Chapter 5 contains a discussion of the musical public sphere in Trinidad in the light of the interventions made possible by Hindi film music from India. The afterword discusses the new directions taken by my research project into the realm of musical practice.

ONE

★ "The Indian in Me":

Studying the Subaltern

Diaspora

> Doh let me catch you in that foolishness
> Trying to reach the Indian in me . . .
> Boy I am Trinbagonian
> I like soca action
> Take your Mohammed Rafi
> And bring Scrunter or Bally
> Only then you be talking to me.
> —Rikki Jai, "Sumintra" (lyrics by Gregory Ballantyne)

> To be an Indian or East Indian from the West Indies is to be a perpetual surprise to people outside the region. . . . You don't go to Trinidad . . . expecting to find Hindu pundits scuttling about country-roads on motor-cycles; to see pennants with ancient devices fluttering from temples; to see mosques cool and white and rhetorical against the usual Caribbean buildings of concrete and corrugated iron; to find India celebrated in the street names of one whole district of Port of Spain. . . . To be an Indian from Trinidad is to be unlikely. It is, in addition to everything else, to be the embodiment of an old verbal ambiguity.
> —V. S. Naipaul, *The Overcrowded Barracoon*

> The term "Indian" was used for more than a hundred years for the inhabitants of any newly-discovered country, and even Africans were so described. There are varieties and species of Indians all over the world. . . . [A]n East Indian means an inhabitant of the *East* Indies. This starts to be bewildering . . . for when we have East Indians born in Trinidad, we should have to call them East Indian Trinidadians. And the people living in these islands are called Westindians. So by definition, what we have here is really an *East Indian Trinidadian Westindian*. Christopher Columbus must be killing himself with laugh.
> —Sam Selvon, "Three Into One Can't Go—East Indian, Trinidadian, Westindian"

> Today I hold no stronger conviction than that the Caribbean is our own experiment in a unique expression of human civilization, and that there can be no creative discovery of this civilization without the central and informing influence of the Indian presence.
> —George Lamming, "The Indian Presence as a Caribbean Reality"

India in the Subaltern Diaspora

I suggested in the introduction that the commonsensical basis for comparative study, in India as in many parts of the formerly colonized world, has been the implicit contrast between Europe (and now North America) and the rest. I went on to suggest that altering the primary reference point might yield new insights into, and fresh perspectives on, our contemporary questions. The altered frame of reference that informs this book tries to bring together two Southern locations in an effort to set up new comparisons.

This chapter explores the possibility of contrasting the formation of the "Indian" in the subaltern diaspora with the hegemonic construction of "Indians" in India, focusing on the indentured migration to the Caribbean in the nineteenth century and the early twentieth century. In this particular attempt at comparative research, the history of the context being compared is profoundly entangled with my own in ways that have been made invisible in the postcolonial present. One cannot, for example, talk about Trinidad without talking about India, over 40 percent of the island's population being of subcontinental origin, the descendants of indentured laborers taken there between 1845 and 1917. The obverse, however, is clearly not true. One can talk endlessly about India without the Caribbean or most other Third World regions, including India's closest neighbors, featuring in the conversation. What difference might it make to how we in India think about our past—and perhaps how we think about our present, as well—to reflect on that which binds India to a west that is not the West?

The special challenge of comparative research when the two contexts are historically linked would be not to show how the cultural-political formations in each are "similar" or "different," but to find out how each situation is actually marked by the other. My attempt in this book will be to seek the kinship between representations of "Indianness" in India and those in Trinidad, but also to argue, sometimes explicitly and sometimes by indirection, that who the "Indian" is in Trinidad is likely to have implications for assertions of cultural identity in India.

My interest in Trinidad comes out of my long-time involvement in the teaching of West Indian literature and dates back to my first serendipitous visit to the island in 1994. I was spending three months in Jamaica, doing research on cultural politics in the Anglophone Caribbean. Having come to understand the West Indies through the reggae of Bob Marley, the poetry of Derek Walcott and Kamau Brathwaite, the cricket writings of C. L. R. James, and through Garveyism and Black Power, I, like many other researchers, saw the Caribbean as profoundly "African," its otherness from my own Indian context framed primarily in those terms. Of course, the demographic fact that Jamaica, the largest West Indian island, is overwhelmingly Afro-Caribbean in terms of its population only confirmed my conviction regarding the culture of the Caribbean at large. Having heard a great deal about Carnival in Trinidad, in the eastern Caribbean, a five-hour air journey away, I decided to make a short trip there to witness the festival. Before I left Jamaica, I was told by friends of the stark differences between that island and Trinidad, the Protestant seriousness of the one contrasted with the Catholic exuberance of the other. But nothing had prepared me for the visual shock of seeing a *Caribbean* population of which nearly half looked like me. In Jamaica, I was—safely—a foreigner, our Third Worldist solidarities undisturbed by conflicts of race or ethnicity. In Trinidad, I felt claimed by the East Indians as a fellow "Indian" and inserted sometimes into oppositional formations that asserted themselves *against* the dominant "African" culture.

I was deeply disturbed at being implicated in this manner, and my first impulse was to disavow all the tacit claims made on me and dismiss the East Indians as a marginal and reactionary group who could only undermine the possibility of conducting dialogue across the South. Much later, however, as I became more familiar with the details of Caribbean history and with contemporary Caribbean politics, I began somewhat unwillingly to recognize the salience of the "Indian" in that part of the world and to perceive how the dominant narratives of West Indianness excluded a large proportion of the population of at least two major countries: Guyana and Trinidad and Tobago. As I see it now, one of the main causes of my discomfort in Trinidad was the encounter with "modern Indians" whose modernity did not seem to have been formed by the narratives of nation and citizenship that were part of my own interpretive and existential horizon in India. What I did not seem to understand in particular was the kind of negotiation with the "West" that Trinidadian Indians had undertaken in producing their modernity. Most disconcerting of all was my interaction with East Indian women, the semiotics of whose bodies and lives I could not read.

This book represents the attempt of a scholar from India to come to terms with the claims made on her by the Caribbean East Indian presence and to make a case for why critical arguments in India should take the East Indian seriously. My subjectivity as a modern Indian woman is tied to the other possibilities that opened up for Indian women elsewhere. More strongly put, I am what I am *because of* who the East Indian woman in Trinidad is. A central concern of this book, therefore, will be to create a space where we might productively bring together the question of women in India with the question of women in Trinidad in such a way as to reposition and add nuance to the frames within which both are customarily discussed.

Studying the Diaspora from India

There are specific problems associated with the study by Indians from India of the older diasporic communities, problems that are now becoming foregrounded as the category of the non-resident Indian (NRI) not only acquires greater importance in the economic, political, and cultural realms, but also comes into currency in academic writing.

It is hard to think of the older diaspora as being "immigrant" in the sense in which Indians in the metropolitan countries can be described today, since the term suggests a certain recentness in the achievement of that status. East Indians, for example, reached the Caribbean as early as 1838 as indentured laborers and kept coming until 1917, when the system of indentureship was abolished. Large-scale Indian migration to the United Kingdom, the United States, Canada, and other First World countries, however, took place from the 1950s onward, to different destinations in different periods. A major percentage of the latter-day migrants to the Americas has consisted of highly educated professionals, usually upper caste and upper class, and their access to a Western-style education is what has facilitated their entry into their new homelands. The links these migrants maintain with the Indian Subcontinent are strong and tangible; in fact, they have, of late, become participants in what Benedict Anderson has called "long-distance nationalism" or "e-mail nationalism."[1] In contrast, the older diasporic groups—although they also participate in the two-way traffic that expanding communication and transport networks have made possible—do not have access to the same kinds of contacts with the ruling elite in India that allow First World NRIs, for instance, to be players in contemporary Indian politics.[2] Indeed, much of the present-day popular discourse on the Indian diaspora is inspired by the visibility and economic success of First World NRIs. As Arvind Das suggests, the role model for upwardly mobile Indians is not the "foreign-returned," as in earlier times, but the "foreign-settled."[3] In the popular imagination, the latter category would include First World NRIs but not, for example, people of Indian origin in Fiji, Mauritius, or the Caribbean.

At a time such as now, when research agendas for diasporic studies in India are being shaped, it may be worth reminding ourselves that those who occupy positions in academic institutions are not exempt from the "common sense" that informs the general interest in NRIs and designates only certain varieties of them worthy of attention. In fact, we might want to reflect on the skewing of research questions in certain directions caused by how we define the NRI, as well as the subsequent lopsidedness in the allocation of funds for research: "There are no Fulbrights to Guatemala," to quote a former student in the English Department at the University of Hyderabad who wanted to study Latin American literature but could not find the finances to conduct research in that region.[4] Relating that concern to the study of peoples of Indian origin, I shall examine the selective disavowal of certain kinds of "Indians" in the process of fashioning the new citizen of India as well as the new Indian in the world at large.

At a historical juncture in which the stakes in defining oneself as "Indian" are being reexamined both in India and in many overseas communities, it seems increasingly important to analyze the many complex ways in which different groups of people in different spaces claim "Indianness" and the various kinds of significance attached to this sort of claim. We would need to investigate the implications of the claim, it seems to me, for Indians both in the location where it arises and in India. I suggest that the construction of "Indian" identities in Trinidad, Guyana, Surinam, Fiji, Mauritius, Tanzania, or South Africa (or even, to mention a different kind of context, in the Persian Gulf countries) is differently relevant to Indians in India compared with the NRI identities being shaped in the metropolitan, postcolonial diaspora located in the United States, the United Kingdom, Australia, or Canada. This is not to deny the class differences between Indians in metropolitan locations, but to emphasize the cultural differences that still exist between the metropolis and the erstwhile colonies. A person of Indian origin living in a former colony like Trinidad would not be viewed with the respect accorded to one living in the United States. At the level of state recognition, this differentiation came to the fore at the 2003 celebration of Pravasi Bharatiya Divas (Day of the Traveling Indian or the Indian Abroad), during which the Bharatiya Janata Party–led Indian government announced the granting of dual citizenship to people of Indian origin from "dollar and pound" countries like the United States, the United Kingdom, and Canada, but not from the other former colonies.

The general argument of this book is that an understanding of the discourses and practices of nationalist modernity, and of the formation of modern subjectivities, in India could be deepened by (1) an investigation of the processes by which subaltern migrants are disavowed; and (2) an inquiry into the contemporary cultural practices of those migrants. I argue that indentureship enabled a different sort of access to modernity for the subaltern diaspora from that which was being consolidated in India in the late nineteenth century and early twentieth century. I draw here on the West Indian thinker C. L. R. James's notion that Caribbean society, with its plantation system based on the carefully regulated labor of slaves that was in place as early as three centuries ago, is in terms of organization of industrial production and ways of living the first "modern" society in the history of the world.⁵ Indentured laborers, both men and women, therefore entered into a capitalist system of production long before most of their counterparts in India. Moreover, they entered a system that had already created, through slavery, modern subjects who were not of Western origin. The composition of postslavery Trinidad society, then, left a significant impress on the forms of modernity that took shape among the East Indian migrants.

Migration through Indenture

When the British took over Trinidad in 1797, it had been a colony of Spain for nearly three centuries. The population consisted approximately of a couple of thousand whites, a few thousand free blacks, and about ten thousand slaves. At the time of the Haitian Revolution, there was a massive influx of French planters and their slaves (after 1782), and French-speakers (or those who spoke French-based patois) came to make up nearly 95 percent of the population. The slaves in Trinidad, as elsewhere, engaged in numerous forms of rebellious activity, ranging from feigning sickness to stealing to burning cane to "maroonage" (running away and forming free communities). After the abolition of slavery, refusing the offer of apprenticeship in near-slavery conditions on the plantations, the ex-slaves settled in villages they established around Port of Spain, along the Eastern Main Road, and in southern and central Trinidad. To meet the shortage of labor in the fields, planters—supported by the colonial government—resorted to promoting immigration, first of free blacks, Portuguese, and Chinese, and later of Indians, this last group being numerically the largest, at a count of over 100,000 laborers coming to more than ten times all the others put together.

As the historian Kusha Haraksingh points out, the kinds of human resources and infrastructure available in present-day Trinidad all came out of the sugar industry. Sugar is a difficult crop, needing labor at a particular time—labor that can be controlled.⁶ When slavery was abolished in 1838, the British colonies expressed a need for sugarcane-plantation labor to replace the freed slaves, who for the most part chose to work elsewhere than on the scene of their former exploitation. A more crucial factor leading to indentureship, some historians have suggested, was the need to depress the wages of free labor in a context in which former slaves had begun to agitate for better wages.⁷ About 8,000 African immigrants were brought over to increase the labor pool and resolve the problem, but many more would have

Cane fields in Central Trinidad. Photo by Tejaswini Niranjana.

been required for wages to come down. Neither increasing African immigration nor initiating immigration from China proved feasible. Eventually, a system was devised for recruiting laborers from the Indian Subcontinent, from areas where long spells of drought and famine had pauperized agriculturists and driven peasants away from their villages in search of work. Between 1845 and 1917, about 143,900 Indians were brought to Trinidad (with a total of over 500,000 to the Caribbean). While about 22 percent of emigrants (Haraksingh puts the figure at one-third) returned to India at the end of their period of indenture, several hundred of these reindentured and went back to the plantations. However, promise of a return passage was part of the early inducement to migrate, and returning migrants' tales contributed to the attractions of employment in the Caribbean. In Haraksingh's own case, his father's father was a soldier who ran away from India after the Mutiny of 1858. After serving his indenture, he claimed his return passage and went home to India but returned to Trinidad to look after his daughter when she was widowed.[8]

Throughout the years of recruitment of indentured laborers, there was a tremendous disparity between the number of men and the number of women. This was mainly due to the planters' reluctance to permit the growth of a permanent community of migrants, a proposition seen as both uneconomic and dangerous. When recruiters attempted to induce more women to migrate for diverse reasons, including pressure from the government of India, they usually were not able to find "the right kind of women," or the docile laborers the planters wanted. So among the people who indentured themselves, not more than an average of 25 percent were women.[9] Migration to the Caribbean took place mainly from northern India. Ninety percent of the migrants were from the "Ganges plain"—that is, from the United Provinces, Central Provinces, Oudh, Orissa, and Bihar. A few were from Bengal in the east, from the North-West Provinces, and from the south (primarily Tamil- and Telugu-speakers). At first there were two ports of embarkation, Calcutta and Madras, but the West Indian plantation owners soon declared that "the Madrasis were inferior both in health and as labourers," and the agency at Madras was closed down.[10] However, as the historian Brinsley Samaroo points out, if a ship was not filled up at Calcutta, it would go down the coast and pick up more laborers farther south, so that a fair number of "Madrasis" ended up going to the Caribbean in later years also.[11]

The system of indenture took several years to formalize. Continual problems of illness, desertion, and destitution of laborers even led to a temporary halt in immigration in 1848–51. However, it was not until 1854 that an immigration ordinance was passed that regularized the pattern of a

Usine Ste. Madeleine: The sugar factory. Photo by Tejaswini Niranjana.

three-year contract with free return passage after ten years of residence in the colony. The contract actually ended up being for a period of five years, with two years being treated as mandatory "industrial residence." For a short period between 1869 and 1880, free lots of Crown land were given to laborers in lieu of return passage, but after 1895 full passage even for those who were otherwise eligible was not paid.

On the estate, there was a sexual division of labor in the sense that certain jobs were done only by men. Women did weeding, manuring, supplying, and cane cutting, and children also did small tasks. According to the Trinidadian feminist historian Rhoda Reddock, however, this division was not constant. Truck loading, for example, was a heavy, men's task, but many women preferred to do it, too. Men earned approximately 50–70 cents per day, and women earned 25 cents, no matter what work they did. Only about 25 percent of the female immigrants were married. The rest had come to Trinidad as single women.[12] But the low wages they earned did not allow them to remain single for long, and most women were compelled to enter into different kinds of domestic and conjugal arrangements.

Working conditions on the plantations were so poor that hundreds of "coolies" took ill and died, especially in the first years of emigration. Those who survived did so in constant poor health, often physically punished when the planters decided they were feigning sickness. Many could not earn enough even to pay for their rations and accumulated large debts to the estate. Laborers were not allowed to leave the estate except for strictly limited reasons. Their living spaces were cramped and unhygienic, having no piped water or arrangements for latrines. Several historians have argued that indenture was just another form of slavery.[13] As Walter Rodney points out, it was "the regimented social and industrial control which caused indenture to approximate so closely to slavery."[14] Antislavery societies in England were in fact among the early opponents of indentureship, but it was only after Indian nationalists in India began a campaign against the system that it was finally abolished, as I discuss in chapter 2.

Even before the system was discontinued, a large percentage of former indentured laborers had decided to stay on in Trinidad. Some of them, having returned to India, had not found the living conditions or future prospects to their liking and reindentured themselves. Children born in Trinidad often refused to go to India with their parents. Two voices from an oral history of the early twentieth century articulate some of these concerns (the glosses in parentheses are mine):

Maharani:
me fadder say
come go
come go india
i say
no
i studying dem cheren (children).[15]

Bharath:
de lady say
whey (where) you gwine india
baytaa (Hindi for son) have hyar
son have hyar
me no having nutting india
all e have have chinedad (Trinidad).[16]

Maharani and Bharath, woman and man, speak of their reluctance to go back to India when everything they have, including their children, exists in Trinidad. Bharath also talks about how even those who went back returned.

Bharath:
everything have hyar
cheren have hyar
india no have notting
all e family dey
all e friend dey hyar
all e family dey hyar
plenty people going come back
two two time.[17]

Indentured communities registered a series of complex changes with respect to caste, especially with the disappearance of untouchability. Another process set in motion was the homogenization of Indian religious practices into "Hinduism" and "Islam," one of the key factors being the impact of a proselytizing Christianity, represented in the early years by the Canadian Presbyterian Church. While some anthropologists and social scientists have emphasized the continuities between North Indian forms of social stratification and those found in Trinidad's East Indian villages, others have criticized this move to study the villages in isolation from larger socioeconomic patterns in twentieth-century Trinidad. Joseph Nevadomsky, for example, who conducted his fieldwork in the early 1970s, emphasizes social mobility among East Indians against both social-science and popular assumptions that "generally hold that norms and values deriving from India provide the conceptual framework for rural East Indian social organization and social stratification."[18] Morton Klass, by contrast, sees village life among Hindu East Indians as a faithful reproduction of village life in northern India. In his classic study of the village of "Amity," Klass declares that the founders of the village "were able to reconstitute social institutions which could be maintained by their descendants, and which functioned as mechanisms for the transmission of their culture and the maintenance of community cohesiveness."[19] Nevadomsky criticizes this "retentionist hypothesis" through his examination of changes in family and marriage, wedding rituals, and occupation, arguing that empirical evidence pointed to significant changes in "traditional" patterns.[20]

Studying the same village, Amity, that Klass wrote about as having social stratification distinct from the rest of Trinidad, Nevadomsky shows that educational and occupational mobility had dissolved earlier systems of stratification. He draws attention to a more general problem for ethnography, where the focus on microlevel community studies seldom makes allowances for processes of social and economic change, thus ending up imputing an "artificial timelessness" to the position of East Indians. John La Guerre's introduction to his pioneering anthology on East Indians, first published in 1974, surveys the existing literature and suggests that generalizations about cultural persistence based on community studies took away attention from crucial developments such as the growth of East Indian elites, urbanization, and the emergence of party politics. La Guerre contends that the "serious neglect" by sociologists of East Indians has allowed the available theses on " 'retentions' and 'persistence' to crystallize into near orthodoxy," marking a failure to see East Indians as part of the wider social structure.[21]

By the end of the nineteenth century, over 90 percent of the Indians had completed their indentures and had gone into independent cane production, rice growing, and cocoa. Often pooling their resources to purchase plots, East Indians soon owned one fifth of the island's cultivated land.[22] While they settled in relatively homogeneous village communities, other communities of Indians began to form in the cities, in Port of Spain and San Fernando, which were racially heterogeneous. The 1921 census shows that although 61 percent of the East Indian workforce was in agriculture, 14 percent was in teaching jobs; 5 percent was in the professions, police, and military; and a substantial number held public office. By the 1940s, a professional class of East Indians, consisting of lawyers, doctors, civil servants, teachers, politicians, and merchants, had begun to emerge. World War II expanded job opportunities, partly due to the labor requirements of the American military base in Trinidad, and East Indians, like other sections of the society, benefited from the economic growth. As Nevadomsky points out, political independence and the 1950s run-up to it, brought universal suffrage, the repealing of discriminatory legislation, bureaucratic expansion, social-welfare programs, and the institutionalization of education. All of these opportunities also helped rural East Indians.[23] There seems to have been a general movement in this time away from the land, with younger family members being discouraged from staying in the village.

Like Arthur Niehoff and Barton Schwartz before him, Nevadomsky demonstrates that caste does not serve a regulatory function among Trinidad Indians. Villagers asked to distinguish between "high" and "low" people used educational and economic markers rather than caste markers to make their classifications. Interestingly, Nevadomsky concludes his study of social mobility and economic change by noting the "marked decrease" in expenditure on religious ceremonies and rituals. He suggests that observance of these rituals "no longer enhances prestige," which instead is sought to be obtained by the acquisition of consumer goods and a modern lifestyle.[24]

A contrast to this interpretation is that of Steven Vertovec, whose 1980s fieldwork focuses on the effects of the oil boom of 1973–82. Adding to the economic growth stimulated by larger oil reserves and higher worldwide oil prices was the rising price of sugar, a major cash crop in Trinidad. Larger cash incomes were now available, and widespread electrification led to newer forms of conspicuous consumption, with stereos and videocassette recorders (VCRs) becoming common. Vertovec argues that the VCR helped to provide "more vivid models of 'Indian-ness'" through Hindi films, which could be circulated more widely through this technology than through celluloid; "splendid sarees" and embroidered kurtas for special occasions became affordable. "And religion, far from dying, became a highly elaborated focus for cultural expression and social interaction." There was a proliferation of family-based rituals—*pujas* (Sanskrit word for worship), Ramayan readings, *yagnas* (another Sanskrit word for worship), all major collective activities.[25] After the oil boom ended, the activities continued but in a pared-down fashion. Vertovec challenges the view that assimilation is "a necessary consequence of development," contending that "shifting social structures and economic advances or setbacks provide new contexts in which institutions can be created or renewed to maintain collective unity and stability, regardless of the exact cultural forms taken."[26] Indeed, the new political opportunities provided by parliamentary democracy brought into being the two main parties that remain to this day polarized along racial lines: the Creole-dominated People's National Movement (PNM), headed at the time of independence in 1962 by Eric Williams, the country's first prime minister, and the Democratic Labor Party of Bhadase Sagan Maraj (supported by the Sanatan Dharma Maha Sabha, the island-wide Hindu organization), which mutated into many forms and has finally provided part of the support base for the East Indian–dominated United National Congress.

The assertion of an "Indian" ethnic identity has sometimes been seen as the manifestation of "Indian nationalism." This term might well puzzle India Indians who cannot see any connection to the politics of their own nation-state. A brief look, therefore, at the significations of nationalism in the West Indies might be in order. Nationalism is a somewhat different entity in the West Indies from that which we find in South Asia, where it is more common to see nationalism as a form of relationship to a nation-state — either one in the making or one that has already come into existence. While Caribbean (particularly elite) nationalism may well take the form of a specifically Jamaican or Trinidadian anticolonial nationalism, all classes of people often represent themselves as Caribbean or West Indian, too. Political movements such as Garveyism in the early twentieth century or midcentury Pan-Africanism, built on perceptions of a shared past of slavery, extended far beyond the Caribbean islands. The short-lived Federation (1958–62) was another attempt to bring together the political units of the region even before the achievement of full independence. The Black Power Movement in the 1970s had African American origins, but it resonated powerfully with Caribbean critiques of elite nationalism — for instance, Rastafarianism.[27]

In spite of the ambiguous nature of the relationship between nation and nationalism in the West Indies, what is evident is the Afrocentric basis of the claim to being West Indian. It is this premise that "Indian nationalism" appears to address, its project not being the creation of an Indian nation-state but one of claiming cultural rights in Trinidad. To me, the most salient factor in the East Indian narratives of Indianness in the Caribbean is not the question of producing and maintaining a "colonial" difference. That is, difference from the colonizing European is not the issue, as it would have been with elite Indian nationalism in India. Rather, the difference at stake is that from the "African" ("the other race," as East Indians say today). "Indians" have a slight demographic edge over "Africans" in Trinidad, making up a little over 42 percent of the population, while "Africans" make up 40–41 percent, and those of Chinese, Lebanese, Latin American, and West European origin make up the rest.[28]

It may be worth emphasizing that the maintenance of distinctions between the "Christianized African Creole" and the "Asiatic coolie" was a matter of some concern for the colonial authorities, as well.[29] After the establishment of the Republic of Haiti in 1803, the specter of successful non-white revolt haunted every European in the Caribbean. Any hint of solidarity between laborers, especially of different races, was sought to be speedily crushed. As the planters faced the prospect of the end of indenture, and the imminent formation of a purely domestic labor force, images of the shiftless, lazy African and the industrious coolie circulated with increasing frequency. The colonial construction of "Indian" and "African" continues to inform the contemporary formations of the two groups' identities.[30]

A late-nineteenth-century visitor to the island, the British novelist Charles Kingsley, wrote about the Indian and African as mutually incompatible:

> [The Negro's] treatment of his children and of his beasts of burden is, but too often, as exactly opposed to that of the Coolie as are his manners. No wonder that the two races do not, and it is to be feared, never will, amalgamate; that the Coolie, shocked by the unfortunate awkwardness of gesture and vulgarity of manners of the average Negro, and still more of the Negress, looks on them as savages; while the Negro, in his turn, hates the Coolie as a hard-working interloper, and despises him as a heathen.[31]

Crucial distinctions were drawn in particular between Indian and African women, and racialized notions of femininity were elaborated, as I discuss in chapter 2.

Thinking about Trinidad in India

At this juncture, it would be important to distinguish between the impulses that animate diaspora studies in metropolitan places (I have in mind especially the theorizing of the black diaspora by scholars like Stuart Hall or Paul Gilroy) and those that might inform diaspora studies in postcolonial "Third World" locations. Gilroy, for example, sees his political and epistemological task as one of reinscribing "diasporic African" identities and practices onto the apparent whiteness of Western modernity. The title of his first book, *There Ain't No Black in the Union Jack*, concisely invokes both the problem and the attempted solution.[32] Gilroy's is an enterprise undertaken at the heart of the metropolis, where the presence and visibility of Afro-Caribbean people enables the emergence of an anti-imperialist politics that foregrounds the question of race.

The situation in India is considerably different. For one thing, the diaspora we are beginning to study is not perceived as racially or ethnically "other" in the sense that the Afro-Caribbean may be in England. Neither are diasporic Indian identities being pressed on our attention because of a large-scale migration of subaltern diasporic people into India; on the contrary, more and more elite Indians are migrating to the diasporic communities in the First World, producing the cultural phenomenon of the NRI who is being emulated in the motherland, not despised. In fact, one sees a number of celebratory NRI stories appearing not only in the popular press in India but also in scholarly accounts, the most recent being televised interviews with successful NRIs and special sections of weekly magazines such as *India Today* devoted to news about non-residents. In the era of globalization and liberalization, these stories—laced with envy and desire—have a potent and homogenizing force.[33] What, then, might be the stakes for the Indian scholar of the diaspora in choosing to study what I have called "subaltern" diasporic communities? For those of us engaged in a sustained interrogation of mainstream nationalism as well as contemporary neonationalism in India, there may be much that an understanding of, say, the formation of the Trinidadian East Indian can offer.

I want to suggest, for instance, that an investigation of "Indianness" in Trinidad can disrupt not only the dominant secular-liberal narrative of Indianness in India that mainstream nationalism endorses; it also disrupts the neonationalist, or Hindutva, critique of that narrative. The geneaology of the earlier nationalism is explicitly anticolonial, while the new nationalism, which looks for an enemy within, is anti-minority. Whereas secular-liberal politics requires a transcendence of caste and religious identities by the "Indian" citizen-subject, Hindutva demands the making visible and claiming of the Hindu identity of this citizen, arguing that post-Independence "pseudo-secularism" has led to the promotion of minorities at the cost of the submergence of the Hinduness of India. To substantiate my assertion that nationalisms in India would look different seen from a Caribbean perspective, for example, we would need to examine the structuring of the claim to Indianness in Trinidad. Once again, Gilroy's work provides a useful point of comparison. As a statement, "There ain't no black . . ." points clearly to the main addressee of the claim to blackness in England: the hegemonic, race-blind, formerly imperial nation. When East Indians in Trinidad make the claim to Indianness, however, their addressee is a divided one. Attempting to *erase* the difference with India rather than to mark it, East Indians assert a racial similarity in relation to the "mother country" and a racial difference in relation to the politically dominant group in their nation-state. The same claim to "Indianness" has to carry the simultaneous burden of this paradoxical address. The further paradox is that some East Indians emphasize cultural continuity with India and cultural difference from Creoles (usually all non-Indians in Trinidad), neither of which is self-evident to India Indians. On the contrary: The tendency of the latter would be not to recognize the East Indian as "Indian," but to see cultural discontinuity with India, on the one hand, and cultural similarity between East Indian and Creole, on the other.

Trinidad cannot be seen as a "post-diaspora" society of the kind that England is. Here, the East Indian claim to Indianness is addressed not to a colonial power at its very center but to two postcolonial nation-states, Trinidad and India, experiencing the aftermath of empire. In this aftermath, the structures of exclusion that mark East Indians have been different from those that mark non-white people in England, as is evident from the ways in which the claim for inclusion in Trinidad, and the politics of that claim, are structured. What the East Indian seems to be asserting is a *shared* history of deprivation and struggle, demanding the recognition not only of this common history but also of its implications for the present.

While some East Indians articulate a claim on India, there are others who wish to call themselves Indian but show no interest in India. One of the women I spoke with about this relationship, a journalist in her twenties, had this to say: "Historically I want to know when we came here, why we came here. I want to understand things about Indian history. I want to understand things Asian, and I want to understand dynamics of where we might have linkages . . . what the feudal system has bequeathed to us, where some of our behavior comes from. I can understand those things in a historical sense, in a scientific sense, but the extent to which I am capable of a psychic exploration I do not know, and I'm not even sure I want to go with it. And I have people telling me you have to go there in order to understand, in order to have a full understanding of where you are now, your contemporary relationship. . . . I don't think I need to do that. India is India, and Trinidad is Trinidad."[34] Another East Indian woman, a former schoolteacher now in her sixties, said: "There was very little interest in India, although things Indian were dear to us—the music, our religious practices, . . . the way you did certain things for weddings. . . . No, India was not real. It was something in our minds, our imagination; it existed, that's where grandparents came from . . . , but I never felt the urge or the need to go to India. . . . It's something remote for me."[35]

The remoteness of India in the emotional geography of many East Indians would inform the nature of their visibility in the Trinidadian public sphere in the post-Independence period. The colonial construction of racial differences notwithstanding, there were different political efforts to avoid polarization of Africans and East Indians. But there were also early initiatives among professional Indians to organize themselves into politically viable entities, such as the East Indian National Association (EINA) and the East Indian National Congress (EINC), formed in 1897 and 1909, respectively, and to protect their interests as East Indians. These two organizations were seen as "communal" and conservative by other East Indians, such as C. B. Mathura, who edited a popular Port of Spain newspaper, the *East Indian Weekly*, in the early 1930s and consistently demanded that Africans and Indians unite in their opposition to colonialism. There was also the African newspaper, *The People*, which appealed to African pride and identity as an anticolonial strategy but never attacked Indians, arguing that allegiance to the working class was what would ensure economic and political action.[36]

The labor riots of 1937 led to the development of trade unions in Trinidad. An East Indian, Adrian Cola Rienzi (born Krishna Deonarine), was the best-known figure in the labor movement, being founder and major office bearer of the Oil Workers Trade Union (OWTU) and the All-Trinidad Sugar Estate and Factory Workers' Trade Union (ATSEFWTU). The unions drew their membership from different races, and the first oil workers' strike in 1937 was seen as a major demonstration of interracial solidarity. In 1938, Rienzi stood successfully for election to the Legislative Council in the constituency of Victoria, where he obtained support from Africans even though his opponent was an African. As Samaroo documents, "*The People* of 8 January, 1938, condemned the supporters of Piper (Rienzi's opponent) for injecting race into the election campaign and the paper advised the workers to support Rienzi in the best interests of the 'two great races, the African and the Indian.'"[37] Analysts like La Guerre present a gloomier picture of the 1933 elections, contending that "labor" and "capital" were slogans but not fully articulated positions and that the race factor loomed large, with socialist fighting against socialist. While it was held that the race question was an economic question, how that complicated attempts to unite the left was not recognized or explored.[38] By 1956, when a new pre-independence constitution was implemented, the PNM, party of the urban African/Creole middle class, was successful in isolating its main rival, Bhadase Maraj's Democratic Labor Party, to what were seen to be "Hindu" constituencies. The 1956 elections brought the race question to the forefront once Trinidad was poised to become self-governing.

Given the relative lack of sociological accounts of interracial interaction in Trinidad, there is only anecdotal evidence to draw on. There are, however, some figures from the late 1960s and early 1970s, cited by Mahin Gosine: Colin Clarke's 1971 data show ethnic endogamy (although religious exogamy was not unknown) among East Indian Christians was 89 percent; among Hindus, 97 percent; and among Muslims, 98 percent. Yogendra Malik's data, published in 1971, show that 93 percent of Hindu leaders, 50 percent of Muslim leaders, and 87 percent of Christians disapproved of marriage with blacks. Ethnic endogamy among blacks according to Clarke was 88 percent.[39] Clarke's study of San Fernando town (1930–70) adds the further information that when Creoles married East Indians, the latter were usually Christians; that while endogamy was the norm, there was the category of *douglas* who "figured prominently in the racially exogamous unions of all other groups."[40] In the village of Debe, however, exogamy was usually religious (Hindus, Muslims, and Christian East Indians marrying each other) rather than racial.[41] Census records of the rate of mixing in the population refers to people with one Indian parent as Indian Creole. In 1911, Indian Creoles were 1.47 percent in relation to "unmixed" Indians; in 1921, the figure was 1.87 percent; and in 1946, it was 4.29 percent. The figure was higher in urban areas, with Port of Spain recording a high of 21.37 percent Indian Creoles.[42] One of the reasons offered by historians for the reluctance of Indians to go back to India was that some of them had racially mixed families (not to mention the fact of marriage across castes that took place in Trinidad), which they feared would not be found acceptable in their home villages. As the calypsonian Hindu Prince sang in "Goodbye to India" (1971), there are many things you can do in Trinidad that you can't do in India, one of them being cohabitation across race: "In India you cyah make dougla children."[43] As a housewife in her seventies put it: "Plenty Indyan chirren go and mix up wid de African."[44]

One of the ironies of postcolonial politics is our mobilization of narratives of racial or cultural purity against one another, narratives that are very similar in structure to those that served to displace us in colonial times. While the purity narrative arguably can serve the purpose of creating a community identity, it is fraught with many problems for the Trinidadian East Indian as well as for those who live in India—problems that should be instructive for both. The East Indian emphasis on indivisibility and unruptured continuity with the motherland only serves to mark off the East Indian as derivative, as having, in V. S. Naipaul's words, "produced nothing."[45] The diasporic cultural form, such as Trinidadian chutney dancing, comes to be seen as inauthentic, as not Indian, *precisely because of* its claim to be Indian. Filiation will be granted only on its own terms by the mother country, which in fact requires the existence of a hybrid form to delineate its own purity by contrast. We can see this logic being worked out in the case of Indian women, as I explain in chapter 2.

As the political scientist Bhikhu Parekh has pointed out, the Indian discourse on the diaspora, such as it is, is neither clear nor coherent.[46] There are, however, some recurrent tropes that configure any kind of discussion—popular as well as scholarly—on diasporic communities. One of these is the trope of derivativeness. Diasporic cultural forms are seen as corrupt, imitative, degraded, a pale reflection of the "original" forms that are only to be found in the mother country. These might be preoccupations specific, though not confined, to the Indian investigator, whose location in a "national" culture prompts the representing of other ("outside") claims to Indianness as inadequate or deficient. The characterization of the claim as inadequate or the cultural form as derivative clearly follows from the characterization of that which is authentically Indian—namely, the "original."

While the conventional contemporary representation of "our" culture in India (our glorious past, our splendid monuments, our ancient literatures) was formulated as part of an anticolonial response, and is informed by the discourses of Orientalism that fed into both colonialist and nationalist frameworks, the invocation of "culture" by Trinidadian Indians appears to partake of a double anxiety. Like all formerly colonized peoples, West Indian East Indians make the claim to a unique (here, "Indian") culture and history as part of the assertion of autonomy from the colonizer, but this claim becomes imbricated with that of the nationalists in India who are claiming sovereignty through nationhood just as it comes to be asserted against other colonized groups. As several scholars have shown, when Indian nationalism began to articulate its anticolonial program, it often redeployed the Orientalist construction of the Indian past, needing to assert the antiquity, authenticity, and continuity of "Indian" culture.[47] So in addition to the anxiety of the colonial subject vis-à-vis the metropolis, the Trinidad East Indian is also caught in the anxiety of the diasporic person vis-à-vis the mother country. Both anxieties center around what the West Indian writer Derek Walcott has brilliantly delineated as the problem of originality and mimicry. Responding to Naipaul's characterization of West Indians as "mimic men," Walcott remarks:

> To mimic, one needs a mirror, and, if I understand Mr. Naipaul correctly, our pantomime is conducted before a projection of ourselves which in its smallest gestures is based on metropolitan references. No gesture, according to this philosophy, is authentic, every sentence is a quotation, every movement either ambitious or pathetic, and because it is mimicry, uncreative.[48]

The belief in the unoriginality of the West Indian (whether of African, East Indian, Chinese, or Portuguese origin), says Walcott, comes perhaps from the idea that there is a line drawn through the Atlantic Ocean that says "this is new, this is the frontier, the boundary of endeavor, and henceforth everything can only be mimicry."[49] Looking specifically at the East Indian in his Nobel Prize lecture, Walcott describes the situation even more vividly:

> Consider the scale of Asia reduced to these fragments: the small white exclamations of minarets or the stone balls of temples in the cane fields, and one can understand the self-mockery and embarrassment of those who see these rites as parodic, even degenerate. These purists look on such ceremonies as grammarians look at a dialect, as cities look on prov-

inces and empires on their colonies. . . . In other words, the way that the Caribbean is still looked at, illegitimate, rootless, mongrelized. "No people there," to quote Froude, "in the true sense of the word." No people. Fragments and echoes of real people, unoriginal and broken.[50]

Social "grammarians" in both India and the Caribbean might indeed perceive the East Indian as unoriginal and mongrelized. What I want to argue for here, however, is the necessity of engaging in a labor of interpretation that will make the Trinidadian Indian *differently* available to the Indian in India so that the former's function will not simply be the confirmation of the latter's superiority. Rather, the East Indian could unsettle profoundly for us the sense of who is "Indian" and why. In initiating this process, the first move might be to detach "Indianness" from the purity claim, which so often ends up being the dominant register in which the claim to Indianness is made, withheld, or granted.

Positioned as we are in India within the story of liberalism-secularism, we are inclined to view any assertion of community identity—as, for example by Muslims in India—as anti-national. When we begin to see that East Indians, for instance, are not refusing a shared future in Trinidad, and that their assertion is not simply anti-national but critical of the formation of the "national," similar processes in our own context might become differently visible to us. We need to pay more attention to how "Indian" in Trinidad has come to be fashioned. And we need to understand that the genealogy of the Caribbean East Indian does not simply duplicate that of the Indian in India.

Different Genealogy

The East Indian is significantly different from the India Indian in terms of one of the most visible markers of social stratification in the South Asian Subcontinent: caste.

The caste-class and religious composition of the migrants reflected, to some extent, the composition in the regions of migration. Historians give varying figures, but aggregates suggest that roughly 15 percent of the migrants were Muslim; there was a small number of Christians, mainly from the south; and among the Hindus, 40 pecent were from the artisanal and agricultural castes like the Kurmi and the Ahir, more than 40 percent were from the "chamar," or what were then called the untouchable castes (dalits in today's India), and about 18 percent were from upper-caste groups like Brahmin and Kshatriya.[51] There is some dispute as to whether the caste composition in the regions of out-migration is accurately reflected in the composition of the indentured recruits. There was active encouragement for agricultural laborers to migrate, and active discouragement of upper castes, leading to occasional falsification of caste status on the part of eager migrants. We must also remember that subsequent to migration there was a complex process of recomposition of castes in Trinidad, as in other colonies. Many people "changed" their caste, often within one generation, and caste endogamy was not strictly practiced because of the scarcity of women.[52] Haraksingh suggests that while the numbers were not adequate and the different caste groups did not come to Trinidad, thus preventing a resurrection of the Indian caste system, a broader, more "collapsed" notion of caste, with the main distinction being one between high and low caste, often functions among the ex-indentured.[53] What is clear, however, is that most of the migrants were either poor or destitute, having lost their land or having never owned any. An intriguing thought is that some of these "Indians" were actually Africans (called Siddis in some parts of India) who had been involved in the Sepoy Mutiny of 1857 against the British and were punished by being shipped to places like Trinidad.[54]

Returning to the study of East Indians many years after his pioneering and much criticized study, Klass conceded that Trinidad Indians had given up features of hierarchy such as caste ranking, marital restrictions, dietary rules, and untouchability but had not yet given them up completely, perhaps suggesting that the caste rules exist in the breach rather than in the observance.[55] Other scholars have stated the case more strongly, such as Schwartz, who argued as early as the 1960s that under indentureship the constant physical contact between members of different castes, food from common rations, crowded accommodations, and the general impossibility of segregation of any kind resulted in a dissolution of caste restrictions.[56] Schwartz also draws attention to what he calls caste passing, a situation in which indentured East Indians assumed a higher caste status than the one they originally possessed, "stimulated" by the circumstances of migration. Pretensions to high-caste status were seldom challenged, especially after indenture, when independent peasant proprietors emerged or Indians migrated to the cities. "Closely related to this caste passing is the fact that high-caste East Indians composed a minority of the indentured laborers," he writes, since emigration agents were explicitly asked not to recruit high castes, who were considered unsuited to hard labor.[57]

A crucial factor that worked against endogamous caste practices was the serious disparity in the sex ratio between male and female migrants. To give a rough estimate, there were 23,093 men to 8,434 women in the period 1851–70, a ratio of three to one. "In addition, the fact that high-caste males married low-caste females, thus reducing the number of 'proper' eligible partners, made the adherence to traditional endogamous practices more difficult for males of the lower castes."[58] With conversion to Christianity and changing economic status, as Nevadomsky also has pointed out, caste affiliation became far less important than religious or ethnic affiliation. Clarke's data indicate that, "for many Hindus, caste presents no great problem. In their working life in town, race and class are infinitely more important to them than caste."[59] Samaroo takes a slightly different view: He argues that caste does function as a means of "social gradation," although it is expressed through an "Arya Samajist" perspective, emphasizing "*guna* and *swabhav* [virtue and nature of the person]" and not birth. "How you are perceived is based on behaviour, merit, deportment," Samaroo said in an interview. "It is a personal ascription." Since most Brahmins in Trinidad are what Samaroo calls "Brahmins by boat" (as opposed to Brahmins by birth), the only two caste categories that are used are "Brahmin" (signifying high caste) and "Chamar" (signifying low caste). According to Samaroo, the *varna* (four-fold) form of caste categorization, which is more common in India, does not work in the Caribbean.[60]

Schwartz's fieldwork in the village of Boodram mentions categories of caste that include both *varnas* and *jatis*, but it is implied that this level of confusion is related to the self-identity of the informants.[61] He establishes that there is no correlation between caste status and economic activity, and that people often come together in groups called *guayap* to help a fellow villager build a house, work in the fields, or thresh rice without payment, at which time they share food and water provided by participating families of different castes.[62] Niehoff's 1960s study of another nonurban area remarked on the diversity of jobs among Indians, which included agriculture (from wage laborers to farmers owning hundreds of acres); storekeeping and business; white-collar jobs; and drivers in oil fields, confirming that there was no connection in Trinidad between caste and occupation.[63]

Another approach to thinking about caste in Trinidad is suggested by Vertovec, who argues that instead of examining the disappearance of caste in relation to the conditions that might work against maintaining traditional caste occupations, such as endogamy, "attention should be turned to how the everyday *practice* of caste in India—involving multi-layered, contextually meaningful identifications together with shifting inter- and intra-group relations—was affected by the sudden move to an alien setting."[64] Agreeing with Gloria Raheja and other scholars that to understand the workings of caste in India one should inquire into particular forms of power relations and not just a purity-based idea of hierarchy, Vertovec affirms that indentured migration separated conceptions of caste from local notions of kingship, sovereignty, and dominance, without which they could not operate.[65] He adds that migration would have led to difficulty of agreement on caste-based interaction and behavior, since the indentured were from different localities in India. Under indentureship, caste *panchayats*, or councils could not be constituted because of jurisdiction problems. Another feature of caste, segregated residence, also did not obtain in Trinidad. Where caste surnames existed, they lost their meaning as status markers, and since in most cases the laborers had no surnames at all, they could in the period after indenture take on any surname of their choice, even those suggesting higher caste status.[66] The disappearance of caste distinctions also had to do, as Vertovec points out, with the creolization of Indian languages into plantation Hindi, which resulted in the loss of specific forms of speech associated with local caste groups in India. Even linguistic components conveying relative caste status changed. So did forms of nonverbal communication, like gestures and mannerisms that conveyed caste attitudes. Other overt symbols of caste status such as specific kinds of clothes also disappeared.[67]

The social anthropologist R. K. Jain raises the interesting possibility of caste having passed into race in Trinidad, giving as evidence the fact that "interracial hypergamous marriages (an Indian male marrying a creole female) do not arouse as much social obloquy as hypogamous ones." He also gives the example of the African who as a child was invited to Hindu pujas and weddings and plied with food and gifts in a separate room before guests arrived, suggesting that this might be similar to the North Indian practice of using a low-caste person in a ritual to avert the evil eye.[68]

Also with regard to the question of community identity, take the example of the Muharram, or Hosay, riots of 1884 in Trinidad: Indians of all religious backgrounds came together, as they always did, to organize processions of the Muslim martyrs' *tadjahs* or *tazias* against the orders of the colonial administration and were massacred by the police.[69] "Indian" in Trinidad today also stands for this kind of figure—one who is not simply Hindu or Muslim or Christian, one who cannot be accounted for by purity narratives premised on religious identity. The historian Prabhu Mohapatra points out that among the eighteen (possibly more) who were killed during the police shootings in the 1884 riots, thirteen were Hindus and five were Muslims. Among the injured were seventy-seven Hindus, fifteen Muslims, and one Christian.[70] As Mohapatra shows, although it was known in the nineteenth century as the coolie festival of the colony, Hosay eventually declined as a community festival because of distinctions made by the colonial authorities between the religious and nonreligious parts of the festival. Muslims had to apply for permission to perform Hosay. In 1929, permission was denied for the St. James Hosay Fesitival (St. James is a Port of Spain suburb) because several Hindus had applied. A group of Muslim youths petitioned for the order to be reexamined:

> It appears sir that it has been represented to the Honourable Inspector General of Constabulary that this festival is to be carried on by the Hindus. We repudiate this fact sir, it is true that there are a few hindus who have subscribed to build the tazia and the moons but sir you will readily understand that we young people now growing up are trying to break down all these distinctions and to remember that we are all east Indians.[71]

J. C. Jha also mentions that from the 1850s on, Hindus participated in the Tazia, Husain, or Hosay festival and procession at the end of Muharram. This festival was seen as the "annual demonstration of Indian feeling." There was evidence that Hindus participated in large numbers and that they were in the forefront of the celebrations. In October 1884, one Balgopaul Singh, a Hindu, was prosecuted by the Trinidad police for taking a leading part in the Hosay riots.[72] As the historian Bridget Brereton points out,

> it was Hosein which became the major Indian festival in Trinidad. It soon lost its special religious meaning as a commemorative rite celebrated by Shi'ite Moslems in memory of the murder of Mohammed's grandson, and became almost entirely secular. Most of the participants were Hindus, not Moslems, and Creoles participated enthusiastically up to 1885. Hosein became a general Indian holiday. John Morton said it was a "fete day" in which Indians joined to remember the old country, while Sir Henry Norman called it "a sort of national Indian demonstration." It

was celebrated chiefly by estate-resident Indians, and was the occasion for friendly rivalries between different estates, which sometimes caused street fights like those of Carnival.[73]

More than a hundred years later, writes an ethnographer, the St. James Hosay is seen by its participants as a cultural rather than a religious performance. Sunni Muslims are known to take part, not just Shias, although some Sunnis have long argued for their withdrawal from what they see as an inauthentic Muslim event. Many participants are East Indian Hindus and Christians, and there are famed *tadjah* builders who are Hindus, with intermarriage between Hindus and Muslims being common in these families. Many older participants complain that Hosay has become an occasion for feteing, not lamenting. Afro-Trinidadians also participate in the procession, often downplaying the religious element.[74]

The celebrated calypsonian Mighty Chalkdust (Hollis Liverpool), exaggerating the uniqueness of East Indian cultural forms, sang in "We Is We" (1972):

> They have no roti [unleavened bread] over in India
> They don't know 'bout curry and kuchela [pickled mango]
> They do not sell oyster by the Croisee
> Or dance our kind of Hosay.[75]

The specific history of Indians in the Caribbean shows that they could never, and cannot simply, be equated with a monolithic entity called "the Hindu." Maybe because of the privileging of racial over religious identity, Hindu-Muslim marriages are extremely common in Trinidad, and it is not unusual for present-day families to have Christian, Muslim, and Hindu relatives. The early migrants brought with them allegiances to many *bhakti* sects (emphasizing nonritualistic and unmediated worship) that were critical of orthodox Hinduism, such as the Kabir Panth, the Aghori, the Ramananda, the Shivnarayan (Sieunaraini), and the Kali worship of the South Indian ("Madrassi"). An earlier, pre-1930 phase of ethnic mobilization saw East Indians forming not only the EINA and the EINC but also numerous Friendly Societies and Literary and Debating Societies.[76] These organizations could be described as social, intellectual, political, and even economic rather than religious in orientation. After about 1930, some of the organizations lost their importance, and their place was taken by a host of religious formations, both Hindu and Muslim. There were attempts to systematize

Temple and mosque side by side. Photo by Tejaswini Niranjana.

and mainstream the diversity of local religious practices in favor of what Vetovec calls a generalized and classically based Hinduism. This form of Hinduism in Trinidad still has a bhakti orientation, which enables followers to maintain dual loyalties—to community-based religion as well as to a particular reformist sect.[77] Carl Campbell speculates that issues of religious and cultural reform came to the fore for East Indians at a time when some of their demands for political representation had been granted (there were in 1929 three elected Indian members in the Legislative Council).[78]

Among the key organizations established or incorporated in the 1930s were the Sanatan Dharma Board of Control (1932), the Kabir Panth Association (1932), the Sanatan Dharma Association of Trinidad (1932), the Tackveeyatul Islamic Association of Trinidad (1932), and the Anjuman Sunnatul-Jamaat Association of Trinidad (1935). As would be evident from the different names, there were already different factions among Hindus and Muslims. The Sanatan Dharma Board of Control objected to the government's incorporation of its rival, the Sanatan Dharma Association (SDA), on the grounds that one of the leaders of the SDA was an Anglican Christian, the Legislative Council member Michael Sarran Teelucksingh. While the orthodox Hindus, or Sanatanists, felt compelled to respond to Presbyterian evangelizing, on the one hand, on the other hand, they also felt challenged by the strengthening of the reformist Hindu Arya Samaj movement, which had already been organizing for a few decades in the Caribbean and had brought many missionaries from India on lecture tours. Some historians, such as Samaroo, are of the opinion that while religious leaders from the South Asian Subcontinent had helped inspire the revival of religious practices among the East Indians, they also brought with them many of the prejudices and conflicts of India, thus denying Caribbean Indians "the necessary opportunity of struggling to find solutions to their problems in the new and very different environment."[79]

The institutionalization of Hinduism also gained momentum because of government recognition and "ecclesiastical grants," the establishment of temples and schools, and the publication of standardized religious literature. The pundits were registered officers licensed to conduct marriages, and their functions began to closely resemble those of Christian priests. Scholars like Vertovec suggest that the completeness of this institutionalization, brought about by the activities of Hindu leaders—in particular, the wealthy and ambitious Bhadase Sagan Maraj—resulted in a carryover into the sphere of secular politics. As Vertovec puts it, "The politicizing of Hinduism further acted to condense Hindu social solidarity, though at the same time secularizing a great deal of religious activity."[80] Ethnic mobilization around religious identity was the central focus of Maraj's People's

View of Waterloo temple with prayer flags. Photo by Tejaswini Niranjana.

Democratic Party (later renamed the Democratic Labor Party), which contested the 1956 elections, winning five seats out of twenty-four to the PNM's thirteen. The Sanatan Dharma Maha Sabha, incorporated in 1952 as a result of Maraj's efforts to link the two major Hindu Sanatanist organizations, backed the People's Democratic Party and campaigned for its victory. However, the renamed party suffered a series of defeats in the post-independence 1960s and lost more support when, during the 1970s Black Power uprising, Maraj advocated a politics of confrontation with Africans.[81] With the death of Maraj in 1971, the activities of the Sanatan Dharma Maha Sabha suffered a major setback, coinciding with the new social mobility of rural East Indians and the diminishing significance of Hindu practices. The situation, however, began to change later in the decade.

It wasn't only East Indian Hindu leaders who were worried about Africans' and Indians' uniting. In 1965, Eric Williams of the PNM sought to prevent the formation of a consolidated trade union. East Indian sugar workers tired of Bhadase Maraj had invited George Weekes, president of the OWTU to represent them, and Williams rushed through an Industrial Stabilization Act, which, among other things, outlawed strikes and set conditions for certification of worker representation. In spite of this, there were further efforts to bring the workers together. On March 18, 1975, several thousand oil and sugar workers set out from the OWTU's office in San Fernando after listening to speeches from their leaders and being "blessed by Hindu, Muslim and Christian clergy." They had not gone far when they were stopped by police wielding tear gas and truncheons. This was the last of the militant mass demonstrations, for by the end of 1975 the oil boom seemed to have helped Trinidad achieve a measure of stability and prosperity.[82]

Anthropologists like Schwartz and Nevadomsky predicted, in the wake of economic and social mobility, the decline of Hinduism along with forms of social stratification encouraged by it, like caste. The oil boom contradicted their predictions, however. In the 1970s, East Indians in general "achieved more prosperity and social mobility than . . . during [the] previous 130 years."[83] The period also saw a "revitalization" of Hinduism, a consequence of perceptions of marginalization by rural Hindus, the alleged state pressure to creolize, and greater racial tension combined with the increased economic well-being of the boom years. A phenomenon like the English subtitling of Hindi films from the 1970s is supposed to have inspired younger, monolingual East Indians' appreciation of "Indian culture," seen by some as contributing to the revival of Hinduism.[84] Even

A temple at home. Photo by Tejaswini Niranjana.

with the downturn in the economy, some of the newly initiated practices continued.

The political mobilization of anti-PNM forces in the 1980s led to the formation of a new kind of government in 1986, by the National Alliance for Reconstruction (NAR), consisting of both African and Indian elements. The expulsion of East Indian leader Basdeo Panday from the NAR weakened its base and eventually led to its defeat in 1991, with the PNM returning to power. Early elections called in 1995 resulted in a victory for a United National Congress–led coalition, and Panday became the country's first Indian prime minister. While he did not necessarily promote himself as a champion of Hindus, some Hindu Indians did see him as their representative. It appears as though when ethnic identity and religious background match, the leader is seen as Hindu. Other non-Hindu Indians, however, support the United National Congress for being an "Indian" party. This particular feature of Trinidadian cultural politics—the mapping of religious identity onto ethnic identity (as the example of the film subtitles so clearly shows)—suggests that Hindu religious practices may be one end of a spectrum of cultural practices asserting "Indianness" in Trinidad. The practices themselves, however, have different kinds of political consequences both in Trinidad and in India.

New Hanuman statue and temple en route to Chaguanas. Photo by Tejaswini Niranjana.

Diasporic Indians in general, and the subaltern diaspora in particular, increasingly have been mobilized since the 1980s in the creation of a Hindu India, their identities both Hindu-ized and internationalized by organizations such as the Vishwa Hindu Parishad (World Hindu Forum), which belongs to the Sangh Parivar, a "family" of right-wing political parties and "cultural" organizations striving to establish their dominance in the Indian public sphere. This contemporary phenomenon points to how the notion of "Indian culture" invoked to legitimize (cultural) minority aspirations in Trinidad incorporates East Indians into a hegemonic formation in India that is constantly deployed to delegitimize religious minorities.

During the World Hindu Conference in 2000, which was held on the University of the West Indies' St. Augustine campus, "Indian-owned" FM radio stations were full of discussions about Hinduism today and interviews with guests from India, some of whom complained about the media's hostility to Hinduism in their own country compared with the favorable reception in Trinidad. Trinidad Hindu ideologists wrote ecstatic reports in the print media about the main speakers in the conference, including Ashok Singhal, president of the Vishwa Hindu Parishad, and Sudarshan, then chief of the Rashtriya Swayamsevak Sangh, an organization with a long history of anti-minority initiatives. In a bizarre sleight of hand, when the "Hindu" intelligentsia in Trinidad draw on ideas of left-inspired critical historiography from India (like the Subaltern Studies series) to endorse their call to Caribbean Hindus to write their own history, they also seem to suggest that the current visibility of political Hinduism in India was made possible by these leftist historians.

Rajnie Ramlakhan, a columnist for the *Express*, a leading Trinidad newspaper, lauded Singhal's description of the new Hindu as "a person who is not inferior, afraid or weak." According to Singhal, "Hindus gave peace, love and unity," whereas "non-Hindus responded with violence and mayhem, driven by a desire to erase Hinduism." Ramlakhan is of the view that Singhal's talk of a "Hindu renaissance within India" was alluding to a new phenomenon: the rise of the strong Hindu. In her opinion, "This change could well have been influenced by the new approach to the writing of Indian history. . . . The new historiography . . . tells of the contributions of ordinary Indians, independently of the elite, to the making and development of Indian nationalism. *This new approach, referred to in the literature as 'subaltern' (inferior ranks) studies is reflected in the mass movement towards Hinduism and Hindu thought (Hindutva).*"[85]

The Subaltern Studies school of Indian historians, authors of a series of volumes from the early 1980s on, draws its political inspiration from the Marxist-Leninist struggles that began in the late 1960s and challenged existing progressive political formations for neglecting the interests of the rural poor. The struggles have given rise indirectly to a hugely diverse set of interrogations of the post-Independence nation-state's welfarism and have inflected, among other things, the influential feminist and dalit movements of the past two decades. In spite of their diversity, these political movements would hold this in common: that it would be deeply problematic to endorse a notion such as Hindutva (Hindu-ness) that for some years underpinned the structures of state power in India and still seeks to inform every institution of civil society. These groups would also assert without hesitation that mobilization around Hindutva would be detrimental to the long-term interests of lower castes, minorities, and women, often loosely called "subalterns." So when we find a Trinidad Indian claiming inspiration from left-wing subaltern historiographers and aligning them with an extreme right politician, it may throw new light on the deployment of the language of minority cultural rights by majoritarian groups in India. What are the conditions that make such deployment possible, and how might the East Indian reemerge as "Indian," reclaimed by Hindutva and renamed Hindu?[86] It is worth speculating that stories of "Hindu marginalization" from Trinidad and other parts of the Indian diaspora will underwrite the Sangh Parivar's claims that Hindus are marginalized in India.

Barely two years after his inspiring speech in Trinidad, Singhal was defending the Hindu attacks on Muslim lives and property in Gujarat in early 2002, after an incident in which a train bogey with Hindu activists was burned in Godhra town. As Prem Shankar Jha put in his column in the newsmagazine *Outlook*, Singhal is an "open and avid admirer of Adolf Hitler." In a public speech, Singhal had hailed Gujarat as a successful experiment: "Singhal is so proud of the way in which so-called Hindus raped, burned alive, and ripped foetuses out of the bodies of defenceless Muslims that he does not mind claiming that the [Vishwa Hindu Parishad] actually planned and executed the Godhra massacre in order to bring the Hindus out 'in defence of their religion.'" Singhal is alleged to have said that it was a "victory for Hindu society" that entire villages had been "emptied of Islam."[87] Trinidad Indians were unusually silent about the carnage in India, except the columnist Raffique Shah, a onetime revolutionist of the Black Power Movement, who pleaded with Trinidadians not to let what he called the horrible religious conflagration affect relations between Hindus and Muslims in their country.[88] Shah's column mentions a debate in Trinidad between Sat Maharaj, a leader of the Sanatan Dharma Maha Sabha, and a Hindu scholar who was attacked by Maharaj for his interpretation of the Godhra massacre. Urging restraint in Trinidad, Shah presents his version of secularism as tolerance of all religions. While this interpretation of secularism has been the official one in India, it has been unable to comprehend either Hindu outrage or Muslim anger, since the premise of secularist policy has been transcendence of religious identity and not the recognition of its significance for many.

The incomprehension and horror of the secular-liberal Indian at the spectacle of one who publicly displays religious identity, such as the Hindu East Indian, is exemplified in the television journalist Vir Sanghvi's report on the 1999 visit to Trinidad of Atal Behari Vajpayee, prime minister of India and leader of the Bharatiya Janata Party, which belongs to the Sangh Parivar. Trinidad, says Sanghvi sarcastically, is "perhaps the one place in the world where L. K. Advani [a key leader of the Bharatiya Janata Party; deputy prime minister in 2002; leader of the Rath Yatra in 1992, which resulted in the eventual destruction of the Babri Mosque; and in 2005 the leader of the opposition] could draw an enthusiastic crowd." He comments that "the ethnic Indian community's unity with the mother country ensures that pop Hindutva would go down well," adding that Trinidadians' version of Hindu culture is influenced by the Hindi filmmaker Subhash Ghai. "And their view of the Ramayan is so vulgar," Sanghvi goes on to say, that it makes Ramanand Sagar's popular TV serial based on the epic "seem sober and restrained." While East Indians greeted Vajpayee reverentially, says Sanghvi, "it was clear that some of them would have been happier if Advani had driven in on his Toyota complete with a film extra dressed as Ram," since that is more consonant with their view of Hinduism. "For the Sangh Parivar that could be good news," concludes Sanghvi, for "if all goes wrong in India, there is a corner of a foreign country that is forever saffron [a color considered auspicious by Hindus]."[89]

I would like to argue that the formation of the Caribbean East Indian actually confounds both the secular-liberal narrative that Sanghvi produces and Hindutva's interpellation of Trinidadians like Ramlakhan and Persad. Sanghvi is full of contempt for a subjectivity whose history of producing its Indianness is strongly mediated by Hindi film (see chapter 5 for an account of East Indians and Hindi cinema), unwilling to grant that the "Hinduism" practiced in Trinidad includes the worship of La Divina Pastora (Sipari Mai), a Black Virgin to whom the first hair of children is offered, and regular visits to African obeah men for healing and magical help. At one level, the East Indians who came to greet Vajpayee are not necessarily votaries of Hindutva but those who might cheer for the visiting Indian cricket team against the West Indies as a protest against their own invisibility in certain public arenas. Their fascination for Hindi cinema, too, may parallel that of nonelite groups in India. Perhaps Sanghvi's problem — or, more broadly, the secular-liberal's problem — is that he is mapping these groups onto the East Indian, thus reproducing old prejudices against lower-caste/class migrants.

As for Hindutva, its present appeal to Trinidad Indians may come from what seems like an invitation to join the global project of Hinduism *on equal terms* with India Indians, a condition unprecedented in the interaction of the mother country with the subaltern diaspora. If East Indians were more skeptical of the basis of this invitation, and of the structuring of the majoritarian claim in India, they might come to understand that their own unique histories would eventually be rendered illegitimate by that claim. Indeed, the shrillness of Ramlakhan's and Persad's call to Hindus to unite on exclusionary and defensive terms may indicate that East Indians in general are not fully convinced by this argument, immersed as they are in other cultural practices such as Hindi cinema or the musical genre chutney-soca. These cultural elements are shared across religion and sometimes across race, which also allows for the making visible of that which is "Indian."

East Indians in Trinidad are indeed claiming a new visibility in all spheres, including that of popular culture. Debates about how to interpret this emergent Indian presence could be seen as contests over definitions of racial identity, ethnicity, and nationality in contemporary Trinidad. Such contests are engaged in and dramatized not just in the arenas of conventional politics but, quite crucially, in domains like popular culture, which are traditionally marginalized in mainstream research. Studying the Indian diaspora from a location in India, we should be careful not to base our analyses merely on the official histories but also—although this would obviously be a much more difficult task—take into account everyday cultural practices in the diasporic communities. In chapter 3, I present in detail the phenomenon of chutney-soca, which has become an important form of musical performance in Trinidad. While there are both male and female singers of chutney-soca (claimed to be a fusion of Indian and African popular-music traditions), it is the female singer who has attracted criticism from those East Indians who see the public performances of chutney as detrimental to "Indian culture." Since my intention is to reflect on the problems posed by the chutney-soca phenomenon to the assertion of "Indianness," my primary interest is not in reconstructing the history of East Indian women in the Caribbean but in investigating the discursive production, historical as well as contemporary, of East Indian femininity.[90]

The chutney-soca controversy appears to center on the refusal of certain East Indians to be "translated," in a diasporic situation where identities already exist in translation, in the sense of "conveyed across." Interestingly, the refusal (or the anxiety over "douglarization," a word that refers specifically to interracial marriage or cohabitation between Indians and Africans) is shaped in the very process of the reconstitution of identities; it is made available as a position through that very reconstitution. The assertion of a separate and unchanging "Hindu" or "Indian" identity is thus enabled in part by the colonial and Indian nationalist reconstructions of ethnic and racial identities—reconstructions in which definitions of women and what is "proper" to them occupy a crucial position. In colonial discourse in

India, the Indian woman came to be defined in opposition to the European woman, whereas in Trinidad she would additionally be defined in contrast with the African woman. Like ethnic identities in the Caribbean, gender identities are formed through a host of colonial stereotypes about different races. An important area of investigation for the diaspora scholar would be the modes of representation of the East Indian woman in literary texts as well as in popular cultural forms such as the calypso.[91] In chapter 4, which deals with the representation of East Indians in calypso, I discuss at some length the construction of the "Indian woman" in a musical genre dominated by Afro-Trinidadians.

Not only is the Indian woman in Trinidad formed by the discourses of colonialism; she is also shaped by the nationalist discourse from India. As I show in the next chapter, part of the nationalist demand for an end to indenture was premised on the alleged prostitution of the East Indian woman caused by the hardships of indentured life. Once again we see the issue of "purity"—civilizational, cultural, personal—as the specific mode in which the entry into modernity is "managed" by elite nationalism in the Third World. The stakes in narratives of purity for those at the margins of national formations would seem to be necessarily different. I indicated what some of those stakes might be in my earlier discussion of race politics in Trinidad and will return to the issue in chapter 3, where I talk about contemporary cultural controversies, especially the one around chutney-soca.

What might it mean for Trinidadian East Indians to rearticulate their claim to "India" and to "Indianness" in the light of subaltern critiques of the formation of nation and nationalism in India? Could we perhaps recognize the popularity of chutney-soca as a marker of a similar, already existing critique that might not only intersect with those being articulated in India but also illuminate the modalities of the latter for people in the subcontinent? If East Indians were to make an assertive claim on India, not a defensive one, they might have to delink the claim from what I have called the narrative of purity. Instead of asking for a place in the dominant narrative of nationhood in India on the terms of Indian nationalism, East Indians might emphasize the specificity of their genealogy and attempt to link this emphasis to questions about the composition of the "Indian" being raised by different subaltern groups in India. Such a rearticulation of the East Indian claim on India might eventually also change the way Indianness is claimed in the Caribbean.

It is precisely at the point of greatest anxiety ("woman's purity") and most intense identification (Indianness embodied in womanhood) that the incoherence of a certain diasporic claim to Indianness comes to the foreground. "Woman," then, might also be seen as the ground for the contestation and transformation of that claim. It would be important in this regard for both East Indians and India Indians, then, not to disavow chutney-soca as derivative or hybrid, but to grant it the name "Indian," for this gesture would inscribe the continuity and discontinuity of such an identity (making it "Indian" and "Trinidadian" at the same time). In clearing a space for an insistent new visibility, the female chutney-soca performer represents an "Indian modernity" in Trinidad that could profoundly challenge the dominant formations of modernity in postcolonial locations.

TWO

★ "Left to the Imagination":
Indian Nationalism and
Female Sexuality

> This business about the women is the weakest and the irremediable part of the evil.... These women are not necessarily wives. Men and women are huddled together during the voyage. The marriage is a farce. A mere declaration by man or woman made upon landing before the Protector of Immigrants that they are husband and wife constitutes a valid marriage. Naturally enough, divorce is common. The rest must be left to the imagination of the reader.
> —Mohandas Karamchand Gandhi, "Indentured Labour"

The aim of this chapter and the next one is to investigate a conjuncture of modernity—"Indianness" and woman that is radically different from the one in India—in the hope that it will defamiliarize that formation as well as throw some new light on the elements that led to its consolidation. This chapter attempts to alter the lens, in both scholarly and popular idioms, through which we have been accustomed to viewing or framing the emergence of that discursive subject, the modern Indian woman. In analyzing the formation of "woman" in India, we often use, almost as if by default, the implicit comparisons with Western or metropolitan situations. I want to ask whether our frameworks might look different when the points of reference include other, nonmetropolitan contexts—in particular, those that are historically imbricated with our own even if in ways that are obscured by later developments.

My investigation proceeds through an analysis of the early-twentieth-century campaign against indentureship in the tropical colonies by nationalists in India. I follow this, in chapter 3, with an investigation of a contemporary controversy around East Indian women and popular music in Trinidad. I have chosen these moments for their foregrounding of the question of female sexuality, an issue that increasingly is being seen as central to the formation of gendered citizenship and to dominant narratives of modernity and nationhood. Historically, the moments are also those of "Indian" political assertion as well as of the availability of new possibilities for "Indian" women. I use the quotation marks for the term "Indian" to signal its double use here: marking in my first "moment," a (future) nationality in South Asia, and in my second, an "ethnic" category in the Caribbean. Much of the writing in the media tends to blur the difference between the two usages, a blurring that could well serve to make Indo-Trinidadians invisible in India as well as in Trinidad, marking them simultaneously as "not Indian enough" in the first location and as "not Trinidadian enough" in the second.

The otherness of the Indian—or, sometimes, "Eastern"—female body is a common enough trope in Orientalisms of various kinds that have been the focus of much postcolonial feminist theoretical intervention in recent years. A more central preoccupation in the women's movement in India in the past decade or two has been to understand the gendered nature of our (non-Western) modernity and its specific concerns with maintaining Indianness or cultural authenticity in the midst of social transformation. Attention has been drawn to the reformulation of patriarchal authority at different moments in the history of anti-imperialist struggle and to the recomposition of "Indian women" through the contests between colonizer and colonized. This process is commonly envisaged as part of an Indian history that unfolds in India. My task will be to show that the constitutive outside of what we in India see today as normative femininity are figures such as the indentured female laborer who was part of the subaltern Indian migration to the Caribbean.[1]

The formation of the Indian National Congress in 1885 signaled the beginning of a new phase of organization in the movement against British rule in India. Accommodating a wide spectrum of ideological strands and reconciling a host of conflicting interests, the congress was able, in the space of the next few decades, to provide focus and direction to the anticolonial struggle, culminating in the final hand over of political power in 1947. Among the many successful initiatives of the nationalists was the early-twentieth-century campaign against indentureship, which contributed in significant measure to building up a moral case against colonialism. However, in the late nineteenth century, indenture did not yet figure as a significant anticolonial issue. On the contrary, as B. R. Nanda points out, in 1893 the leading nationalist M. G. Ranade actually wrote an article titled "Indian Foreign Emigration," in which he argued that emigration provided some "relief" to the growing population of India and that the expansion of the British Empire could be seen as a "direct gain" to the masses of this country.[2] Eventually, however, due in significant measure to the efforts of an Indian involved in agitations in South Africa, Mohandas Karamchand Gandhi, a figure who was to rise to great prominence in the nationalist struggle, indentured emigration became an important issue for Indian nationalism.[3]

Born in India and educated as a barrister in England, Gandhi had gone to South Africa in 1893 to work as a lawyer for a prominent Indian business family and ended up staying there for nearly twenty-one years.[4] Although the early agitations initiated by Gandhi did not involve indentured workers in Natal, many of them came to participate in Gandhi's passive-resistance (satyagraha) campaign against the various legal disabilities imposed on Indians in South Africa. Closer interaction with the indentured increased Gandhi's awareness of their specific problems, which he tried to bring to the attention of nationalists in India.

The satyagraha, stretching from 1906 to 1914, was for Gandhi a direct ancestor of the anti-indenture agitation. When Gandhi began the satyagraha campaign in South Africa, the Imperial Indian Citizenship Association, a group which expressed explicit concern for Indian immigrants, was founded in Bombay.

From the 1890s on, Gandhi attempted to enlist the help of the Indian

National Congress leaders. Gopal Krishna Gokhale in particular supported his endeavors. In 1894, Gandhi drafted the first petition protesting against the indenture system. After constitutional reforms in 1909, a Legislative Council with Indian members was formed in India and was dominated by the Indian National Congress. As a member of the Legislative Council, Gokhale in 1910 moved a successful resolution to stop the recruitment of indentured labor for Natal. In spite of his failing health, Gokhale not only visited South Africa on Gandhi's invitation but also aroused public opinion in India. "Eventually all India was deeply stirred, and the South African question became the burning topic of the day."[5] The focus of Gandhi and his European Indophile colleagues (C. F. Andrews, William Pearson, Henry Polak) was hardship among the indentured in Fiji and South Africa, and while Indian indentured laborers in the West Indies seldom got special mention in this narrative, it was usually assumed that they were included in the criticism of the British Empire's government-controlled labor migrations.

Indentured Women in the West Indies

The nationalist description of the situation of indentured women drew from missionary accounts, government of India and colonial administrators' reports, and firsthand accounts of sympathetic Europeans such as Andrews, who wrote about Fiji. The central concern of all these writers seemed to be the "immorality" caused by the disparate sex ratio of the immigrant laborers. There was also more than a suggestion that the inconstancy of Indian women could be traced to the social composition of the female migrants.

Women evangelicals of the Canadian Presbyterian Church, which began proselytizing among the Indians in Trinidad in 1868, interacted closely with the indentured women and recorded their impressions of what they saw as barbaric "Indian customs" and the reprehensible behavior of the women in particular:

> There are no zenanas [women's quarters] in Trinidad. Our women immigrants are not recruited from the class that in India are shut up in zenanas. In Trinidad they find themselves of added importance through the small proportion of their sex. They have great freedom of intercourse and much evil example around them. Sad to say they often shew themselves to be as degraded as they are ignorant. On the other hand many are beautiful and

lovable, faithful to their husbands and devoted to their children. This, however, is by no means the rule.[6]

While the planters did not want a permanent community of laborers at first, preferring young male workers who would return to India at the end of their indenture period and make way for a new batch, colonial officials recommended that a certain proportion of women to men be maintained to avoid what they saw as social complications. For a variety of reasons, however, recruiters were often unable to obtain a sufficient number of women.

Rhoda Reddock addresses the implications of this problem in her important early work on women under indentureship. Modern historians, according to Reddock, do not pay sufficient attention to the disparate sex ratio, although it was a crucial point of contention during the entire period of indenture. In 1884, Act 21 of the government of India authorized the resumption of emigration to the West Indies after a long break, laying down as one of its conditions that at least 12 percent of the emigrants should be female—a legal proportion, says Reddock, that was rarely enforced. She points to how, in a period of twenty-two years between 1857 and 1879, the recommended ratio of women to men changed about six times, "ranging from one woman to every three men in 1857 to one to two in 1868 and one to four in 1878–79." Reddock is of the view that these changes in the proportion of men to women reflect the contradictions in recruiting "the right kind of women." She concurs with other historians that as early as 1851 there was a recognition of the need for women as a "stabilizing factor" on the male laborers, and that by the late nineteenth century, planters were convinced that they needed a stable workforce that would not return to India and were therefore willing to create the conditions for the reproduction of Indian families in Trinidad. This need for domestic units coincided, as we shall see, with the Presbyterian initiatives regarding education for Indian women and the range of housewifely skills they were expected to acquire. Among the efforts to increase the number of female emigrants was the 1890s reduction of the indenture period for women from five years to three and the promise to recruiting agents of an increased commission for women, sometimes 40 percent higher than that for men. Emigrants were also encouraged to take female children, preferably between age ten and fourteen.[7]

As historian K. O. Laurence suggests, one of the reasons for the lack of women was that few wives emigrated, since their husbands preferred leaving them behind in the protection of their joint family to taking them to a strange country, especially since the indenture period was presumed to be a short one.[8] The government of India tried to set the proportion of women to men at 50:100, but that was opposed on various counts, including the argument that it would, according to a former emigration commissioner, result in recruiting "bad women" who would "do more harm than good."[9] The concern about immorality arising because of the small number of women seemed to go hand in hand with the idea that these women were innately depraved to begin with and that the real solution was to obtain enough virtuous wives to offset the other kinds of women, who seemed most likely to want to emigrate.

If we look at the number of married women among the female emigrants, it becomes obvious that they were often a minority. Here are some random figures for Indian female immigrants registered as married on arrival in Trinidad from 1882 to 1900, taken from G. I. M. Tikasingh's tables from the General Registers of Immigrants and the Register of Indian Marriage. In 1882, the total number of female immigrants was 662, among whom 133, or about 20 percent, were married. In 1890, of 713 female immigrants, 291 (40.8 percent) were married. In 1891, of 1,091 female immigrants, 470 (43 percent, the highest figure in the period under consideration) were married. And in 1898, of 371 female immigrants, 59 (15.9 percent, the lowest figure) were married.[10] In 1900, at the beginning of the new century, of 188 female immigrants, 46 (24.4 percent) were married. The rest of the women, from 57 percent (in 1891) to nearly 84 percent (in 1898) were single, being unmarried, widowed, or deserted. Family legends are often invoked in present-day Trinidad to trace the history of foremothers. A woman now in her seventies who was born in Trinidad told me that her parents had migrated from India. Her father was a young Muslim who spent his time doing "kusti" (wrestling). One day he went to a dance and was waylaid by recruiters who treated him to *channa* (chickpeas) and lured him to migrate. "Dey fool dem from Indya and bring dem to Trinidad," she said. Her mother was Hindu, of the Chattri caste. She had lost her husband and was being taken to have her head shorn—to "cut hair and break bracelet," as befitted an upper-caste widow—when a recruiter got her to go away to Trinidad. She felt that her parents would never accept her if she went back and decided to stay on in Trinidad, even though her second husband was keen to return. She also converted to Islam. "All o' dem come dung on de same wite man estate, and so she met my fader," the woman said.[11] Another woman, a young telecommunications worker, claimed that she was "a descendant of the Mughals. . . .

Indentured Indian woman. Collection of Eric Scott Henderson.

[S]ome of those who came to Trinidad were stolen or some of them were sold by their own relatives and my great grandmother, she was a Mughal princess and she eleven years old and she was being transported back from her home to her husband's house. Her brother-in-law was taking her and she had all her jewels on and everything and she was going and he took her and sold her. She got away and she was captured and sold again and when she came to Trinidad, she didn't know how to work."[12]

    The planters demanded not only more women but the "right kind of women," who would be not only productive laborers on the estates but also faithful wives to the male workers. In response to these demands, the recruiters pointed out that a better class of women could not be induced to emigrate and that, in any case, they would be no good as field laborers. As an emigration agent in Calcutta put it in 1915: "In considering this matter it must be borne in mind that genuine field labourers such as the planters require can be obtained only from among the lowest castes, i.e. from among the non-moral class of the population. A more moral type is found higher in the social scale, but such women would be useless in the fields."[13] Recruiters also warned that if more women were demanded, they would be sending "non-effective" ones or "objectionable characters."[14] As Basdeo Mangru points out in the case of British Guiana, Trinidad's neighbor, "Criticisms regarding the type of women imported had not been wanting. Immigration officials and others often referred to their 'loose and depraved character' and condemned the Emigration Agents for shipping 'the sweepings of the Bazaars' of Calcutta and other large Indian cities."[15]

Evidence from another destination of indentured emigrants, the Dutch colony of Surinam, suggests the diversity of occupations of the women who decided to migrate. An emigration agent for Surinam wrote in 1877–78 about the recruits gathered in the depot prior to departure: "Their number was considerably augmented by a batch of dancing girls and women of similar description with their male attendants. These people laughed at the idea of labouring as agriculturalists." Other descriptions of female migrants to the same colony indicate close similarities with the British West Indies. The protector of emigrants, writing in 1880, says, "The class of women willing to emigrate consists principally of young widows and married or single women who have already gone astray and are therefore not only most anxious to avoid their homes and to conceal their antecedents, but are also at the same time unlikely to be received back into their families."[16] James McNeill and Chimman Lal, authors of a 1915 report on the situation of the indentured, state that the female migrants "consist as to one-third of married women . . . the remainder being mostly widows and women who have run away from their husbands or been put away by them." They go on to say that a small number of the women were "ordinary prostitutes." Given this general profile, it was difficult for the commissioners to "elicit from the women themselves a full and frank account of their antecedents."[17]

Oral histories of early-twentieth-century Trinidad provide the story of Maharani, a young Brahmin widow who ran away to Trinidad, fearing ill treatment in her in-laws' house:

Maharani
I married
    me husband dead.
. . .

Indentured woman (1890s). Collection of Eric Scott Henderson.

> Milk boiling
> > dem go want de milk to eat
> an ah cat coming to drink
> > an ah hit im an de milk fall down
> I say dem go beat me
> > because I getting too much lix [beatings]
> I say dem go beat me
> > well I run
> I no tell nobody I leaving
> > only me modder-in-law.[18]

Given the disparity between wages for male and female laborers, young women like Maharani often found it difficult to manage on the small amounts that they earned. To avert indebtedness to grocers and traders, the agent-general ordered in 1879 that rations be given to all first-year immigrants, to be deducted from their wages. (On some estates, the rations were given free of charge.) However, as Judith Weller points out, "The immigrants, especially women, frequently embarked on the second year of their apprenticeship saddled with a considerable debt for the first year's rations. The newly-arrived immigrant was the 'fag' and given the hardest work to perform."[19] There were skilled "men's" tasks (millwork, forking, truck loading) and less-skilled "women's" tasks (such as weeding, manuring, supplying, and cane cutting, which were also the lowest-paid tasks). Even when women did heavy men's tasks like truck loading, they were paid the same as other women. In 1870 and 1875, a fixed minimum wage was set for men at 25 cents; for women, it was always less.[20] Low wages drove women to increased dependence on male partners, although they sometimes were able to negotiate the terms of such dependence.

Maharani, the Brahmin widow, for example, did not particularly want a partner but was pressed to acquire one:

> An e carry me go
>   e carry me he room
> I no want nobody
>   I say
> I stop alone
>   but she fadder say
> I like you
>   but I say
> me nuh like you
> [but he takes her all the same].[21]

Missionary Travails

The Canadian Presbyterian missionaries who came to Trinidad to work with the indentured Indian laborers were the first to build schools for them.[22] Access to Western-style education was accompanied by exposure to Christianity, to which the missionaries often found the Indians quite resistant. A Girls' Training Home was established in 1890 "for the protection and training of Indian girls." Christian girls age twelve and older were admitted to the home to be instructed so that they would become good wives for "our helpers" (Christian teachers). At the home, apart from Hindi, English, arithmetic, and Bible classes, the girls were taught "washing, ironing, starching, scrubbing, gardening, sewing, and all the housewifely arts."[23] While some of them turned out to be apt pupils, other Indian women presented a puzzle to the Presbyterians, as the following extracts from the Mortons' (the missionary couple among the first Canadian Presbyterians to come to Trinidad) writings[24] show:

> The women, as a rule, are quite as wicked as the men and more ignorant and prejudiced; thus their influence for good or evil is very great.

Soobhie knocked at Juraman's (two Indian converts) door and was taken in. Both had become Christians. Subsequently, in March 1878, she wanted to leave him and live with another man on the estate. Despite the intervention of the Mortons and others, Soobhie finally went to live with the other man:

> She must be crazy as well as wicked. Some of these Indian women are hard to understand and I fear are not much good when you do understand them. But then it is the result of long ages of ignorance, mistrust, and degradation. And we cannot hope to raise them in a day. . . .

> July 1878 — Soobhie wishes now to come back to Juraman, but he will have nothing to say to her. [She never returned to her husband.]

The following extracts, most likely dating from 1893, indicate the difficulties the Mortons had to deal with:

> S. E. M. — The loose notions and prevailing practices in respect of marriage here are quite shocking to a new-comer. I said to an East Indian woman whom I knew to be the widow of a Brahman, "You have no relations in Trinidad, I believe." "No, Madame," she replied, "only myself and two children; when the last [immigrant] ship came in I took a papa. I will keep him as long as he treats me well. If he does not treat me well I shall send him off at once; that's the right way, is it not?" This will be to some a new view of women's rights.

> S. E. M. — . . . A group of women newly returned from field work salute me thus: "Your disciple is going to church now." There is a spice of malice in this, for the woman indicated [as a disciple was not baptized with us and] has left her married husband for another. I answered, "That will do her no good unless she change her living." "What can she do?" says one, "This husband takes better care of her than the other one did."

S. E. M.—A few weeks ago a poor little girl was deliberately stabbed through the heart by her would-be husband; he said he had paid $200 to get her, and since she would not live with him no one else should have her. [These are extreme cases, but it will be understood that there was great need for improvement in the conditions of home life among the people.] A woman who had left her husband because he had taken another wife, said to me in the calmest possible way, "You know, it would not be pleasant for two of us in one house." "And where are you now?" Unhesitatingly she mentioned the name of her newly-adopted husband. "And where is your boy?" (Quite cheerfully) "With his father." But enough; or you will be thinking Trinidad the hell the East Indians sometimes call it.

It should be added that in some Indian nationalities women are treated with much greater consideration than by others, and that in more than one Sanskrit drama, read and sung every day by the priests among the people, and reverenced by all Hindoos, beautiful and touching love stories are related with pictures of unspotted purity and supreme devotion in married life.

And from a report from 1891:

S. E. M.—In connection with our Bible class I have read and explained each day to the girls, in Hindi, a lesson from the Zenana Reader, used by lady missionaries in India, each chapter containing a separate lesson on some subject suitable for wives and house-keepers. . . . Nothing but the power of the Word could ever have subdued the evil passions that made the experience of the first few months the most soul-trying we have ever gone through.

A new girl of about seventeen, who had studied in a mission school in Calcutta and could read Hindi and Farsi, came to the home. She was married off to a teacher and taught sewing in the Presbyterian school in Arouca. Once, in a rage, she took a broomstick to her husband:

That broom-stick, however, was a grave source of dissatisfaction around; it was feared that other wives might hear of it and do the same.
Sad to say Rachel left her husband permanently; he was proved to have been unkind to her. We last heard of her in Venezuela.

About the difficulty of training Bible women:

> It must . . . be remembered that, with few exceptions, Indian girls are married at a very early age . . . and also that moral conditions in Trinidad render it altogether inadvisable, if not unsafe, for young women to visit from house to house, nor are the husbands willing.

About a teacher who was Christian but disregarded the clergy and "took unto himself a wife and a heathen to boot":

> With a sad heart I had to dismiss him. In three months' time she had become another man's wife. After due repentance and full confession of his wrong-doing he was taken back into the school.

Marriage and Morals

The rapidity with which Indian women formed new relationships in Trinidad was a matter for comment by contemporary writers as well as later historians. Late-nineteenth-century visitors to the West Indies like Charles Kingsley tended to see women's behavior as stemming from practices like child marriage, which Kingsley called "a very serious evil" but attributed to customs brought from India:

> The girls are practically sold by their fathers while yet children, often to wealthy men much older than they. Love is out of the question. But what if the poor child, as she grows up, sees some one, among that overplus of men, to whom she, for the first time in her life, takes a fancy? Then comes a scandal; and one which is often ended swiftly enough by the cutlass.[25]

Kingsley talked of child brides, although many of the examples in the missionary writings are those of older women who seem to have constructed for themselves spaces of negotiation to offset their lack of privilege in the wage system of the plantation.

As Tikasingh remarks, the most common type of union was the "keeper union, . . . whose stability depended primarily upon the satisfaction of the female partner." He cites the legal case of a woman named Mungaree, who had an arrangement with a man named Namoomarlala on Orange Field Estate. Namoomarlala had given Mungaree one hundred fifty dollars in clothes and silver, and she had lived with him for eight years. She then went to live with another man, Nageeroo, "with the understanding that she could return to her former keeper at any time." Subsequently, at the time of the court case mentioned here, she was living with yet another man, a shopkeeper. "As soon as females were ill-treated by their 'papa,' . . . they were quite ready to break the existing union and form another."[26]

Speaking about British Guiana, Mangru points out that the "paucity of women made polyandry almost an acknowledged system. Very often an Indian woman was found to have two husbands and to be unfaithful to both."[27] That these kinds of relationships were also common in Trinidad is borne out by the experiences of Sarah Morton and other missionaries. Mangru cites official correspondence that expressed concern about the "loose domestic relations" among the indentured laborers: "It is not uncommon for a woman of this class to leave the man with whom she has cohabited for another, and then for a third, perhaps for a fourth, and sometimes to return to one of those she had previously deserted; and this she does in most cases with impunity."[28] Citing the work of B. L. Moore, K. O. Laurence gives the 1887 example of a woman at Bush Lot, British Guiana, who was "married with Hindu rites to three different men in a single year." He also points out that "in Guiana polyandry with two or three, sometimes even four men became fairly common. Similar situations were also known in Trinidad, though probably not widespread. Keeper unions however were very common there."[29] Evidence from Fiji and South Africa, other destinations for indentured laborers, indicates that there, too, women entered into the sorts of relationships described by commentators on the Caribbean.[30]

The Anti-Slavery Society in England proposed banning the recruitment of single women to avoid what it saw as inevitable immorality, but it was pointed out that, to circumvent this rule, recruits would pretend to be married to each other at the time of emigration. In any case, some opponents of indentureship believed, as Gandhi did, that marriages between recruits were often fictitious. The point is not whether the marriages were false or real, or whether single women were entirely responsible for "immoral relations," but why critics and commentators chose these as the causes of a situation clearly related to the displacement of men and women into a diasporic condition. In the diaspora, new opportunities would have presented themselves to married people as well as unmarried ones. Colonial officials, however, persisted in seeing the "notoriously lax morals" of the indentured as due to the significant proportion of "sexually permissive women" on the estates, where they claimed the general "level of sexual morality" was lower than in a typical Indian village.[31]

Wife Murders

The prevalence of "wife murders" by indentured Indians in Trinidad and British Guiana in the nineteenth century was represented as due to the inconstancy of the women. David V. Trotman presents the following factual information: Between 1872 and 1880, 27 percent of all murders in Trinidad were committed by East Indian immigrants; subsequently, East Indians accounted for 60 percent of the murders between 1881 and 1889 and 70 percent between 1890 and 1898. Tikasingh gives figures between 1872 and 1900 of 87 murders of Indian women, of which 65 (74.7 percent) were murders of wives.[32] The majority of the murderers were men, and those killed were women who were wives, concubines, or fiancées. Although there are quite a few court cases involving men who had killed their child brides whose fathers had promised them to several men for a hefty bride price each time, many of the cases were against men who had murdered their wives for having taken up with another man. It was also not uncommon for Indian women to form relationships with overseers and white estate managers, as depicted, for example, in A. R. F. Webber's 1917 novel *Those That Be in Bondage*.[33] Trotman contends that the women received very little sympathy, in spite of their difficulty in resisting the advances of their employers, most officials choosing to blame "the very loose character of the majority of coolie women, and the temptations to which men in the positions of managers and overseers are subjected."[34]

"Wife murders," D. W. D. Comins wrote in 1891, "form the foulest blot on our whole immigration system."[35] A variety of explanations was offered for this phenomenon, ranging from the cultural (wife murder as proof of the moral depravity of heathens as resulting from "Asiatic idiosyncrasies" or from the "constitutional jealousy of Orientals") to the materialistic (Indian men outraged at having the woman they had paid for become the wife of another man), the psychological (envy, jealousy, rage, and revenge), and the demographic (the disparity between the numbers of men and women). Whatever they saw as the causes of wife murder, the only possible remedy for the problem, according to some colonial officials, was the introduction of larger numbers of women.[36]

Other colonial officials, however, refused to accept the idea that the shortage of female recruits was at the root of the trouble, suggesting that "it was a question of quality rather than numbers: that the women were of such 'low class' that the men regarded them as chattels and treated them as such. Much was ascribed to 'Asiatic ideas' of the low value of female life."[37] Prison authorities in Trinidad were of the view that, "so long as there shall be in the Colony a large body of Asiatics who live as a race distinct from the rest of the labouring classes, keeping their own style of dress and observing their own peculiar traditions, it is useless to expect that the mere risk of death upon the scaffold will prevent their holding in Trinidad the same views with regard to their womankind that exist in the country from which they come."[38]

Kingsley seems to concur: "Wife-murder is but too common among these Hindoos, and they cannot be made to see that it is wrong. 'I kill my own wife. Why not? I kill no other man's wife,' was said by as pretty, gentle, graceful a lad of two-and-twenty as one need see. . . . There is murder of wives, or quasi-wives now and then, among the baser sort of Coolies — murder because a poor girl will not give her ill-earned gains to the ruffian who considers her his property."[39] There is an additional hint here, perhaps, that the woman's "ill-earned gains" may be money obtained from a man other than her husband.

Oral histories confirm the prevalence of wife murder, as in Fazal's testimony in *The Still Cry*:

> If e run way nex man daughter
>   e go beat e arse too
> if you have to run way wid man wife
>   leave one time
> dat man go kill e wife
>   kill two a dem.[40]

Much of the information about the nature of the relationships that led to wife murder comes from anecdotal sources. It is not easy to obtain statistical data about wife murder, since, as Judith Weller suggests, the crime was often recorded as murder only when a conviction was obtained, and very often there was not enough evidence to convict the murderer.[41] It is perfectly possible to imagine, then, that the incidence of wife murder was even higher than the records indicate. Early punishments for those caught enticing women away from their husbands included flogging, shaving, transfer of guilty parties to other estates, fines, and imprisonment, but the penalties did not bring down the number of wife murders.

The eventual solution to the problem was sought in legislation about marriage, not just in punishment on the scaffold. Colonial authorities and the immigrant men seem to have agreed on this score. Take, for example, a petition from Indian immigrants, signed by 274 Indians and witnessed by the Canadian missionaries Reverend Morton, Reverend Grant, and Reverend Christie, seeking enactment of an ordinance for registration of Indian marriages. The purpose of the registration was to enable "any person . . . [to] prosecute an unfaithful spouse and their partner in guilt either in the Magistrates' Court, the Complaint Court or the Supreme Court, according as damages are laid at [ten pounds], at [twenty-five pounds] or upwards, with provision for imprisonment if the damages be not paid, for the imprisonment of the wife if she refused to return to her husband, and also for the continued prosecution of the parties if the offence be persisted in."[42] Interestingly, the petitioners did not demand divorce but "the preservation of their households." Ordinance 6 of 1881 was passed to make the necessary provisions for the marriage and divorce of Indian immigrants. This applied only to Hindus and Muslims among the immigrants, since Christians were already covered by the existing laws of the colony.[43] Tikasingh, however, speaks of the problems connected with registration under the Immigrants' Marriage and Divorce Ordinance 6 (1881) and Ordinance 23 (1891), suggesting that part of the difficulty lay in the framing of the ordinances. "For example, the marriage ordinance of 1881 was really concerned mainly with the prevention of wife-murders rather than with the recognition of Indian marriages." He goes on to say that "the act of registration itself was subject to numerous difficulties such as the age of the bride, *the lack of accurate information concerning the former marital status of either party*, and the refusal or neglect of either party to apply for registration of the marriage."[44]

Other kinds of solutions were also sought. In 1879, for instance, William Young, acting governor of Trinidad, demanded measures to improve the "moral status of the Coolie woman." Only by recognizing their traits of character, among which he included thrift and industry, and initiating measures to develop them, Young contended, could "civilization and morality" be substantially improved among the Indian population. He maintained that the Indian woman was not strong enough for strenuous plantation labor but could exert a "civilizing and humanizing influence" if she devoted herself to domestic duties.[45] This impulse coincided with that of the Canadian missionaries who started the first schools for Indians in 1869. The schools had distinctly different curricula for boys and girls. The schools for girls focused primarily on the production of housewives.[46] Just a couple of years before Young's statement, the planters had passed a resolution asking for the indenture-free importation of Indian widows and "betrothed women" who had lost their intended husbands. This proposal had been suggested by the emigration agent in Calcutta, who commended the "pure and blameless lives" of these women; other colonial officials agreed that bringing in a higher class of women would ameliorate the cause of the problem of wife murder: the immorality of immigrant women. This new scheme of emigration did not find support among recruiters in India and eventually had to be dropped.[47]

The shameless Indian woman was being increasingly represented as a matter of grave concern not just to colonial officials but also to Indian men, as can be seen in a letter written by Mohammed Orfy, the author of numerous letters to the secretary of state for the colonies, the Indian government, and other authorities "on behalf of destitute Indian men of Trinidad": "Another most disgraceful concern, which is most prevalent, and a perforating plague, is the high percentage of immoral lives led by the female section of our community. They are enticed, seduced and frightened into becoming concubines, and paramours to satisfy the greed and lust of the male section of quite a different race to theirs." Having mentioned the women's susceptibility to seduction, Orfy goes on to say that "they have absolutely no knowledge whatever of the value of being in virginhood and become most shameless and a perfect menace to the Indian gentry."[48]

Between Sarah Morton's comment about the Brahmin widow who took a new "papa" and the reasoning of educated East Indian men as exemplified by Orfy, the difference might not be that the first stresses the wilfulness of the Indian woman and that the second is inclined to emphasize her susceptibility to "enticement," as did the colonial authorities who framed the marriage laws. Both Orfy and the colonial authorities were in agreement on the lax morals of the female Indian immigrant. We could see the emerging East Indian middle class in Trinidad and the colonial rulers as complicit in the reconstitution of patriarchal structures that had become visible by the early twentieth century.[49] However, it might not be accurate to assert, as Reddock appears to do, that "Indian tradition" simply comes to the fore once indentureship ends.

I will now briefly examine two approaches to the culture of Indians in Trinidad. The pioneering work of Morton Klass, discussed in chapter 1, typifies one approach, in which classical anthropological paradigms prevail and indenture is seen as a temporary disruption in well-established patterns of living. The emphasis here is on cultural persistence and survival, since culture is framed as that which continues through time and includes characteristics of people—for example, the supposed docility and submissiveness of Indian women (a prevalent stereotype even today among Afro-Trinidadians and other Creoles). The work of Rhoda Reddock typifies the second approach, which employs a consciously historical paradigm and, in her case, provides a nuanced understanding of women's lives under indenture. The emphasis, however, is on the twentieth-century reconstitution of the Hindu and "Indian" family, with all its patriarchal features, including prescriptions for women. The suggestion here is that "tradition" won out in the end and was able to subjugate women, so that their options today are not much different from those of women in India who have not shared their history. The stories about immoral Indian women result, in Reddock's analysis, in the construction of a new patriarchy and to the closure of the question of women's agency, or "freedom denied." The implicit argument here concerns East Indian women in the present and Reddock's perception that, like women in India, they do not live lives that are "free."

It is interesting to note how historians and anthropologists are able to document changes in areas such as caste, religion, and customs but seem to insist that with regard to women there were no changes at all, or that if they did occur, they were eventually reversed. Commonly, they make a series of culturalist assumptions, where "Indians" no matter where they are continue to manifest certain behavior patterns. Against both these approaches, I argue that the displacement caused by indenture brought about irreversible transformations. The discursive deployment of the East Indian woman in the realm of popular music that I discuss in chapters 3 and 4, for example, is an indicator of some of these changes.

Abolishing Indenture

In 1896, Gandhi, who was still living in South Africa, met with Gokhale to try to interest him in the cause of overseas Indians. In 1901, Gandhi again spent time with Gokhale, who was to become one of his earliest admirers and supporters in India. On Gandhi's urging, in February 1910 Gokhale piloted a resolution through the Imperial Legislative Council, of which he was a member, calling for a complete ban on the recruitment of indentured labor. In 1911, a ban was imposed on recruitment for Natal, and finally in 1917 it was extended to all overseas colonies, but not before a large-scale campaign had been mounted against indenture by Gandhi and a host of other nationalists.

As historian Hugh Tinker points out, the campaign was in fact Gandhi's first big political intervention in India. He gave anti-indenture speeches all over the country, wrote about the topic at length in newspapers, and was able to get an Anti-Indenture Resolution passed at the Lucknow Congress meeting in December 1916. By 1915, "The indenture issue became the central question of Indian politics."[50] Even as emigration itself declined for a variety of reasons, there was widespread nationalist protest, with meetings organized in Hyderabad, Sind, and Karachi (then in northwestern India); Allahabad (in the central region); Madras (in the south); and parts of Bengal (eastern India).[51] The agitators called for an end to a system that they said was a "moral stigma" for the country. As Reddock reiterates, issues of low wages or poor working conditions were of far lesser importance than "women's moral condition" in the campaign to abolish indentureship.[52] The historical significance of the anti-indenture campaign, Tinker suggests, lies in the fact that "this was the first major Indo-British political and social issue to be decided in dependent India, and not in metropolitan Britain."[53]

An examination of the nationalist discourse on indenture would reveal the crucial place occupied in it by the question of women's sexuality, helping us understand why it was believed to be something unspeakable, and why—paradoxically—it needed to be spoken about so interminably. Given this campaign's centrality to nationalist thought, it would be interesting to see how women were represented in the criticism of indentureship. I will take as my point of departure some aspects of Partha Chatterjee's well-known argument about the nationalist resolution of the women's question. Chatterjee has tried to account for the relative insignificance of the "women's question" in the late nineteenth century by suggesting that nationalism was able to "resolve" the question by this time in accordance with its attempt to make "modernity consistent with the nationalist project."[54]

In constructing a new woman—the middle-class, upper-caste *bhadramahila* (Bengali for bourgeois lady)—nationalism in India was able to produce and enforce distinctions between the material might of the colonizer and the spiritual superiority of the colonized. Chatterjee suggests that the distinctions were embodied in new oppositions between public and private, the "world" (*bhaire*) and the "home" (*ghare*). In the former realm, the Indian man acquired English education and took on the manners and dress of the

British, while in the latter realm the Indian woman took on new markers of ethnicity and new responsibilities for maintaining the sanctity of the home, which was now also seen as a refuge from the world in which the colonizer held sway, a point also made by Sumanta Banerjee in his study of nineteenth-century popular culture and the emergence of the *bhadralok* (the respectable classes).[55] Although both Chatterjee and Banerjee write about the Bengal case, there are enough parallels in relation to women and nationalism in other areas of India directly ruled by the British. The new woman envisaged by nationalism was "modern" but not heedlessly Westernized. Neither was she like the uneducated, vulgar, and coarse lower-caste or lower-class working woman.[56] The lower-caste woman would be a central figure in the labor migrations of the nineteenth century.

The processes of differentiation of the upper-caste woman from the lower-caste woman unfolded in a variety of spheres as the qualities assigned to each were naturalized. A comment in a nineteenth-century *Brahmo Samaj* newspaper opposed a proposal to educate respectable Bengali women so they would become self-reliant, saying, "They did not have to be self-reliant since they were being looked after by their menfolk." The writer then added, "Only among the women of the lower classes in this country, we come across some sort of self-reliance."[57] Banerjee's argument is that throughout the eighteenth century, lower-caste groups in Bengal climbed up in the social hierarchy in the process distancing themselves from their poor or rural kinfolk and becoming a new middle class through their access to English education. "The stratification was ideologically buttressed by the *bhadralok* concept of *itarjan* and *chhotolok*—the pejorative terms used to describe the lower orders and evoke the picture of a lifestyle that was to be scrupulously avoided by the educated and privileged Bengalis."[58]

Among the features of a lifestyle to be avoided by the educated bhadralok was the close interaction between middle-class women and the wandering female artistes from the lower castes who were a source of entertainment and education for those confined to the inner space of the courtyard. There was a concerted attempt by the bhadralok in the late nineteenth century, for example, to eliminate from the *andarmahal*, or women's quarters, the *panchalis*, or folk songs described as "filthy" and "polluting" by missionaries. This description was echoed by Indians, too, like Shib Chunder Bose in a book titled *The Hindoos as They Are*: "The Panchali (with female actresses only) which is given for the amusement of the females . . . is sometimes much too obscene and immoral to be tolerated in a zenana having any pretension to gentility.... Much is yet to be done to develop among the females a taste for purer amusements, better adapted to a healthy state of society."⁵⁹ By the end of the nineteenth century, panchali performance had disappeared. We may speculate whether the deskilling of large numbers of performers led some of them to join the indentured migration to the Caribbean and elsewhere, as shown by the report on the dancing girls and their troupe waiting to embark for Surinam. The historian Kusha Haraksingh remarks that as late as the 1960s, one could hear village women in Trinidad referring to each other jocularly as "*randi.*"⁶⁰ The earlier etymology of this Hindi word can be traced to a variety of courtesan in the precolonial kingdoms, while the later meaning in several Indian languages is "prostitute."

That the making of the bhadramahila involved a new domestication is evident from the effort to dissuade women from attending public recitals of epics, or *kathakata*. It was feared that descriptions of the erotic affairs of the gods, as in the Krishna-leela, for example, would be a bad influence on respectable women. According to a commentator in the Bengali journal *Somprakash* in 1863:

> Since it [kathakata] has become a source of so much evil, it is not advisable for bhadraloks to encourage it. Those who allow their ladies to go to kathakata performances should be careful.... If, during kathakata performances, women stay home and are provided with opportunities to listen to good instructions, discussions on good books and to train themselves in artistic occupations, their religious sense will improve and their souls will become pure and they will be suited to domestic work.⁶¹

The geneaology of the domestic woman has been traced in Indian contexts other than Bengal, as the nationalists attempted to fashion a purified civilizational essence in the face of missionary and colonialist criticism. As Susie Tharu and K. Lalita argue:

> In India... the middle-class woman's propriety was also to be vindicated under the glare of the harsh spotlight focused right through the nineteenth century on what was described as the moral degeneration of the Indians. Bureaucrats, missionaries, journalists and western commentators of various kinds filed sensational reports about Indian culture and made authoritative analyses of Indian character, which was invariably represented as irrational, deceitful and sexually perverse. The ultimate thrust of these decriptions... the situation in India was so appalling that

it called out for intervention by rational and ethical rulers [such as the British].⁶²

Tharu and Lalita wrote this in the context of the controversy about reprinting *Radhika Santwanam* (Appeasing Radhika) by the eighteenth-century Telugu poet Muddupalani, a *ganika* (courtesan) at the royal court of Thanjavur. In 1911, another learned woman in the tradition of Muddupalani, Bangalore Nagaratnamma, reprinted her predecessor's poem, only to be charged with obscenity. The poem that Nagaratnamma appreciated so much described the relationship of Radha and Krishna and the nature of their intimacy, and it was considered a fine literary work in its time. Copies of the book were seized and their sale forbidden. In an earlier edition of the poem published in 1887, Venkatanarasu, a linguist and associate of the lexicographer C. P. Brown, had removed verses regarded as sexually explicit and obscene. Nationalist initiatives led by the upper castes such as the construction of the good Indian woman sometimes found unlikely allies, such as the non-Brahmin Self-Respect Movement, which in the 1920s provided support to the "anti-nautch" campaign, which was also setting up as normative "the virtuous domestic woman."⁶³ The anti-nautch campaign, which reached its peak in 1911, had been initiated by Western-educated reformers in the early 1890s, who wrote about the degradation of women and the "threat posed by *devadasis* [temple and court artists]," who were often derogatorily referred to as "nautch girls," to the purity of family life. The bill prohibiting dedication of women in temples was finally passed in 1947.⁶⁴

Another figure that evolved to complete the picture of virtuous womanhood was that of the upper-caste widow. The historian Tanika Sarkar contends that the Hindu widow emerges as a significant figure in nineteenth-century Bengal because her "purity," chosen consciously, "becomes at once a sign of difference and of superiority, a Hindu claim to power." Women's monogamy, then, makes possible the existence of the Hindu nation.⁶⁵ As Srinibas Basu, a contemporary writer, puts it: "This so-called subjection of our woman produces this sacred jewel of chastity which still glows radiantly throughout the civilised world despite centuries of political subjection."⁶⁶ Sarkar argues that the ascetic widow was seen as gaining moral and spiritual energy through her "voluntary abdication of all earthly pleasures," thus ensuring "a reservoir of spirituality in each home and for the Hindu order as a whole."⁶⁷

Although in the nineteenth century and later various forms of remarriage and cohabitation were prevalent among widows, ascetic widowhood and sometimes *sati* (immolation with the husband's corpse) came to be seen as the norm in nationalist discourse. This would serve to illuminate Sarah Morton's annoyance and bewilderment at the behavior of her prospective Indian converts in late-nineteenth-century Trinidad who seemed so far removed from ascetic upper-caste norms.

The period in which indentured emigration to the other colonies began, the 1830s, is also the period of the initial formation, via the social-reform movements, of nationalist discourse in India. Since for the nationalists official modernity came to be produced through the project of the future nation, there was no room for formations of modernity other than those that involved as its subjects middle-class, upper-caste Indians. The problem with indentured laborers, both men and women, was that their geographical displacement and the new context they came to inhabit was enabling them also to become "modern." The transformations caused in the lives of the indentured by displacement, the plantation system, the disparate sex ratio, racial politics, and so on had to be made invisible by nationalist discourse so that the indentured could be claimed as authentically Indian. This was accomplished, I suggest, by erasing the difference between the agricultural laborer in Bihar and the one in Trinidad ("Chinitat," as the indentured called it) or in other parts of the subaltern diaspora and imaging the agricultural laborer in Trinidad in particular as victimized, pathetic, lost, and helpless. Even when the changes in the emigrant were acknowledged, they were criticized as "artificial" and "superficial," loss rather than gain. Gandhi writes that the laborer came back to India "a broken vessel," robbed of "national self-respect."[68] Any "economic gain" he might have obtained could not be set off "against the moral degradation it involves."[69]

The indentured woman in particular could not be accommodated in the nationalist discourse, except as a victim of colonialism. By 1910 or so, when the campaign against indenture was gathering momentum, nationalism had already produced the models of domesticity, motherhood, and companionate marriage that would make the Indian woman a citizen of the new India. The question of what constituted the modernity of the Indian woman had been put forward as an *Indian* question, to be resolved *in India*. What, then, of the Indian women who were "becoming modern," but elsewhere? For nationalism, their modernity would have to be considered an illegitimate modernity because it had not passed through, been formed by, the story of the nation in the making. By the late nineteenth century, the route to modernity—and emancipation—for the Indian woman in India was a well-established one: education, cultivation of household arts, refinement of skills, regulation of one's emotions. The class-caste provenance of this project, and of the new woman, should require no further reiteration here.

What sort of ideological project, then, did nationalism envisage for the indentured female laborer who was shaping her own relationship with the "West" in a distant land? Reform was not practicable. Disavowal of this figure would not have been possible while the system of indenture still existed. The only solution, therefore, was to strive for the abolition of indenture. The manifest immorality and depravity of the indentured woman would not only bring down the system but also serve to reveal more clearly the contrasting image of the virtuous and chaste Indian woman at home. As Gandhi asserted, "Women, who in India would never touch wine, are sometimes found lying dead-drunk on the roads."[70] The point is not that women never drank in India and started doing so in Trinidad or British Guiana. It is that, for Gandhi and others, this functioned as a mark of degraded Westernization and "artificial modernity." The nationalist reconstitution of Indian tradition, I suggest, was a project that was still incomplete when the new phase of the nationalist struggle, marked by the anti-indenture campaign, was inaugurated.

Although, according to Chatterjee, the nationalists had "resolved" the women's question without making it a matter for political agitation, with the anti-indenture campaign there seems to have been a refocusing on women. At the end of the first decade of the twentieth century, a political campaign was undertaken—mobilizing "a wider public than any previous protest"[71] against the colonial rulers—to dismantle a system that was said to be turning Indian women into prostitutes.[72] As Gandhi wrote, "The system brings India's womanhood to utter ruin, destroys all sense of modesty. That in defence of which millions in this country have laid down their lives in the past is lost under it."[73] The nationalist discourse on indentured women's sexuality, however, veered time and again from denouncing the women as reprobate and immoral to seeing them as having been brought to this state by colonialism.[74] The Indian nationalists were joined by the European critics of indenture, led by C. F. Andrews, Gandhi's associate, who had worked with Gandhi in South Africa and had been mobilized by him to prepare a report on Indians in Fiji. As the anthropologist John Kelly puts it, Andrews and others "portrayed indenture . . . as a degenerating force and blamed it for the moral condition of the 'helots of Empire.' But they accepted the claim that the 'coolies' were degraded, and they agreed especially about what we might call the 'harlots of Empire.'"[75] Gandhi's focus on the alleged sexual availability of women can also be read as a strategic move to counter the colonial administrative reports, which, as Susan Bayly puts it, defined "the dependent status of unclean menial groups . . . in terms of the sexual availability of their womenfolk."[76] In this case, by ending indenture and providing the conditions for chastity, women would cease to be available, for instance, to their white employers in the colonies. Thus, nationalism could refuse menial status for Indians versus the colonizer.

The nationalist campaign to end indenture was supported by a series of developments in Trinidad. By 1870, voices were being raised in the Creole press against importing Indian laborers. There was public criticism of the size of the subsidy for immigration, especially by cocoa interests (who used free labor, as opposed to the sugarcane planters, who used indentured) and the professional middle class. The Creole middle class also sought to diminish the influence of the planters during the campaign for constitutional reform in the mid-1880s. Creoles who feared the influx of Indians into the political system they hoped to capture found new reasons to attack the system of immigration.[77] After the Hosay riots of 1884, when Muharram processionists in Trinidad were killed by the colonial police, the interest of the Indian press in the conditions of indenture began to grow. The Anti-Slavery Society in England, which had long criticized indenture, renewed its attacks after the 1884 riots.[78]

On March 4, 1912, after immigration to Natal and some other countries had been stopped, Gokhale moved in the Legislative Council that indentured emigration be wholly prohibited. He spoke eloquently of the misery of the immigrants, of the "immorality" resulting from the disparate sex ratio, and of the blow to national self-respect. The agitation to end indenture was fueled by the publication of reports from Fiji. An Anti-Indentured Emigration League was formed in 1914. "Centred in Calcutta, it organized public lectures and the distribution of pamphlet against emigration and tried to discourage recruits on their way to Calcutta from continuing their journey. Soon it also began to operate in the United Provinces."[79] Leaflets were distributed in towns and villages; recruiters were molested; and relatives were brought to Calcutta to secure the release of recruits from the depot.[80]

In 1915, Gokhale died, but Gandhi had returned from South Africa by then to provide leadership to the agitators. On March 20, 1916, Pandit Madan Mohan Malaviya's motion was discussed in the Legislative Council. He listed all of the evils of the immigration system, drawing extensively on the situation in Fiji, and spoke of indenture as "a horrifying record of shame and crime," demanding that "the system . . . be abolished root and branch."[81] In February 1917, Malaviya sought permission to introduce a bill for immediate abolition, which was disallowed. Unable to obtain a clear assurance from the government about ending indenture, Gandhi toured the country and addressed public meetings, demanding that the abolition be announced before the end of July.[82] Large demonstrations were held in Madras and Bombay. The viceroy was "pelted with telegrams," and his wife received many "asking her whether she approves of Indian women being converted into harlots and imploring her to help." Attempts were made to mobilize the opinion of Indian women. An appeal by Andrews to Indian women was printed in several languages and widely distributed in the United Provinces.[83]

As the final phase of the campaign against indenture gained momentum, among the delegations that met Viceroy Charles Hardinge to press for action were several organized by Indian women's associations. At a meeting between representatives of the Colonial Office and the India Office on May 9, 1917, James Meston, representing India in the War Cabinet, spoke about how "the women of India" felt "deeply on the question [of indenture]." Satyendra Sinha, the other India representative, declared that "there was an intensely strong feeling of concern, . . . [which included] ladies who lived in purdah, but read the news."[84] In spite of Englishmen such as Alfred Lyall, governor of the North-West Provinces, and G. A. Grierson, who reported on emigration from Bengal and recommended it for its benefits to women, giving a chance for a new life to "abandoned and unfaithful wives,"[85] Hardinge was not willing to keep supporting a system whose "discussion arouses more bitterness than any other outstanding question." Hardinge was convinced that Indian politicians firmly believed that indentureship "brands their whole race . . . with the stigma of helotry" and condemns Indian women to prostitution.[86]

By mid-1917, the end of indenture was certain. Historians tend to see indenture as an issue that brought a new focus to nationalist politics in India and gave it a wider base. I would argue that it was not simply that. We need to reframe the indenture question so it can be seen as marking the consolidation of the early national-modern; a setting in place of new (nationalist) moralities, new ways of relating between women and men, appropriate "Indian" modes of sociosexual behavior, the parameters for the state's regulation of reproduction as well as sexuality, and the delineation of the virtues that would ensure for Indian women citizenship in the future nation. It should be obvious that the historical formation of these virtues, for example, and the contemporaneity of their description was obscured by the nationalist presentation of them as the essential, and "traditional," qualities of Indian women.

While it is evident that the immigrant woman was an important figure invoked by Indian nationalism in India, the centrality of this figure to "East Indian nationalism" in Trinidad has not yet been systematically elaborated.[87]

With regard to the indentured woman, too, the immediate contrasting image for the colonialist was the African woman, the ex-slave, the urban *jamette* of Carnival whose sexuality was othered, and sought to be regulated, by the European ruling class.[88] The jamette was seen as vulgar, promiscuous, loud, and disruptive, and the removal of this figure from Carnival and related activities became part of the project of creating a new urban middle class in Trinidad. Charles Kingsley, visiting Trinidad in the late nineteenth century, sketched his impressions of African and Indian women: "[The] average negro women of Port of Spain, especially the younger . . . their masculine figures, their ungainly gestures, their loud and sudden laughter, even when walking alone, and their general coarseness, shocks, and must shock." In contrast to the "superabundant animal vigour and the perfect independence of the younger [African] women" is the picture of a young Indian woman "hung all over with bangles, in a white muslin petticoat . . . and green gauze veil; a clever, smiling, delicate little woman, who is quite aware of the brightness of her own eyes."[89]

Much of the elite's anxiety about the jamette, or even about the rural Creole woman, seemed to hinge on the fact of her being seen as independent in both sexual and economic terms. The East Indian woman in postslavery society, then, brought in to compensate colonial planters for the loss of captive labor, had to be imaged as completely different from the African woman. For this, "Indian tradition" was invoked by different groups, and the lack of conformity of indentured women to the virtuous ideal of Indian culture was deplored. In post-indenture society, the need to differentiate between the African and the Indian woman would take on a new kind of urgency, both for the emerging Indo-Trinidadian middle class and for the dominant Creole imaginary. One important mode of differentiation would have to do with denying the obvious similarities between women of all races in Trinidad and emphasizing instead the similarities between indentured women and women in India. However, as I have argued, the indentured woman was a figure that the nationalist construction of Indian womanhood had to disavow precisely to ensure its own coherence. If one set of reasons for the disavowal arose from the non-upper-caste provenance of the indentured woman, another set had to do with her incorporation into Creole modernity. But clearly it was not one set of reasons *rather* than another but the combination of both that placed indentured Indians outside the normative frameworks that were being assembled in India.

Thinking about Trinidad might be interesting to those of us investigating the processes by which contemporary feminism in India comes to rest on the historical disavowal of lower-caste and lower-class women even as it claims to speak for them. The Trinidad example shows that for Indians in India this also involves a disavowal of other forms of modernity that have not passed through the anticolonial struggle or participated in its inevitable outcome. As Mrinalini Sinha contends, "The nationalist construct of the modern Indian woman also created the climate both for women's reforms and for women's entry, under male patronage, to the male-dominated public sphere."[90] Sinha describes the early initiatives of Indian feminists as being linked to the "unprecedented mobilization of middle-class women" in the nationalist movement, manifested, for example, in the all-India women's organizations of the early twentieth century,[91] many of which would have petitioned the viceroy in support of the campaign to abolish indenture. While nationalism provided the language and the spaces in which the middle-class woman could become modern, it also made her a representative—one who spoke for all other Indian women; who became, as Sinha puts it, "the transmitter of the fruits of modernization."[92] The indentured woman in the subaltern diaspora could never be seen in India as this kind of figure, given her caste-class characteristics and the tangentiality of her modernity to the project of the future nation. It is not just the notion of the woman in India today, therefore, that rests on a disavowal of the indentured woman. The feminist has also crucially been implicated in the project of nationalism even as she tried to formulate a critique of it.

In this chapter, I have tried to suggest that present-day critical interventions in relation to the formation of the Indian national-modern might be strengthened by an examination of its illegitimate and disavowed double: "Indian" modernity in the Caribbean. I hope that this exercise will also yield

83
★

unexpected benefits for those intervening in issues of modernity and gender in Trinidad, providing for analysts a different purchase on the production of normative femininities and their complicity with discourses of racial difference.

And what of Trinidad? A popular calypso (some called it a soca because of its lilting rhythms; others called it a chutney because of its extensive use of Hindi) sung during Carnival 1996—the first Carnival after the political victory of the East Indian-dominated United National Congress over the African-led People's National Movement in late 1995—was "Jahaji Bhai" by Brother Marvin, an Afro-Trinidadian who also claimed some Indian ancestry. The music for the song, drawing heavily on East Indian rhythms and instruments, was arranged by two other "Africans," Carlyle "Juice Man" Roberts and C. B. Henderson. The song dramatized the notion of fictive kin, or "brotherhood of the boat" (in Hindi, *jahaji bhai* means "ship brother") invented by the indentured laborers who formed communities of friendship on the long journey from India across what they called *kala pani*, or the black waters. The burden of Brother Marvin's song was to demonstrate that Indians and Africans shared, in a metaphorical sense, an ancestry; that "Ramlogan, Basdeo, Prakash [East Indian men's names] and I / Jahaji bhai." Although the calypsonian came under sharp criticism from many Africans and Indians (see chapter 4), the song was also appreciated by many across political boundaries. But some people, even while applauding Brother Marvin's attempt to envisage a common past and future for the two major racial groups in Trinidad, asked the question: "Where are the women in Brother Marvin's story? Were there no *jahaji behen* (ship sisters)?"

The intention in relating this concern is not to suggest "adding women" to an already well-defined story. Rather, it is to underscore that projections of racial harmony in Trinidadian popular music seem to rest on the possibility of men's friendships across race, whether in Brother Marvin's song or in "Sundar," a tribute to the chutney singer Sundar Popo, by Black Stalin's (Leroy Calliste) or Black Stalin's and Rikki Jai's "My Brother My Friend." When East Indian women take the initiative to create new music out of the combination of African and Indian rhythms, their effort is seen as a threat or disruption to relationships between the races. In the next chapter, I investigate the controversy around chutney-soca and its diva Drupatee Ramgoonai, taking the discussion from indentured women and nationalism in India to the descendants of those women and their invocation by Indian nationalism in Trinidad.

THREE

★ "Take a Little Chutney,
Add a Touch of Kaiso":
The Body in the Voice

"Going to Trinidad? You must check out those Indian women there dancing up a storm." It was in Kingston, Jamaica, in 1994. My new friends, Hubert Devonish from Guyana and Pat Mohammed from Trinidad, were telling me what I might find on my visit to the eastern Caribbean. I gathered that the dancing women constituted an early-1990s phenomenon that had enraged East Indian men in Trinidad. At the time I had no way of knowing why this should be a scandal, working as I was with a notion that all Caribbean people regardless of ethnic origin loved music and dance. "You don't understand," said my friends. "There are only women there, and even the singer is often a woman." During my short stay in Jamaica, I had been exposed to the controversies around dancehall music, where at downtown venues the mostly female dancers "carried on bad" in their responses to the male singers. I wondered if something like this was happening in Trinidad to arouse the ire of middle-class moralists. Apart from this fuzzy notion that the chutney singing represented in some sense a women's space, I did not know anything about the music, its lyrics, or its performers when I first went to Trinidad.

My main purpose in going to Trinidad was to witness the Carnival that has assumed such mythical proportions in Caribbean literature, in calypso music, and in the tourist trade. I went to watch the incredible spectacle with a couple of new acquaintances, an "Indian" woman and an "African" man. Dazzled by the brilliant colors and costumes, my ears filled with the thumping Road March music, I had no eyes for the differences between the "mas" players who were "wining" down the streets.[1] In hindsight, one could tell that there were not many "Indians" out there, but this did not seem strange, since I had mistakenly assumed that they were in the minority in Trinidad. There in the Carnival music, and in the pageant of winners I attended a few days later, I looked out for the chutney I'd been told about, but none of the performances that year sounded even remotely Indian (assuming I knew what that was).

Later, while questioning the women at the Caribbean Association for Feminist Research and Action, I acquired some information about what they told me was called "chutney-soca" and about the controversies surrounding the singer Drupatee Ramgoonai in particular and the phenomenon of chutney dancing in general. I listened to an East Indian male academic's fulminations about the denigration of Indian history and culture; about how Africans in Trinidad were trying to insult the notion of the grandmother—"Nani"—which all Indians held in love and veneration, by encouraging Indian women to sing about their "nani," which in Trinidadian street slang was another word for vagina (punanny). I remember thinking fleetingly that Indian women in India were highly unlikely to sing in public about vaginas and that "Indians" in the Caribbean clearly occupied a different expressive register. A Trinidad Indian woman who had studied in Europe and had a classmate from India mentioned in passing, but with some puzzlement, that her friend had been very different from her in terms of her sexual choices and constraints. The Indian women I saw on the streets of Tunapuna, St. Augustine, and Port-of-Spain seemed different from me, although I couldn't immediately grasp why that was so. Clothing, I thought: In India, one would not see so many older women in "Western" clothes. But it was more than clothing that constituted the difference. A complicated semiotic of facial features, complexion, movement, and speech positioned the Trinidad Indian woman as unlike her counterpart in India. These were not things obvious at first glance; they insinuated themselves gradually into the naïve gaze of the amateur ethnographer.

My hosts sent me to Rhyner's record shop in Port of Spain to buy Trinidadian music. After I had stocked up on all the Carnival hits of the year, I asked for chutney and was shown an audiocassette of Drupatee's songs, including a number called "Lick Down Mih Nani." Guessing that this song was at the center of the chutney controversy, I purchased the tape immediately, although I didn't get to listen to it until I returned to Kingston some days later. What, then, might have drawn me to chutney-soca even before I had heard the music? An anticipated sense, I suppose, of its outrageousness, its sauciness and irreverence. An awareness of the controversy, in which so many women's groups had participated. The possible significance of the form and expressive space for African-Indian relations configured differently than the persistent rumblings about racial tension seemed to suggest.

When I bought the audiotape, I had no idea that most chutney singers were men, although as I found out much later there were many more female singers in chutney than in the African-dominated calypso. I listened to "Lick Down Mih Nani"—to Drupatee's rich, exuberant voice reaching out into the audience, a voice filled to the brim and spilling over; the gaiety of her intonation; the sheer wickedness and humor of both her words and the mode of rendering the song; the infectious rhythms; the distinctive Trinidadian dialect and lilting accent; the musical beat remembered from Carnival and post-Carnival performances (the soca beat, here combined with "Indian" drums). Clearly here was a woman who had what African Americans would call "attitude." The thought of hundreds of women dancing to this irreverent song, an ostensible lament for a grandmother's accident that conveyed in its tone a totally different meaning, was a delightful one. I had a vague idea then that the dancers might be a bunch of teenagers, trendily dressed and middle class, somewhat like the young women students I had seen on the University of the West Indies' St. Augustine campus.

I had also brought from Trinidad a copy of the slim book *Women in Calypso*, with profiles of a handful of Trinidadian singers, including Drupatee.[2] Seeing a picture of her on stage, dressed in shimmering green, I remember asking myself: "What on earth is she wearing? What kind of clothes are those?" Diaphanous, shiny, sequined, and "Oriental," the costume did not seem like anything that a leading singer in contemporary India would wear. On a subsequent visit to Trinidad, I saw young Indo-Trinidadian women in similar outfits at the Indo-Caribbean Music Awards function, the grandest and most formal cultural occasion I ever witnessed there. It seemed to signal an attempt to connect not to an alien present-day India but to a history that was now insistently being inscribed on the dominant "Creole" imaginary. In the late nineteenth century, furious letters to the editor had complained about the Indians' supposed fondness for their native clothing. As the historian G. I. M. Tikasingh puts it, "One writer advocated fines to compel the Indians to wear 'Creole clothing' rather than 'the wild indecent costumes of the East.'"[3]

This chapter and the next two analyze the invocation of the "Indian" in Trinidadian popular music in the context of debates about sexuality and cultural identity. The music ranges from what has come generically to be called "chutney" (including folk-derived Bhojpuri lyrics and rhythms at the one end and Trinidadian English and Afro-Caribbean beats at the other) to calypso and soca. East Indian women, whether as performers or as narrativized characters, are central to this music, with their centrality being commented on, criticized, or celebrated by the various interlocutors in the discussion.

Tracking Chutney-Soca

Chutney-soca eludes definition, partly because there are so many different varieties of song called "chutney" in Trinidad. Especially in the aftermath of the widespread success of chutney-soca in the 1990s, any Caribbean music with even a hint of "Indian" rhythm or a couple of Hindi words is likely to be labeled chutney, a tendency about which many of the practitioners of the music complain.

Calypso, which emerged in the late nineteenth century as a mode of social-political commentary, is one of the most popular musical genres, making its seasonal appearance around Carnival. Sung, with a few rare exceptions, solely by Afro-Trinidadian men, calypso engages in explicit discussion of current, often highly local, politics. However, there has always been an important strand in calypso that comments on relations between women and men. Several Afro-Trinidadian calypsonians have also sung about East Indian women, who appear in the songs as exotic objects of desire.[4]

In the 1980s, a new form called soul-calypso, or soca, emerged, claimed by its inventor Lord Shorty (later Ras Shorty I) to have its inspiration in East

Indian music. Shorty's songs "Indrani" (1973) and "Kelogee Bulbul" (1974) provided the genesis of the soca, marking clearly the Indian influence on calypso.[5] In "Kelogee Bulbul," East Indian instruments like mandolin and dholak are used. The Trinidadian sitarist Mungal Patasar, an important experimenter with fusion music, provided this background:

> Soca really originated from chutney. Ras Shorty I, who is the father of the soca, was singing calypso, and he went to practice in the bandroom, and the music arranger was playing reggae, and when he asked him how come you playing reggae, because there is a little thing about reggae and calypso, reggae taking over in Trinidad, although reggae originated in Trinidad. That much I can tell you, if you study the beat. Anyway, the guy say "Calypso is dead now, man, let's go for reggae." And that hurt him [Shorty] in a way, so he went back home. But he grew up amongst Indians, and he had a neighbor who used to play dholak and dhantal and ting. And he called me—that time I had a band called Sangam Sangeet in La Romain—and there's a drummer named Robin Ramjitsingh who used to play dholak, and he called me and asked for a dholak player, and I sent Robin, and he did his first recording with Robin Ramjitsingh. The bass guitarist was trying to imitate the dhol, the left side of the dholak, and in trying to do that they created the beat with the bass guitar out of the dholak, and that's what they call "soca." The word was "so-k-a-h," the soul of calypso and an Indian beat. They used the word "kah" because it is the first letter of the Indian alphabet. . . . The Africans try to say it is "soul" and "calypso." But it is not that. It is soul of calypso and Indian chutney. That would be the definition of soca.[6]

Shorty, too, spelled the name "s-o-k-a-h" to indicate the East Indian influence, but the spelling did not stick, and other singers and those who wrote about music—disinclined to mark the East Indian input and suggesting instead a derivation from the African American musical genre soul and from calypso—assigned the new form the name "soca." Soca is different from calypso in that it is usually seen as music to dance to and for the most part, and unlike one of the key strands of calypso, does not talk about the political situation.[7]

An important popularizer of chutney was Sundar Popo. He was one of the early singers to use a good deal of Trinidadian English along with some Hindi, a trend reflected in some of the folk music derived from wedding songs sung by East Indian women in Trinidad. One of the first of these

East Indian music group. Collection of Eric Scott Henderson.

women's songs sung in English went: "Rosie gal, whey [what] you cookin for dinner / She makin' *choka*, it ent [doesn't] have no salt." (*Choka* is any mashed cooked vegetable, like tomato or eggplant, with seasoning.) Already we see the suggestive connection made by the singer between cooking and eating and sexuality, a theme prevalent in much of the subsequent music, as well.

Confusion often reigns in the media and public perception about chutney. There are some who argue that soca comes out of chutney, while others decry what they see as the movement of chutney (according to them, a purely East Indian form) toward soca (a Creole form). Those who condemn chutney—and, in particular, chutney-soca—often seem to be criticizing the lyrics and the behavior of the audience, not the form of the music itself. One can speculate, however, that the form is also contentious, even when the objection appears to sideline this issue. I return to this point later in the chapter.

Chutney draws from the folk forms brought to Trinidad by the indentured laborers from rural northern India. It is related especially to the ceremonies of the *maticore* or *matti korwah* (which refers to the act of "digging dirt" and burying betel leaves with flowers and *sindur*, or auspicious vermillion powder, for the gods on the Friday night before the wedding; most East Indian Hindu weddings in Trinidad are held over an entire weekend); the cooking night ("farewell night" before the actual wedding); and *laawa* (Sunday morning of the wedding; *laawa* is parched unpolished rice exchanged during the marriage ceremony). All of these were occasions for singing and dancing by women. The participants in the ceremonies were all female, except for the young boys who played the drums, and the songs and "performances" (like miming the sexual act with a prop like a melongene or aubergine) were known to be full of humor and sexual explicitness. The ostensible reason for this was to assist the sexual initiation of the bride. Contemporary chutney draws its melodic and textual inspiration from these ceremonial songs.[8]

One of the early pieces of scholarly writing on the topic seems to share the prejudices of the present-day East Indian urban middle class. In a thesis titled "Some Aspects of Hindu Folk Songs in Trinidad," Niala Maharaj makes the following observations:

> In all of the jokes there are overtones of sexuality and some often come close to being obscene. But a certain laxity in these matters (as far as conversation is concerned) prevails on this occasion which is normally absent from Hindu family life. [Here the reference is to the ritual teasing of the bridegroom by the bride's female relatives.] These intrusions of the sexual element occur at several points during the drawn-out wedding preparations especially at all-female rituals such as the "matte (dirt or soil) korwah" and "going for kwah" occasions, where normally quite reticent women, stimulated by the drums (and sometimes alcohol) depict the sex act in dance and sing sometimes quite obscene songs. But this sexuality is of such a customary and institutionalised nature that modesty is at these times at a minimum and different standards of behaviour obtain.[9]

Another young scholar points out that, after the rituals for the bride and bride's mother were completed, women "erupted into erotic folksongs, accompanying themselves on the dholak." Old lyrics were sung with relish: "Boom, boom tack, tack, doh bite me in meh pomerack," or "Higher the mountain cooler the breeze / Sweeter the lover, tighter the squeeze."[10] A

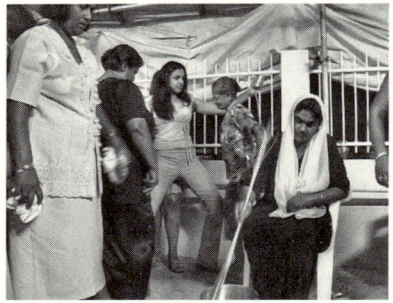

Hindu wedding. Surabhi Sharma/R. V. Ramani.

former plantation worker now in her eighties could remember lyrics that went: "I beatin' my drum / An' singin' mih song / De only ting missin' / Is a bottle of rum."[11] Other lyrics could be in Bhojpuri Hindi, such as the following: "Deeya mange batti aur batti mange tel / Ankhan mange jebanwa mange khail (The lamp wants the wick and the wick wants the oil / Man's eyes are heavy and want to sleep but the breasts need fondling)."[12] A seventy-year-old woman, well known for her singing prowess at weddings, gave the example of the song "Mor laawa tor laawa eke me milaawe" (roughly translated as mixing together the parched rice from the girl's side and the boy's side), which is a "bad song" with "real cuss": "When yuh have your drum, and shak shak, and two drinks inside, yuh can really sing."[13]

Lyrics similar to those made famous by the controversial "Marajhin" series by Mighty Sparrow (Slinger Francisco) were also first sung at weddings:

> Gimme the pepper
> Make sure the *sada* [plain roti] have plenty *choka* [hot oil seasoning]
> Put *ghee* [clarified butter] and *jeera* [cumin] and make it sweeter
> Then ah want you leggo fire in meh *kutiya*.[14]

Mungal Patasar says that the wedding and childbirth lyrics come from the songs of the *hijras* (eunuchs) who in India would have sung on these occasions. These songs later came to be known as chutneys:

> When you make a mango chutney, you grind mango and you put dhania leaf in it and plenty pepper and garlic and that makes the spicy thing we are talking about. Chutney only means masala, and the word originated only twenty or thirty years back. My father was a singer, and I recall they used to sing whole night for a wedding. And when it's about one-two in the morning, and the people started feeling sleepy, they would sing what is called a breakaway. Meaning breakaway from the classical traditional sort of songs, and that also became chutney later.[15]

The eminent Trinidadian musicologist Narsaloo Ramaya writes that in the 1940s, women sang *sohar* after a child was born. Sohar songs were like lullabies, "delivered in a slow tempo with measured beats and rhythms." The sohars were followed by "spicy" songs, called chutney because of their faster beat.[16] Helen Myers, an ethnomusicologist who did fieldwork in the Trinidadian village of Felicity, comments that, according to her informants, "hot" songs, chutney, and lachari have a "nice taste."[17] A contrast to these "bawdy and abusive songs known in different districts [of India] as lachari, lachi, nakata, and jhumar" are the *byah ke git*, "the serious wedding songs, relating events from the [Hindu epic] Ramayan." On all three days at different times there were dancing and lachari. On the Sunday afternoon, there was even an exclusive Ladies' Party.[18] It would be difficult to reinscribe here in an unproblematic way the ethnographic present tense that is found throughout Myers's text on "Hindu music" in Felicity.[19] The space that chutney music now occupies is considerably different from the private and domestic sphere of the wedding, and we need other kinds of information to understand the larger context in which the phenomenon of chutney-soca emerged.[20]

The broader musical and performative context of chutney-soca would have to include the calypso, Carnival, Hosay (drumming and dancing at the Muslim festival of Muharram or Hosein), Phagwa (dancing at the Hindu spring festival of Holi or Phagwa), Mastana Bahar (the East Indian talent show and TV program launched in the 1970s), "Indian dance" (dance dramas based on mythological themes and solo performances inspired by Hindi cinema), Indian and Hindi films (which have been showing in Trinidad since the 1930s and are immensely popular among East Indians), Hindi film music (which is immensely popular over the radio and has influenced some aspects of chutney singing and calypso in terms of both melody and instrumentation), Ramlila (the performance in the weeks before Divali, the festival of lights, showing the victory of good over evil, Rama over Ravana, from the Indian epic the Ramayana), and Indian tent singing (presumably inspired by the Carnival-season tents for calypso music).

In the early twentieth century, East Indians began to settle in areas like Barataria and St. James and some parts of Port of Spain that traditionally were controlled by French Creoles and their ex-slaves. This was the beginning of their exposure to urban cultural forms after many decades in the canefields of rural Trinidad. While calypso and steel band dominated the national cultural stage and provided entertainment to all Trinidadians, East Indians also had access to other kinds of performance, including "Indian" dance drama ("film dance" in which the most famous names were Alice Jan and Champa Devi until the 1950s), instrumental music played on the dholak, dhantal, harmonium, and, later, the sitar; and, of course, the drumming and dancing involved in various Hindu and Muslim festivals and religious rituals such as weddings.[21] The constant stream of popular Hindi films from India from 1935 on was seen as one kind of inspiration for the emergence of distinctly Trinidadian East Indian cultural forms, although not all East Indians think of the films as a positive influence. There was also local classical Indian dance and music, many of whose proponents had training in India, sometimes under scholarships from the post-Independence government of India.

Popular East Indian music that was not confined to the domestic space began to take shape with the advent of the widely appreciated *Mastana Bahar*, started in August 1970 by the Mohammed brothers, well-known promoters and impresarios, as a half-hour TV show on Trinidad and Tobago Television. The popularization of the name "chutney" is in fact attributed to Moean Mohammed by singers such as James Ramsewak and Cecil Funrose. The show encouraged local compositions, and through the 1970s Indo-Trinidadian folk songs with English lyrics became common.[22] But in 1971, only five of the eighty-eight compositions at a *Mastana Bahar* audition were local; the others were renditions of Hindi film songs. This was the situation in which Sundar Popo began to make his mark. Popo's music had precursors in Suriname, where the singer Dropati had released her 1968 album *Let's Sing and Dance*, with songs like "Gowri Puja (special worship for a Hindu goddess)" and "Laawa" (a reference to the parched-rice ceremony at a wedding), to major popular acclaim. Dropati's album followed the 1958 release of her compatriot Ramdeo Chaitoe's *King of Suriname*. Both albums had many religious songs, accompanied by the strong beat of the dhantal and dholak, but, as commentators suggest, their wide circulation fueled the need for popular nonreligious music.[23] Although chutney shows became widespread only in the 1980s, chutney as a public dance phenomenon might well go back to 1963, when the Mohammed brothers organized well-attended performances by Drupati and Chaitoe, whose fast-paced songs became popular in Trinidad.[24] Sundar's first album was *Nani Nana* (1969); on it, he used instruments like the dholak, dhantal, guitar, and synthesizer to back catchy lyrics such as, "Nana smoking tobacco and Nanee cigarette / The rain started falling the both of them got wet / Nanee tell meh Nana old man ah feelin cold / Give me some white one to warm up me soul." The song, which drew on local chutney as well as Indian film music, became a big hit in Guyana and Trinidad, and Sundar Popo began to be called the King of Chutney.[25]

The phenomenon represented by Sundar would not have been possible without Harry Mahabir, leader of the British West Indian Airways National Indian Orchestra.[26] Using Western musical instruments, Mahabir tried to play melodies that were recognizably non-Western. Through the *Mastana*

Bahar TV show, Mahabir extended his support not just to Popo but to many other East Indian singers. Along with the Western instruments, notes the journalist and music critic Kim Johnson, there was "some characteristically Indian instrumentation, tassas or a harmonium. Lyrics, even when in English, were sung in the nasal way of Hindi phrasing. Certain melodic lines had a distinctive Indian flavour, but even when they didn't they could be played with an Indian lilt." Johnson does not elaborate what "Indian flavour" and "Indian lilt" refer to.[27] These broad descriptions seem to have a specific reference in Trinidad and are used by East Indians and others.

Popo's songs, some of them his own compositions, were in Trinidadian English and in Bhojpuri Hindi; he recorded "traditional" wedding songs and several others about Indo-Caribbean life. Sharda Patasar, also a musician, points out that "generally any man singing chatti or sohar songs [post-childbirth, on the sixth day and the twelfth day] together with the women was branded as leaning towards homosexuality. It is however interesting to note that it is from these very tunes that the present Chutney songs have evolved and are sung by men in a public forum. . . . As children, boys learnt these songs which they later gave expression to in public. Sundar Popo said that he was unable to compete with the classical singers so whenever he got the opportunity he would sing these songs. He was chastised by the classical singers who called him, amongst other things, 'dog.' He learnt these songs from his mother and *mausie* (mother's sister)."[28]

Another important input for the formation of chutney and chutney-soca came from the Indian singer Kanchan and her husband, Babla, the well-known arranger of film music from Bombay. Having first visited Trinidad with the renowned Indian film playback singer Mukesh in 1967, Babla returned to Trinidad to do music shows with his singer wife Kanchan and his orchestra. Introduced to Sundar Popo's chutney songs, Kanchan and Babla started doing versions with added instrumentation and melodies from the musical circuit of Hindi films, generally smoothening out Popo's "folk" style.[29] Kanchan sang "Kuch Gadbad Hai" in calypso style in the early '80s, using the calypsonian Arrow's hit song "Hot Hot Hot," a song that became popular in India, as well. Babla and Kanchan remained frequent visitors to the Caribbean and gained fame as chutney performers across the Caribbean diaspora. Their remixes (compiled, along with a few of Babla's own compositions, in something like fifteen albums) became so well known as "Caribbean" songs that most audiences did not know the duo were actually from India.[30] The Revue and Sparrow's Young Brigade calypso tents tried to employ Kanchan to sing with them during the 1985 Carnival season, but not until Drupatee Ramgoonai's career took off did Trinidadians see an "Indian" woman on the Carnival stage.[31] By the end of the 1980s, several East Indians, including the versatile Drupatee, began to perform on stage their own blend of Indian folk music and soca, which has come to be known as chutney-soca. (Drupatee's 1989 hit, "Indian Soca," contained these lyrics: "Sounding sweeter / Hotter than a chulha / Rhythm from Africa and India / Blend together in a perfect mixture.")

One way to trace the growth of chutney-soca is to see how it derives from chutney; another is to look at the history of its relationship to calypso and soca. According to both Gordon Rohlehr and Zeno Obi Constance, calypso has had a long history of the incorporation of "Indian" elements. Winsford "Joker" Devine composed the "Marajhin" series for Mighty Sparrow, with songs that are heavily backed by Indian melodies and instruments. Devine also composed "Indian Party" for K. D. in 1981. Then there were ghostwriters such as the Indo-Trinidadian Mohan Paltoo, mentioned earlier, who wrote hits such as "Raja Rani (King and Queen)" in 1986 for Baron and "Roti and Dhalpouri" in 1989 and "Bombay Ladkee (Bombay Girl)" in 1991 for Sugar Aloes. The final ingredient, says Constance, was khimta, or chutney, "into the already douglarised soca," referring to the Indian-African mix, as in Drupatee's "Chutney Soca" in 1987.[32] Another beginning for chutney-soca is in the recordings of tent singing by Windsor Records in the 1970s. Albums such as "Tent Singing by Abdool 'Kush' Razack," "Tent Singing by Yusuf Khan," and "Tent Singing by Sharm Yankarran" later became a kind of Indian soca.[33]

In the 1980s, chutney came to be performed in public, sometimes with five thousand or ten thousand people present, both men and women, and with many of the women dancing to the music.[34] That this sort of spectacle did not always obtain is evident from the account of Hardeo Ramsingh of the village of Felicity, who writes that until the 1980s, public dancing by women in Felicity was taboo despite the exploits of performers like Champa Devi, Baby Susan, and Baby Sandra. In the period from the 1880s to the 1960s, says Ramsingh, there were male drama, singing, and dancing troupes that performed at weddings, Ramleelas, Hosays, and Carnivals. There were also "court" dances ("Sarwar/Neer type") and caste dances, such as Ahir, Kaharwaa, Dhobi, but none of these had female dancers.[35] In the mid-1980s, the Mohammed brothers began to organize weekend chutney dancing "fetes" that attracted hundreds of participants, including a large number of women. Once a segregated dance form, chutney now became a public event. Instead of a performance watched by an audience, like the older forms of "Indian dance," chutney turned dancing into a public participatory form for both men and women. "Long time we used to have real Indian singing, with all these old ladies singing, but now nobody don' sing dem kind of song again. The younger gyuls ain't wan' to learn to sing, dem only wan' to go and jump up," said Miriam Gajadhar, who still sings chutney at weddings.[36] Drupatee Ramgoonai, the first female Indian singer in the calypso tents, became one of the most popular singers of chutney-soca. Like those of other well-known East Indian singers, her repertoire spans chutney, Hindi film music, and chutney-soca. Unlike them, but like her colleague Rikki Jai, Drupatee also sings calypso.

It has been suggested that after the Black Power Movement of the 1970s more space appeared for black women to sing calypso, the exposure of the "talent and beauty of black women" being upheld as part of the agenda of a wider political movement. After the advent of soca, the participation of women in calypso increased even more in the late '80s, with women of varied races finding the calypso arena more accessible. Women like Denyse Plummer, who is French Creole, and Drupatee Ramgoonai came onto the calypso stage for the first time. It is possible that soca, with its focus on danceable music, destabilizes the male and Afrocentric perspective from which calypso is usually composed and sung, thus making room onstage for other kinds of performance.

Drupatee had had a long singing career before she came to chutney-soca: "From small, I started singing. My mum used to play de drum, and sing those folk songs at weddings, and she used to tag along me."[37] Although she never took formal lessons in music ("it came natural to me"), she did work with Ustad James Ramsewak, who sang Indian "classical songs." At age twelve, Drupatee sang in school choirs and with religious groups at weddings and functions, as well as for Charleau Village in the Best Village competition, and she was a backup singer with Sundar Popo on prizewinning songs for the Indian Cultural Pageant and for *Mastana Bahar*. "If Sundar Popo asked me to do chorus, he knew I could sing," says Drupatee with some pride. The experience of working with Sundar helped her get used to being on stage. "It made me more show off myself," she says. She experimented with *parang* soca (soca with Latin American strains) in Harry Mahabir's orchestra. In 1983 and 1984, Drupatee won the competition at

Mastana Bahar, the Indian Cultural Pageant, singing in chutney style. Referring to her mother and aunts who sang at weddings, Drupatee commented on the element of masquerade that goes into cooking-night frolic:

> She would be putting on hat, and big shirt and big pants. Only ladies used to be upstairs, and they used to have their singin' and their jokes. I never like how they used to dress up, I never never like how they do those things. I didn't like how my mother danced. I used to swell up mih mouth when I saw them. Now I know how they used to enjoy themselves, I now find myself with all de old ladies doing de same ting!

In 1987, Drupatee sang "Chutney Soca" and "Nau Jawaan," composed by Kenny Phillips, both of which brought her some success. "Chutney soca, yeh chutney soca / Is dat weh hav' mih winin' fe so," sang Drupatee. "Nani say don' party in Arima / I decide not to listen to her." With this song, Drupatee claims to have invented, and named, the genre chutney-soca, with the credit shared by her schoolteacher husband and her producer, Kenny Phillips.

Drupatee's first big hit was the single "Pepper Pepper" (1987), which presented the travails of an East Indian housewife seeking revenge on her husband for his lack of interest in their marriage. According to the song, the wife will solve her problem by putting pepper in her husband's food so that he will say, "Pepper, I want Paani [water] to cool meh, Pepper I want plenty Paani." The hapless husband screams:

> Pepper burning me—all in meh eye
> Pepper burning me—making me cry
> Pepper burning me—all in meh nose
> Pepper burning me—look take off meh clothes.

Although the song did very well on the soca charts, it brought Drupatee the criticism of conservative East Indians. In the following year, Drupatee sang "Mr. Bissessar, or Roll up the Tassa" (1988), composed by Wayne MacDonald, which reached the top position on the soca charts in "every country in the English speaking Caribbean, from Antigua to Guyana" and repeated the success in the United States, Canada, and England.[38] The song enabled Drupatee to become the first East Indian soca best-seller. She was also voted Top Female Recording Artiste of the Year in 1988.[39] When she was young, Drupatee watched the Carnival competitions on television and told herself

Drupatee Ramgoonai in concert. Surabhi Sharma/R. V. Ramani.

that she would be singing there one day. Although she did not participate in the contests until much later, she became a regular performer in the Carnival calypso tents. "I have my biggest audiences in Port of Spain—all mix-up people. All de Negro, all de African people acceptin' me. The people really really love me. They like how I does move."[40]

Curiously, Drupatee has always been a central target in the attacks on chutney-soca, although she doesn't compose the music or write the lyrics to the songs she performs. The attacks may indeed be associated with her role in performing these songs, and with her exuberant performing style, which includes dancing to her own music. The last section of this chapter will propose a hypothesis that attempts to account for Drupatee's success as well as the outrage she has provoked.

"Lick Down Mih Nani, or Careless Driver" (1988), the double meanings of whose central term, "Nani" (grandmother and vagina), has scandalized some East Indians, also plays on the term "lick," which can mean both to give a blow or beating and to lick with the tongue.[41] The ballad-like narrative tells of a grandmother's accident at the hands of the careless driver of a maxi-taxi, the common mode of public transport in Trinidad:

> The driver was ruthless and drivin too hard
> He bounced down mih nani right so in she yard.

While the main text of the song relates the details of the accident in gruesome detail (grandmother's leg was broken, she's now in a coma, etc.), the refrain, sung by the female chorus, is fast-paced and almost joyous:

> I-man lick up mi nani
> I-man lick up mi nani oi
> I-man lick up mi nani
> I-man lick up mi nani oi.

Adding to the suggestiveness of the refrain is the repeated call to the protagonist's "neighba": "Neighba come and see what he do to me nani"; "Neighba you ent see [haven't seen] what he do to meh nani"; "Neighba you ent see what e [his] maxi do to she." The sexualization of the older woman draws on an established tradition in the calypso, a precursor to Nani's being Lord Shorty's insatiable old East Indian woman in "Indrani" (1973). The song ends with the whole town hearing about Nani's accident:

> All over town
> De talk around
> Nani get jam
> From maxi man.[42]

Drupatee's manager, Simone Ragoonanan, has talked about the double meanings in chutney and chutney-soca. She says that, because Trinidadians don't speak Hindi or Bhojpuri, "most of the people . . . don't have a clue what's in the song; but when they hear it in English they get mad," suggesting that "Nani" was not very different from the cooking-night songs. Drupatee herself insists laughingly that the phrase is "lick down mih nani" (although the chorus sings "lick up mih nani"), but, she admits, "it's double meaning," adding that "the audience love that song."

Drupatee's other major hits, "Mr. Bissessar" (1988) and "Hotter Than a Chulha (Indian Soca)" (1989), both repeatedly draw the listener's attention to the unique and unprecedented form of the music. "Mr. Bissessar," a tribute to a tassa drum player, is a song about an actual "Indian" fete where a new kind of music is being played and sung. In addition to tassa, dholak, and tabla, the drum set or trap set was used for instrumentation. Here the chutney-soca stands as a performative; it is the very thing it sings about. There are frequent references to how the event is a "soca tassa jam":

Drupatee Ramgoonai at home, with manager and songwriter. Surabhi Sharma/R. V. Ramani.

> A section from Debe
> Join and start to play
> Indian lavway
> And dey jammin de soca, jammin de soca.

The dancers don't want the drummer to stop playing ("hear how people bawl / Bissessar don't stop at all"); everyone is wining and sweating ("Is first time they gettin dis kinda soca tassa"). As Drupatee herself puts it, "When the song came out, no one would stand still. Every [radio] station had it playin,' from the Indian to the English." Here, too, there is a Nani "getting on bad," and Phagwa (Holi or Spring Festival in the Hindu calendar), Hosay, and laawa all invoked as occasions for the tassa to be played.[43]

"Hotter Than a Chulha" declares that Indian soca is sweeter than conventional soca, since in this new form, "Rhythm from Africa and from India / Blend together in a perfect mixture."[44] Addressing her audience directly, Drupatee sings:

> Cos we goin an interfere wid de soca
> And we add a little curry and some jeera [cumin]

And you know you goin to like me wid dis style
It go send you wild.

From the hills of Laventille, the "African" slum near Port of Spain that gave birth to the steel band, the song continues, the skills of the pan man (steel-band player) must "spill into Caroni," the rural sugarcane belt in Central Trinidad, which is predominantly East Indian:

For we goin and cause a fusion wid de culture
To widen we scope and vision for de future
And the only place to start is wid de art.

Why this seemingly innocuous call for racial harmony and cultural "fusion" should arouse so many different reactions will be discussed later.

In the brief period from 1995 to 1999, more chutney and chutney-soca artists and albums appeared than in all three of the previous decades combined. As the success of the new form spread rapidly throughout the Caribbean, it came to include several singers of African origin, with "Khirki Na Din" (1996),[45] performed by the Afro-Trinidadian singer Cecil Funrose, earning the second highest amount ever.[46] When the privately sponsored Chutney-Soca Monarch Competition was instituted in 1997, about a third of the audience and half the performers were non-East Indian.[47] Kim Johnson suggests that "the coupling of chutney and soca is like a dance, drifting now in the soca direction, now in the chutney direction, the partners none too skilled as yet. In the calypso season they move, in numbers such as Drupatie's [sic] 'Mr Bissessar,' towards the Afro-creole side of the floor (although that's changed since Sonny Mann's 'Lotay La'). As Rikki Jai sang in a tune which was, like 'Bissessar,' written by an Afro-Trini, 'Hold the Lata Mangeshkar, give me soca.' Other times, at the large chutney shows in Central and South [Trinidad], in the music of men such as Anand Yankaran and women such as Geeta Kawalsingh and Prematie Bheem, the movement drifts towards the Indian side."[48] Appreciation of chutney-soca, it would seem, includes the fact that it is *not* calypso or soca or even folk-style chutney. It reminds you of all these forms even as it disavows them.

The resemblance between chutney and soca is asserted by some Afro-Trinidadian singers, however—for example, by Delamo in "Soca Chutney" (1990), with its strong refrain about "the same jam":

When the synthesizer ramajay in the key—
The same jam . . .

> And the dhantal man—the same jam
> With the iron in hand—the same jam
> An interesting similarity. . . .
> People doh [don't] understand
> Chutney and soca go hand in hand
> You wine up and grind up ingredients
> Like a chulha
> But the spicy, spicy chutney
> Is the same as soca.[49]

Another example is a song written by Ras Shorty I for Leon Coldero (no date available), with its injunction to "squeeze them tighter" and "wrap them up closer" sexualizing the creation of the new music:

> Take the rhythm of India, then take some of Africa
> Take the dhantal and tabla, with the fine bay
> And dambala
> Join them together, one with the other
> And squeeze them a lil tighter,
> Wrap them up closer, closer, closer and closer
> And call that chutney soca.[50]

The acclaimed calypsonian and soca singer David Rudder is supposed to have remarked that saying "chutney-soca" was actually saying "double chutney," because soca is already chutney to begin with.

Chutney and Soca: Beat and Structure

There are differing interpretations of the musical structure of chutney. According to Helen Myers's informant Amar, the *kirtan*, or devotional songs on which the chutney beat is based, are short and repetitive, with a fast tempo, usually *kaharwa tal* (rhythmic cycle of eight beats divided into 4 + 4) or *dadra tal* (six beats divided into 3 + 3).[51] According to the musicologist Peter Manuel, the chowtal, which exemplifies East Indian folk song, relies more on "linear intricacies than on African-style simultaneous layerings of interlocking patterns. One common feature of Indian music is the use of 'additive' meters, often involving measures of odd-numbered beats." Chowtal uses such a rhythm, also common in North Indian styles and in Indo-Caribbean *tan* singing (*tan* is an idiosyncratic version of North Indian classical and semiclassical genres). "The *chowtal* meter," says Manuel, "can be regarded as in seven beats, divided into three plus four (hence the term *additive*). You can get the feel of it by counting '<u>one</u>-two-three-<u>one</u>-two-<u>three</u>-four' repeatedly, clapping on the underlined beats." The *chowtal* is commonly sung during the Phagwa or Holi festival and has received new impetus in a competition for original English-Hindi compositions organized by the Hindu Prachar Kendra. Manuel also points out that, "in studios and concerts, the rather sparse chutney instrumentation is sometimes jazzed up with soca rhythms and instruments (synthesizers, pressure drums, and whatnot). The soca beat mixes quite easily with the funky, heartbeat chutney rhythm (what Indians would call *kaherva*), and the result is called 'chutney-soca.' While generally lacking calypso's textual interest, chutney-soca has a flavor quite distinct from mainstream soca because of its Hindi lyrics, ornamented vocal style, often minor-sounding modal melodies, and the thumping and pumping *dholak*."[52] Since the 1990s, however, there is increased use of English lyrics and the soca beat, which might eventually affect even the structure of the old-time chutney.[53] There is also the difference in approach to chutney singing and presentation between singers like Heeralal Rampartap, who come out of an East Indian singing tradition, and Rikki Jai, who comes out of calypso.[54]

Some scholars argue that there is nothing "new" about the kind of fusion represented by chutney. Kusha Haraksingh says that every Indian village always had a band that played chutney and included one or two Africans to play guitar and drum ("their" instruments). So the musical mixing has been going on for a long time, although it is only now being "recognized" by Creole society. What is different about the contemporary scene, he says, is the commercialization of chutney and the lack of embarrassment about being "Indian," the ability to "wear your culture on your sleeve" that marks the emergence of the East Indian into "so-called larger society."[55]

Audience, Language, Industry

The commercialization of chutney in the 1990s has led to its wider availability as recorded music and in the form of regular stage performances. New state policies allowed the establishment of privately owned Indian-oriented radio stations in the mid-1990s, and East Indian music and dance forms found a space for the first time in events like Carifesta, the official pan-Caribbean festival of the arts. Chutney-soca cassettes and CDs can now be found not only in music shops in "Indian" areas but also in "African" dominated Port of Spain. It has been noted that earlier audiences were almost homogenously East Indian and that many of them were lower class. The majority of female chutney patrons are older and working-class women, "cane cutters, hucksters in the market, doubles [fried dough sandwich with chickpea filling] vendors, domestics, cleaners and suitcase traders."[56] Writing in the early '90s, Sharon Syriac observed that chutney attracted a "predominantly female audience," although she also noted that more young adult men recently had started attending chutney fetes, saying that they "come to see the women 'wine.' " Syriac's research also revealed that, in rural areas, the audiences consisted more of families who came in groups and that near urban areas there were more young adults. She proposed that chutney offered "social and mental release for the working class East Indians," since underprivileged Indians participated only marginally in an event like Carnival, which, according to Syriac, served a cathartic function for other groups in Trinidad.[57] The question that can perhaps be asked here is why a chutney fete, and not other cultural forms, should serve this function. Why can only a form parallel to the Creole Carnival be represented as offering "release" for East Indians of different class backgrounds in Trinidad?

There is indeed some evidence indicating changes in the class (and for some time, race) composition of the chutney audience. I have been told that in the late 1980s and early '90s, chutney performances had plenty of wild dancing by everyone present. Men often danced with ("wined on") men and women with women, and most of them were working class. Since the late '90s, however, chutney has been sought out also by the East Indian middle class, although at special performances where chairs are provided (such as Mother's Day concerts) this kind of audience will sit without dancing. At other venues, such as Skinner Park, which hosts the Monarch competitions, the audience—which can sometimes reach twenty thousand people—does not sit still but dances, waves, and cheers on the singers.

The increased legitimacy gained by chutney has resulted in public recognition of its performers. The past few years have seen the institution of the Chutney Monarch Competition, the Chutney-Soca Monarch Competition, and the Indo-Caribbean Music Awards, all of which honor contributions to the development of East Indian Caribbean music. Chutney and chutney-soca fetes are now held almost every Saturday night in predominantly East Indian areas. These areas are mainly in central and southern Trinidad, where performances are held at the Rienzi complex (Couva), the

Hi-way Inn (Charlieville, Chaguanas), the Himalaya Club (San Juan), Lall's Cultural Complex (Debe), Simplex Cultural Centre (New Grant, Princes Town), and other venues.[58] The anthropologist Daniel Miller has written about the capacity crowds on Sunday that gather at shopping malls in areas of East Indian concentration such as Chaguanas, where the public spaces are turned into auditoriums for music events.[59]

The lyrics are now as often sung in Trinidadian English as in Bhojpuri or Hindi, which accounts for their greater accessibility to people outside the East Indian community—and, indeed, to young East Indians, most of whom do not speak any "Indian" languages. Earlier in the twentieth century, both wedding songs and religious music such as bhajans were likely to be in Hindi and its dialects, such as Bhojpuri, Braj, or Avadhi. However, by the 1970s, chutney songs in English were becoming common. Another turnaround is observable by the 1990s, when Bhojpuri or Hindi seemed to witness a sort of revival—spearheaded by singers such as Anand Yankarran and Sonny Mann—alongside the popularity of English-language chutney-soca.

Some people hold strong opinions on the language of chutney, especially purists such as Satnarine Balkaransingh, a well-known dancer and teacher. In a recent essay, he remarked: "The current presentation is a mishmash of Trinidad English dialect, some Indian Bhojpuri dialect, and some Hindi words. Ignorance of the language has led to incorrect pronunciations, hence incomprehensible meanings and sometimes the introduction of nonsensical words in the text of the songs." Balkaransingh claims dismissively that the music is plagiarized from Hindi films, religious songs, and old folk tunes, without giving any credit to the improvisatory quality of chutney (and chutney-soca) and the inventiveness of its practitioners.[60]

Debates about what really is chutney sometimes pivot on the language question, with the amount of English and Hindi in a song determining what is chutney and what is not. In 1996, when the popular hit "Jahaji Bhai (Brotherhood of the Boat)" by Brother Marvin (Selwyn Demming), to be discussed in chapter 4, was excluded from the Pan Chutney Festival on the grounds of not being a chutney song, Marvin explained: "Chutney/soca is more chutney music mixed with soca, while soca/chutney is a soca song mixed with a little chutney. It is like *anchar* and *kuchela* [sweet mango pickle]. They are the same thing, yet different. One has a big piece of mango and the other has the mango shredded."[61] Others, like Vijay Ramlal, who is quoted in the same article, argue that "Some Hindi in a song doesn't make it a chutney," while Carl "Beaver" Henderson, the producer of "Jahaji Bhai," had this to say: "Chutney is just the beat you put to a song. Chutney is a hybrid and is still in transition. Who among us has the musical authority to hear a song and say it is not now or cannot be a chutney?"

If soca can pass for chutney, then sometimes chutney passes for soca. The surprise hit of Carnival 1996 was a Bhojpuri chutney song about a man seducing his sister-in-law, "Lotay La": "Roll, roll, roll de Bhowji, roll nicely / Bhowji took up a piece of soap / And bathed me for a long time / When Bhowji drinks and gets high, she rolls me."[62] Its singer, Sonny Mann, reached the National Soca Monarch finals. Mann's detractors argued that people did not object to the obscenity of the lyrics of "Lotay La" because the words were not understood by the general public, including most East Indians.[63] Afro-Trinidadian calypsonians like Denise Belfon and General Grant did immensely popular "re-mixes" of Sonny Mann's song, which was also used in the 1995 general election campaign of the People's National Movement, the African-dominated party. This was the election, incidentally, that brought to power for the first time an Indian-dominated party, the United National Congress, and its leader, Basdeo Panday, who became prime minister of the country in late 1995.[64]

More than one commentator has pointed out that the return of a predominantly East Indian government in Guyana in 1992 and the ascendance of East Indians to political power for the first time ever in Trinidad in 1995 led to different kinds of cultural manifestations, including a "tidal wave" of recordings in which the performances of hundreds of local artists in both countries began to circulate on tape.[65] Commentators have related this phenomenon, and the increased popularity of chutney-soca, to the growing Indo-Caribbean communities in the United States and Canada, which have established their own record companies, such as the enormously successful Jamaican Me Crazy (JMC) records and many others. New Caribbean nightclubs in New York and Toronto have become significant outlets for the music. It has been pointed out that about a third of all Indo-Caribbeans now live in Canada, the United States, and the United Kingdom. However, Peter Manuel, writing in the early 1990s, commented that the Indo-Caribbean recording industry was in its infancy, being "merely an appendage to the live performance scene," especially the wedding and chutney show circuit.[66] Manuel has mentioned elsewhere that most cassettes sell about a thousand copies, with hits selling up to five thousand copies.[67] Figures for 1992 indicate that five thousand to six thousand cassettes of chutney as a broad category sold in the domestic market, and an equal number sold abroad. Since this figure includes different kinds of Indo-Caribbean music, from chutney to chutney-soca, it would be somewhat difficult to disaggregate it. Some shopowners quote ten thousand copies (domestic) for well-known artistes. This number is equal to, and sometimes surpassing, calypso and soca sales.

Chutney Performance

CHUTNEY SHOW AT THE TRIANGLE, ARANGUEZ, AUGUST 30, 1998
It is the Independence Day Special soca and chutney jam at "D" Triangle, Aranguez (San Juan). We reach at 8:15 p.m. Families with little children and lots of teenagers, overwhelmingly East Indian. A few dougla children seen.

From the time we enter, 6–7 items are Hindi film songs—one bhangra, sometimes preceded by rap. Then a chutney dance with an African-looking girl with braids, wearing red and black (colours of national flag). Followed by five young girls—the Cutie Kuchi dancers, approx 7–12 years old, in white and sequins, dancing to Rudder's Carnival 1998 hit "High Mas." Then the Shiv Outar dancers—three tall East Indian women, one very fair, dance to a chutney song with much wining.

After this is a "winer competition," where the audience is invited onstage. Half a dozen young girls in their early teens go up and start wining. All the girls are East Indian. In the middle is the African chutney dancer. The winner is a girl with a long plait, looks about 12 or 13, white sleeveless tank top and blue jeans with no make up. Winner is given $100 by someone in the audience. She holds the note in both hands and shows it off to the audience. Her face is completely expressionless throughout the wining.

Marcia Miranda comes on stage (a well-known singer of mixed race, from Tobago)—sings about the Hindu god Krishna. Then a chutney called "Bulwasie." The programme runs on as follows—Hindi film songs and bhangra; chutney with dancing, including a hijra [trans-gendered person]; romantic American pop; Jamaican dancehall.

The audience dances in the same fashion to all the music—a little faster to the dancehall beat. An old couple, the man at least 65, the woman in her 50s, wearing the same designer shirts with big alphabets on them, hold each other and dance slowly to the pop songs and the old Hindi film songs, and facing each other—faster—to the rest. A Surinam family, very light skinned, one woman has permed and dyed blonde hair, facing the stage and drinking whisky out of paper cups—they keep reaching out to touch the performers—especially the blonde, to upcoming young singer Richard Ramnarine.[68]

The Controversy

The flurry of discussion in the early '90s about the East Indian woman and chutney-soca kept coming back to issues of female sexuality, much like the discussions about indentured women in the nineteenth century. Today one cannot speak of how the sexuality of the East Indian woman in Trinidad is constituted except through the grid provided by discourses of racial difference (the question of "the opposite race"); cultural and ethnic difference (the supposed cultural attributes of the "Indian" woman as opposed to the "African" woman),[69] and caste-class or "nation" ("low nation" and "high nation" are terms I have heard older Trinidadians use to refer to what they see as caste differences).

These discourses intersect in various ways with that of "East Indian nationalism," which is often seen as being at odds with "Trinidadian" or "West Indian" nationalism. Unlike in the nationalist discourse in India in which East and West were thematized by the race and culture of the colonized and the colonizer, respectively, in Trinidad the presence of the "Afro-Saxon" (the term used by some Trinidadian scholars, such as Lloyd Best, to refer critically to the culture of the ex-slave society, which is part Anglo-Saxon and part African) indicates that in many ways, the "African," who had been in contact with the West a couple of centuries before the Indians who migrated to the Caribbean, came to stand in for the West as far as the Indians were concerned.[70]

We may speculate that contact with the European in India did not affect labor to a great extent partly because the Western master belonged to a different social class, and his ways of life were not part of the milieu of the Indian laborer. In Trinidad, however, the African (already part of the "West" in the New World) was presumably of *the same class* as the Indian, occupying a similar social position. The transformations among Indians, therefore, had to do with finding ways to inhabit, and change, their new home through a series of complex negotiations with other racial groups, the most significant of which was the African. Exposure to "Western" ways,

Chutney dancers. Surabhi Sharma/R. V. Ramani.

therefore, came to the Indian through interaction with the Afro-Caribbean rather than through contact with the European. Even today, when Trinidad Indians speak of Westernization, they often treat it as synonymous with "creolization," the common term for the Afro-Trinidadian still being "Creole."[71] It is not surprising, then, that the controversy over the phenomenon of chutney-soca tends to be structured in terms of creolization and the consequent degradation of "Indian culture."

As the cultural critic Gordon Rohlehr points out, to be "visible" in the Caribbean is literally to be on stage, to perform.[72] When East Indian *women* take to the stage as singers or dancers, or as politicians, the protracted struggle over "culture" and "authenticity" takes a new turn, not only in the national arena between different ethnic groups, but also among East Indians themselves.[73] In the chutney-soca controversy, which may have provoked some rethinking of what the claim to Indianness involves in Trinidad, the singers, and the participants in the chutney dances, have been denounced by many East Indians for what is termed their "vulgarity" and "obscenity."[74] The objection has been directed partly at the spate of "Nani" calypsos, starting with "Dolly Nanee" in 1972, sung by Clipper (of East Indian descent), a song about his girlfriend's habit of not washing her genitals. The word acquired new popularity in the mid- and late 1980s, with "Nanny" (Scrunter, 1985), "Love Meh Nanny" (Sharlene Boodram, 1987), "Nani Wine" (Crazy, 1989), "Nanny" (Oliver Chapman, 1989), a host of songs with or without sexual connotations, and, of course, Drupatee's controversial "Lick Down Mih Nani."

Prominent East Indians have indicated that their objection has to do with the display in a public space of a cultural form that used to be confined to the home. The public sphere here is considered to be an "African" realm, so the making public of chutney (and its rendering in English) necessarily involves making it available to the gaze of Afro-Trinidadians. The disapproval of "vulgarity" can be read also as an anxiety regarding miscegenation, the new form of chutney becoming a metonym for the supposed increase in relationships between Indian women and African men. When Drupatee sings in "Hotter Than a Chulha" about the blending together "in a perfect mixture" of African and Indian rhythms, it is almost always assumed by her critics that she is talking about interracial marriage.

The East Indian responses to the public appearance of chutney have been diverse. "Chutney is breaking up homes and bringing disgrace," proclaimed a letter writer in the Sunday Express.[75] "Culture means refinement, and this is not culture," declared a participant in a seminar on the chutney phenomenon.[76] The Hindu Women's Organization (HWO), a small but vocal urban group, demanded that the police intervene at chutney performances and enforce the law against vulgarity. The "Indian secularist" position, however, was that chutney was "functional," that it represented "Indian cultural continuity and persistence." Social interaction between boys and girls in an "exclusively Indian environment" was only to be encouraged, argued the self-identified "secularist." Not only was chutney an East Indian alternative to Carnival, it was also a way of establishing "cultural unity with India."[77] Others accused the "Muslim producers" of some chutney festivals, an obvious reference to the Mohammed brothers, for using tunes from Hindu bhajans, an act they considered sacrilegious.[78] A few East Indian men expressed alarm at what they called the "creolization" and "douglarization" of "Indian culture" and alleged that African men were writing the songs for the chutney performers in such a way as to "denigrate" East Indian cultural values. One letter writer who had attended the opening ceremony of the World Hindu Conference protested against "the lewd and suggestive behaviour of the female dancer" during the chutney part of the cultural program. "This standard of behaviour," he said, could not be sanctioned by Hinduism, which he claimed had "high moral and spiritual values."[79] In a hurt response, the dancer in question, Sandra Beharry, said that for her chutney dancing "is a very sensual dance which involves the use of every fibre of the body from eyes, neck, shoulders, waist, hip and feet either separately or together." Although it was a dance with "hot and spicy movements," it was not "a vulgar dance.... [V]ulgar dancing is when the dancer strips herself. I do not strip myself when I dance."[80]

Others stated flatly that "no Indian woman has any right to sing calypso" or that "Indian women have been a disgrace to Hinduism."[81] An acerbic writer proclaimed that "for an Indian girl to throw her upbringing and culture to mix with vulgar music, sex and alcohol in Carnival tents tells me that something is radically wrong with her psyche. Drupatee Ramgoonai has chosen to worship the God of sex, wine and easy money."[82] Practitioners of "classical" cultural forms, like the well-known dancer Rajkumar Krishna Persad, described chutney in contrast to their own style of performance. In an interview, Persad said, "[You] wouldn't want to send your child to do any old kind of dance. You want to send your child to do something of class and people realised that I was trained so they send their children by me. They realise is no wining down thing, no chutney thing, disgracing yourself like prostitutes: you are going to do something of class."[83]

While one writer contended that chutney represented a unique new Trinidadian cultural form,[84] yet another argued that it was self-deluding to think of chutney as creative or unique: "No creation whatsoever has taken place in chutney. The form and content have simply moved from the private domain to the public and from a female environment to a mixed one."[85] "Indianness" is seen in many of these responses to be inextricable from cultural purity, which in turn is seen to hinge on questions of women's propriety and morality. In the global context of the reconfiguration of a "Hindu" identity, the chutney phenomenon is inserted by elite Trinidadian Indians into the process that disaggregates Hindus from other "Indians" while redescribing a "Hindu" space as inclusive of all that is Indian, as being identical with Indianness. Curiously enough, this formation of elite Trinidadian Indian identity today is facilitated not only by religio-political organizations such as the Vishwa Hindu Parishad (World Hindu Forum) but also by the professedly secular Indian state, which intervenes in Trinidad in the academic and cultural spheres.[86]

A news item in the *Trinidad Guardian* of April 22, 1991, reports the speech of Pundit Ramesh Tiwari, president of the Edinburgh Hindu Temple, who says that "the concept of the liberated woman" has created a "crisis in womanhood" that threatens the Hindu religion, which is "taking steps to reintroduce values to the Hindu woman." Indrani Rampersad, a leading figure in the HWO, writes that it is "Hindus" (and not "Indians") who form the largest ethnic group in Trinidad. The HWO condemned chutney performances for their "vulgarity," claiming that "as a Hindu group the HWO is best placed to analyse the chutney phenomenon from [a Hindu] perspective, and as a women's group they are doubly so equipped."[87] The HWO, however, was not supported by some who otherwise shared their position on chutney-soca. The East Indian academic and senator Ramesh Deosaran elsewhere questioned one of the objectives of the HWO, which was to "advance" the status of women. Deosaran objected to the use of this word in a context of "increasing sexual freedom."[88] This freedom, he argued, had resulted in such things as the "intense gyrations" of chutney dancing, "a serious cause for concern by members of the Hindu and Indian community."

Taking issue with this kind of position are some East Indian feminists who see chutney-soca as a positive development, symbolic of the attempts of women to overcome inequality in many spheres.[89] The feminist activist and scholar Rawwida Baksh-Soodeen urges middle-class and upper-class East Indian women not to take the stand taken by their men against chutney, which she sees as "clearly a movement by lower class Hindu women against male control, and towards greater personal and communal freedom." She suggests that all Indian women will benefit from "the independence of women expressed in chutney dancing," which represents that "my body and sexuality belong to me, and nobody has the power to prevent my expression."[90] This appears to be an assertion made against the stereotyping of East Indian women described this way by the anthropologist Aisha Khan: "Many depictions of Indo-Caribbean women have tended to implicitly (or otherwise) assume docility, obedience, shelteredness, and being ruled with a vengeance by a socially anachronistic patriarchy."[91] However, Baksh-Soodeen's view of feminism is criticized by another writer who also calls herself a feminist—Indrani Rampersad of the HWO—who wrote in a column in the *Trinidad Guardian*, "If the ability to manipulate the pelvic area were any indication of the independence, freedom and happiness and control that women have over their lives, then the . . . chutney gyrators in TT [Trinidad and Tobago] would be amongst the happiest in the world. . . . Superficial outward actions of showing the body to be free to make all kinds of movement is not necessarily linked to a similar freedom in the condition of women."[92] Here is an incipient debate on what constitutes women's autonomy that may well be taken up not just by Indo-Trinidadians but also by the larger women's movement in the Caribbean.

In the wake of the chutney-soca controversy, a Pichakaree Competition was started in 1992 by the East Indian theologian Raviji, with the aim of encouraging local compositions as an "Indian alternative to Carnival music."[93] The competition was hosted during the Phagwa or Holi (Spring) festival. Use of the "Indian language" was encouraged, although it was not specified what that referred to, with the preference being for "limited and imaginative use rather than bulk," presumably intended not to discourage listeners who for the most part did not understand Hindi or Bhojpuri.[94]

Going back twenty years in the newspaper archives, one finds the following letter about Phagwa not being like Carnival, although the writer also adds: "A sad thing, there were men and women who participated in the Phagwa celebrations who were disgustingly drunk. Young boys and girls were not far behind."[95] The same author wrote elsewhere that everyone was to be blamed for low sexual standards: "It is true that Indian girls in particular are today 'singing songs of love in the mud,' for which there is no forgiveness. Formerly fathers, grandfathers, husbands and brothers would let young wayward Hindu females know they are misbehaving."[96] Continuing the complaint against the unacceptable behavior of East Indian girls, another letter writer had this to say: "In recent *Indian Variety* and *Mastana Bahar* shows, I have seen girls in maxies [ankle-length dresses], but with their necks, arms and backs exposed. I do not think this is right for any girl who participates in Indian culture. To me it looks too unfeminine. Therefore, I would appreciate very much, if the organisers of these Indian programmes, could encourage our Indian girls to dress in a more decent and graceful manner."[97]

Talking to a range of Indo-Trinidadian women of different ages, I came across several negative responses to chutney and chutney-soca, focusing in particular on Drupatee, the most visible female Indo-Trinidadian performer:

> I do not like Drupatee. I don't know if it's the way she expresses herself or the way she sings. . . . But her stage performance, I don't like what she performs as an artist. It's not appealing to me then. I believe it's more the way she carries on . . . the way she wines . . . is more chutney, and I don't like chutney music from the time I was a young girl growing up. I never danced to that type of music. (Mabel, in her forties)[98]

> My family is very, very religious, and they would not approve of going [to a chutney-show]. . . . They would just call it a waste of time, but I have a lot of friends who just live to go to a "chutney" where they could party and drink and have a good time. It's no big deal, right? My mom, she really, really finds Drupatee distasteful—the way she dresses and carries on, on the stage gyrating, and this woman, she has no respect for herself. And there are other women, other people who enjoy her and appreciate her and think she's really, really a great performer. Personally, I didn't appreciate her. (Vashnie, in her twenties)[99]

At the beginning of the new century, the discussion still finds purchase. In an article titled, "Carnival Not for Indians," Kamal Persad argues that "Carnival is *adharmic* and cannot be condoned by Hindu spirituality. The chutney challenge to Carnival is real. For those Indians in pursuit of pleasure (*kama*), chutney is providing that alternative to Carnival fetes and the Carnival culture. It heralds Indian cultural solidarity and the Indian withdrawal from Carnival. . . . Carnival is hostile to Indians."[100] The idea of a hostile Carnival seems to find resonance among the ideologues of the "neo-Indianists," such as Kumar Mahabir (formerly Noor Kumar Mahabir) and Rajnie Ramlakhan. In contrast to the viewpoint that chutney has to be posited against Afro-Trinidadian and Western music is the daily auditory experience of many young Indo-Trinidadians who listen to and enjoy several kinds of music. These young people claim to like chutney-soca for its innovative beat and English lyrics as well as for the possibilities it provides for interactive singing.[101]

Speaking out against these fans of the music, the columnist Indira Maharaj, invoking the Nani figure, writes that "Soca chutney [is] sinking":

> *Refrain:*
> Nanee, nanee, run for yuh dignity,
> Is again time for Soca chutney.
> . . .
> Lang time we coulda complain
> About dem calypsonian
> But what we go say when we hearin worse
> From we own Indian!
> . . .
> Dey cyah go beyon de bailna [rolling pin], de Bhougie [sister-in-law] an de Nannie!
> . . .
> Ah tink ah de tears ah meh Nannee.
> Ah tink ah de anger ah meh Bhougie. . . .
> Wit dis kinda ah Chutney Soca, Ah worried
> about we culture.[102]

Maharaj launches an attack on "Carnival culture" in an article titled "The Wining Must Stop." Referring to what she calls Carnival and calypso culture, she contends that "the expression and exhibition of female sexuality, wining, has been an acceptable part of that culture." Indian women adopted this from the "hegemonic culture," so much so that it has become a matter of pride for "young Indian females to say 'who tell yuh Indian cyah wine [who said Indians cannot wine]?'" Maharaj further suggests that this imitative hedonism has the support of certain feminists in Trinidad: "A western, feminist stream of thought which sees the expression of female sexuality in the public domain as legitimate, as a woman revelling in her own sexuality, is also conducive to Indian women wining in the public domain."[103] Critical of this approach is the Indo-Trinidadian feminist Sheila Rampersad, who sees it as an expression of upper-caste "Brahmin culture":

> In fact chutney music is incredibly popular among Indians, and among young people who go because chutney allows them to behave in a Hindu or Indian framework in the way they really would want to behave. And if they're in Carnival they'll say you're being bastardised or something. . . . You are doing it in your own context and this is the context we have evolved to do it in. So there is a class discussion that must happen there, there is the generational discussion that must happen, . . . because those are the kind of dynamics influencing chutney. Nobody's stopping to say all these things. Why is it so popular? What is it moving in people? Nobody has stopped to ask those questions and that's where our analysis will have to be directed. It really is an outlet for people. And to celebrate in the way we see Africans celebrating. We wanted to celebrate and have not had the framework to do it.[104]

Rhoda Reddock points to the ambivalences in the upper-class East Indian denunciation of chutney:

> A few years ago, Sat Maharaj [head of the Sanatan Dharma Mahasabha, which claims to represent Trinidadian Hindus] said that chutney dancing was worse than carnival dancing. But when Sundar Popo died, he grabbed the whole limelight of Sundar Popo's funeral, took it over. I remember Mahasabha was organizing the funeral, to the shock of everybody. He spent his whole life saying chutney was wrong and bad, and now he took over the funeral and decided who could sing and who could go and who couldn't go. So people were writing in the newspapers saying, what is this? We can't believe this! . . . So, on the one hand, there's this ambivalence . . because [chutney] presents a crisis of representation, in that it represents Indian women as just . . . like African women, liking to dance and wine, and liking sex, and so like everybody else. But at the same time, chutney is a symbol of their location and their contribution in the local space. So it's a Catch-22 situation. And I think that there's no doubt that especially women, grassroots women, identify with chutney. They are the vast majority going to these big events. And even though the men dance, it is the women who really become totally absorbed and enthralled and carried away with the music.[105]

The Body in the Voice

In this chapter I have provided a historical analysis of chutney-soca both as a musical genre and as a cultural practice. Listening to the songs, or seeing them performed, impels us also to construct a conceptual frame that plots the relation of the listener to the voice. What do we hear when we hear chutney-soca? I suggest that Roland Barthes's distinction between pheno-song and geno-song, from the essay "The Grain of the Voice," could be usefully deployed here.[106]

But first we should look at the "cultural body" of the East Indian woman —or should we say, the encultured body—and ask what proliferating discourses converge on chutney-soca. The controversy seemed to indicate an intimate connection between the musical form and the East Indian woman's sexuality. I would argue, however, that chutney-soca does not express or provide a statement of an existing sexuality. Instead, it represents the point of convergence of a multiplicity of discourses around sexuality, serving in turn as a node from which such discourses proliferate. Further, the sexuality question cannot be separated from the question of racial difference.

A series of popular conceptions about "Indians" and "Africans" circulate in the performative space of chutney-soca, just as they do in other aspects of the public sphere in Trinidad. One idea is that of the rampant sexuality of the Indian woman. "Ride an Indian or walk": A non-East Indian woman told me that this was a phrase commonly used among Trinidadian men, referring to the Indian woman's allegedly insatiable sexual appetite as well as her sexual skills and suggesting that if you hadn't slept with an Indian woman, you didn't know what you were missing. This notion may have a history that goes back to the days of indenture and some of the representations that prevailed then of the promiscuous Indian woman. Another idea relevant to an understanding of both calypso-soca and chutney-soca is the supposed liking of the Indian woman for "*kilwal*" (Creole or Negro), where the representational tradition includes 1950s calypsos like Killer's "Moonia" ("What's the matter beti [daughter]? / That kilwal standing like jankey [donkey] / You got am speed / So you like am that nigger breed") and Sparrow's "Marajhin" calypsos of the 1980s. A related idea, discussed in chapter 4, is that of the emasculation of the Indian man and the corresponding enhancement of the African man's sexuality, especially that of the calypsonian. Then we have the notion of the African woman's threatening sexuality (the Afro-Trinidadian calypsonian's endless complaint is about the woman from whose attempts at entrapment he must escape) as also stories about the sexual appetite of young East Indian women. (As one of my interviewees told me, these girls behaved "worse" than "the other race" in order to appear "modern.")

The reactions to chutney-soca obliquely invoke all of these intersecting notions of sexuality. Without separating out the semiotic elements of chutney-soca—music, lyrics, body language of dancer and performer, voice—and operating therefore what Barthes in a different context called an "expressive reduction," we might want to ask why chutney-soca as it is performed arouses such varied reactions from its audience, which range from the ecstatic to the hostile, from the celebratory to the denunciatory. But the answer may not be as obvious as the media controversy suggests, especially since the most successful chutney-soca songs all seem to refer to chutney-soca itself, reflecting on what it is and what it does and on its physical, cultural, and political effects.[107]

Barthes regrets the inability of language to interpret music except by piling on adjectives and argues for a displacement of the "fringe of contact between music and language."[108] To achieve this displacement, he proposes a distinction between pheno-song/text and geno-song/text so that the "grain" of the voice can emerge as a signifier. While the pheno-song includes the rules of the genre, the performer's interpretive style, the mode of communication and expression—in short, the "tissue of cultural values" that involves tastes, fashions, and so on—the geno-song refers to the "volume of the singing and speaking voice" and the generation of signification from the very materiality of language.[109]

How might chutney-soca work at these two levels? The "grain" of the voice, according to Barthes, would be the friction between the music and the particular language (not the "message"). In chutney-soca, the music is the fusing of *tassa* (a goatskin drum) with trap-set and keyboards and of *dhantal* (long iron rod hit by a curved piece of iron) with horn (saxophone). The language is Trinidadian English and Bhojpuri-Awadhi-Hindi, with a few stray Punjabi words thrown in—the vocabulary of Trinidadian English being shared with other communities in the society, such as African, Chinese, French Creole, Portuguese, Syrian, with different cultural-social histories. Given that the majority of the population, including the East Indians, know very little Bhojpuri or Hindi, the "signifying play" of the use of this vocabulary is clearly unrelated to "communication" or direct ex-

Cassette cover: The "Nani" tape.

pression.¹¹⁰ Rather, it is an attempt to let the melody and language work at each other.

Unlike in the monolingual French context of which Barthes speaks, in Trinidadian chutney-soca we have the coming together of English and Bhojpuri, with the former language being more widely understood. The "grain" of the song, then, would be "the materiality of the body speaking its mother tongue; perhaps the letter, almost certainly *signifiance*."¹¹¹ Here the mother tongue, I would argue, is Trinidadian English and not Bhojpuri, just as the cultural/encultured body of the female East Indian is not simply an "Indian" body. This could be a plausible explanation for why the English-language chutney and chutney-soca songs are so much livelier than the songs sung exclusively in Bhojpuri or Hindi, languages that are rarely spoken now in Trinidad. A puzzle—not just to be put down to my lack of immediate understanding of the lyrics—is why conventional chutney as a genre is so monotonous, so musically and textually lacking in innovation. Taken out of the context of worship or wedding ritual, detached from the functions it seemed to serve, East Indian music seems somewhat static.

But listen to Drupatee's "Lick Down Mih Nani," "Mr. Bissessar," or "Real Unity" (with Machel Montano), in which the "volume of the singing and speaking voice" fills the head, the room, the auditorium. What Barthes calls the "voluptousness of [the] sound-signifiers" is evident in Drupatee's voice as it "sways us to *jouissance.*"[112] As we hear "Lick Down Mih Nani" it is not just the double entendres that pleasure us, but something spilling over, perhaps—as Barthes would have it—into pure signification.[113] For Barthes, "grain" is the body in the singing voice, marking the passage of work into text.[114] From the fixable meanings of the bounded song, we move into the space where meanings are fluid and resist capture. Perhaps this is far more threatening than the literal or textual meaning of the chutney-soca song. In cultural spaces in which identities are being refigured with some urgency, and new boundaries are being drawn, the body in the voice disrupts mere mellifluousness, and the seemingly simple referentiality of the song begins to gesture at the possibility of meaning itself.

Reading Indenture and Chutney-Soca

I wonder how much my feeling of strangeness and difference in relation to East Indian women has to do with the unfamiliarity of bodies and tongues. South Indians were approximately only 5 percent of immigrants, and their original languages, which would have made some sense to me, disappeared long ago into plantation Hindi. The bulk of the immigrants were from northern India, and the dialects of these communities, which sometimes surface in the chutney songs and words from which might lurk in Trinidadians' everyday speech, for the most part are unintelligible to me, trained as I am only in school-level, homogenized Hindi. To my eyes, Trinidad Indian women's bodies are not encoded like Indian ones; neither are they Westernised. (The Indo-Euro-American tonalities are familiar ones to us in India because of the continuous contemporary migration to North America and some parts of Europe.) Perhaps, as suggested earlier, modernity for the East Indian has been Creole and not Western modernity. Consider the possibility of the encounter of Indian indentured female laborers of varied castes (predominantly the middle and lower castes) with the West refracted through the "Creole," and consider what formations of "Westernization" it might result in, as opposed to the upper-caste-dominated professional migration to the West and the resultant convergence of Indian elite subjectivities with Western habits and aesthetics.[115] I think of the Indian computer engineer from Madras (now Chennai) who studied in Canada in the 1970s and dated Indo-Trinidadian girls, there being a substantial Trinidadian population in that country; he said it took him two years to figure out they were "not Indian."

The resemblance between the vocabulary of the anti-indenture campaign, discussed in chapter 2, and that of the critics of chutney-soca may allow us to conclude rather misleadingly that what is asserting itself in both is "Indian patriarchy." This is misleading because, as phenomena, elite nationalism in India in the early twentieth century and elite assertions of "Indian" ethnic identity in late-twentieth-century Trinidad are somewhat different from each other. Although there may be a historical connection between Indian nationalism and indentured labor in the British colonies, the analysis of contemporary Trinidadian discourses of East Indian women's sexuality has to be placed in the framework of the predominantly biracial society of the island. Indian tradition (and Indian women) in Trinidad come to be defined as that which is not, cannot be allowed to become, African. While the assertion of a separate and unchanging "Hindu" or "Indian" identity in Trinidad is enabled in part by the colonial and Indian nationalist reconstructions of ethnic and racial identities in which definitions of women and what is "proper" to them occupy a crucial position, such an assertion is today part of a Trinidadian reconstruction of such identities, a process whose participants include both "Indians" and "Africans." And while the chutney-soca controversy could be read as marking an attempt to reconstitute East Indian patriarchy, perhaps it could also be read as a sign of patriarchy in crisis. The East Indian attempt to "resolve" the question of women, just as Indian nationalism in the early twentieth century sought to do, can be seen as aligned with the effort to consolidate the meanings of cultural and racial identity at a time when the new political visibility of "Indians" is providing newer spaces of assertion for women as well as men. Both of these projects, however, are rendered impossible precisely because of the need to continually refigure the distinctions between the two groups, signified as "Indian" and "African," that dominate the postcolonial space of Trinidad. The next chapter looks at the representation of East Indians in calypso and soca, where the majority of performers are Afro-Trinidadians. My attempt will be to analyze how notions of African masculinity depend on characterizations of East Indian women, as well as of East Indian men, and to emphasize the significance of representing the "Indian" to political-cultural assertions of Creole nationalism.

FOUR

★ Jumping out of Time:

The "Indian" in Calypso

I will do anything to make you happy
So if you think its best
I change my style of dress
I will wear a kapra or a dhoti...
I'll learn to grind massala and chonkay dhal
And jump out of time to sweet pan soca melody.
—Mighty Sparrow, "Marajhin"

In chapter 3, I sought to investigate the East Indian reinvention of the calypso. This chapter examines the processes by which Indians have been represented in calypsos sung by Afro-Trinidadians. While East Indian differences from the Creole tend to be stereotyped in cultural practices dominated by Afro-Trinidadians, the question to ask would be how they are constructed and why. I set out to examine not the "images" of East Indians we get from the calypsos but, rather, to ask what the calypso's mode of signification suggests about the specific configurations of the "Indian" with the "African" formed by Trinidadian history. As I elaborated in chapter 1, African Trinidadians seek to define themselves in opposition to East Indians. In no cultural practice is this process of definition more obvious than in the calypso. My attempt will be not to set a knowledge of the "real" Indo-Trinidadian against the stereotypes in calypso, but to raise questions about the changing historical functions of the "Indian" in a musical form dominated by Afro-Trinidadians.

In this chapter, which looks at calypso music from the 1930s to the early twenty-first century, I try to understand how in the calypso, a cultural practice that is crucial to Trinidadian nationalism—although one that is often critical of the government in power, if not of the nation-state itself—the question of the "Indian" sometimes comes to occupy center stage.[1] From being exotic creatures whose dress, language, and customs appeared as objects of ridicule as well as fantasy, East Indians at the beginning of the twenty-first century in Trinidad, finally (although tentatively and intermittently) holders of political power, are key figures in the ballads directed by calypsonians against a supposedly elite group, as they also are in reinterpretations of Trinidadian history (Brother Marvin's "Jahaji Bhai") or celebrations of Trinidadian multiculturalism (Machel's and Drupatee's "Real Unity").

The musical form that has come to be called calypso emerged in the early part of the twentieth century, when singers produced social commentary in the newly hegemonic English language, albeit with a Trinidadian twist. The beginnings of public singing and entertainment in Trinidad have been linked by scholars such as Gordon Rohlehr, Errol Hill, and others to stick fighting and Carnival, popular practices among the slaves of African descent before and after Emancipation in 1838. Documenting the origin of these practices in colonial times, Rohlehr points out that planters viewed the dances of slaves—held on Saturdays and Sundays—"with a mixture of suspicion and tolerance," since they were thought to provide "therapy for the enslaved" even if they sometimes provided the opportunity for plotting rebellions. The occurrence of the dances on Sundays especially attracted in all slave societies the criticism of the church, which denounced them for being sacrilegious and sexually suggestive.[2]

Both the former slaves and the indentured Indians who replaced them on the plantation had many encounters with the colonial rulers over their cultural practices, all of which were viewed with hostility, whether it was the Hosay festival of the East Indians or the practice of obeah, or Shangoism, or the Shouter Baptists, or Carnival, all of which attracted mainly lower-class black people, both men and women.[3] Carnival in particular became the focus of tensions around the maintenance of class boundaries in post-Emancipation Trinidad. Needless to say, in such a society, class distinctions were closely related to racial ones. Before the 1830s, whites celebrated the period of several weeks before Lent (for Roman Catholics, a time of penance, fasting, and abstinence) as the time for Carnival, when they masqueraded, played jokes, held dances, and visited friends. Most of these activities excluded even the free blacks. After the abolition of slavery, Blacks turned Carnival into a major celebration, with loud music and revelry, attracting the disapproval of the colonial government, which tried in various ways to regulate or ban aspects of the festival.[4] The stick fighting, or calinda, that was an important part of Carnival had as its exponents both East Indians and Africans, as eighteenth-century paintings and illustrations reveal, although the two communities may not have occupied the same social spaces. In the post-Emancipation period, thousands of migrants from other parts of the Anglophone West Indies ("small islanders") settled in Trinidad. By 1881, the year of the Canboulay Riot, they numbered about ten thousand—about one third of the population of Port of Spain—and were ready to join forces with the "equally explosive and exploited East Indian workers."[5] The term "canboulay" itself is derived from *cannes brulees*, French for burned canes, referring originally to acts of arson caused by slaves on plantations and subsequently to the procession of ex-slaves with lighted torches, or *flambeaux*, that were incorporated into Carnival.[6]

Rumors about the colonial authorities' suppression of Carnival circulated regularly, especially after 1860, when *jamet/jamette* Carnival took shape. The terms were French patois for those men and women who were part of the underworld, beneath the *diametre* of decent society,[7] and who were joined by the growing slum-dwelling black working class of the city. There was also serious unemployment in the city by 1880, and the newspapers carried complaints from "respectable people" about the lawlessness of vagrants. Until the beginning of the twentieth century, it was the urban black underworld that had taken over Carnival.[8] The revelers formed into bands whose members dressed up in different kinds of rich costumes and had their own stick fighters and *chantuelle* (female lead singer), accompanied by a female chorus.[9] An official report on the Canboulay Riot includes the following:

> From the time these bands took part in the Carnival, the riot and disorder greatly increased as well as the obscenity and indecency attending

these exhibitions. It is common during Carnival for the vilest songs, in which the names of the ladies of the island are introduced to be sung in the streets, and the vilest talk to be indulged in which filthy and disgusting scenes are enacted by both sexes, which are beyond description and would be almost beyond belief were it not that they were vouched for by witnesses of unimpeachable credibility.[10]

The main function of the violently denunciatory language of this report would presumably be to legitimize the retaliatory actions contemplated by the government, among whose members were the European and Creole elites who resented the Africanization of Carnival. The colonial anxiety about "riot" and "disorder" is often linked to "obscenity," even in the critique of the East Indian Hosay, which, like Carnival, provided a space for diverse groups of subaltern people to come together.

Some amount of antagonism existed in Carnival between bands that represented different African groups—in particular, those of the post-Emancipation nonslave immigrants (including a large group of Yorubas, who, although they intermarried with other African groups such as the Kongo and Hausa, tried to keep alive a distinct cultural identity) and those bands formed by Trinidad-born Creoles or immigrants from other West Indian islands. While the various African languages became creolized or gradually disappeared, their songs and religious chants were incorporated into the secular songs of the early Carnival singers, especially into the "satire-cum-boast tradition," with its combination of *picong*, or provocation, and *mepris*, or scorn. The opposite of this iconoclastic tendency, also seen in calypso, would be a form of social reprimand.[11] A related process occurs with East Indian music in a different and much later period, with public entertainment coming to consist of songs originally composed for ritual contexts. While there is no extensive documentation regarding the East Indian participation in *mas'* (short for masquerade, the term refers to the costumed Carnival processionists), many informal accounts testify to a substantial Indian presence, both in Port of Spain and in central and southern Trinidad. Indian men often played mas' dressed as "jab jabs" (and referred to as coolie devils), "with their whips, bright colors and bells which Indians would have understood as 'ghungroos' [ankle bells used in Indian folk and other dances].... Indians also played red or wild Indian ... and were also deeply involved in the stickfight."[12]

The basic tunes of calypso, numbering from a dozen to fifty depending on the cataloguer, are constantly recycled, whereas the lyrics—humorous, satirical, lewd, full of *fatigue* (sharp teasing)—form the original component of the song. The language of the calypso moved from patois to English after 1898, when Norman LeBlanc sang a satire on "Jerningham the Governor." The structure of the calypso often included a call-and-response pattern (traced to Yoruba songs by scholars like Warner-Lewis). Early stanzaic patterns would be based on the calinda/stick fight antiphon (couplets); expanding on these would be four-line stanzas drawing on French, English, and Scottish balladic traditions or even church hymns. Inputs for the calypso form also came from the African dances prevalent in late-nineteenth-century Trinidad, such as the Jhouba, the Bel Air, and the Bamboula, with their distinct rhythms (duple/quadruple as well as triple time in the Jhouba; the balladic structure of Bel Air into which the Jhouba became assimilated; the frenetic and repetitive rhythm of Bamboula, associated with stick fighting).[13]

As I discussed in chapter 1, the 1880s were a time of unrest among the East Indian indentured laborers, whose Hosay festival, originally celebrated as part of Muharram by the minuscule minority of Shia Muslims (but that very quickly included Sunni Muslims and Hindu Indians, as well as black drummers) had become an occasion for revelry, drinking, and dancing. In 1884, there was an incident of police firing at Princes Town during Carnival; that same year, workers defying an ordinance confining them to their own estates during Hosay marched toward San Fernando town by the thousands and were fired on by the police, resulting in the massacre of eighteen people and injuries to dozens. The planters and the colonial government increasingly sought to prohibit both Carnival and Hosay, using a series of interim measures such as a ban on drums and on stick fighting that applied to both festivals. Historians note an increase in the verbal violence of the calypso during this period, which, they suggest, came to substitute for the physical aggression of stick fighting. The ban on drums led to the introduction of the tamboo bamboo—bamboo tubes of different lengths either struck against the ground or against each other—to provide percussion. This remained the main form of accompaniment until the late 1930s, when the first steel drums emerged. While Mighty Chalkdust emphasizes that the steel band derived from the tamboo bamboo, other scholars have suggested that the East Indian tassa drum was part of the musical genealogy of the steel drum.[14]

Calypso or cariso/kaiso singing eventually acquired middle-class and upper-class patrons, who sometimes provided prizes and other kinds of sponsorship.[15] By the first decades of the twentieth century, bamboo and *cocoyea* (coconut branch) tents were being set up around Carnival time where the singers competed for the audience's attention. Picong was the order of the day, and criticism of the ruling class was ritually voiced, as were praise songs for Empire. By this time, the associated dancing and masquerade for Carnival had also come to acquire the aspects of "pretty mas" that today predominate in the image of Trinidad Carnival recognized worldwide. The Sans Humanite calypso, which flourished as an oratorical tradition in the period from 1900 to 1920, later merged into the *cariso*, the female banter song; the self-aggrandizement of the Sans Humanite song changed to include social and political issues, sometimes adopting a ballad-like narrative structure. When in 1941 the United States established military bases in Trinidad, American servicemen went to the calypso tents looking for "bawdy sexual themes," not social commentary, leading to a revival of the sexual banter of nineteenth-century singers. Calypsonians also moved from tent to tent from the 1920s to the 1950s in search of competitions organized by "coloured and East Indian merchants."[16]

While the impact of the East Indian Hosay drum (the tassa) had been felt for decades, references to Indian cultural practices came into the calypso only in the 1930s. We may speculate that this appearance of the Indian in an urban musical form like the calypso is related to the increasing visibility of East Indians in cities like Port of Spain and San Fernando by this time, as they consolidated their positions in occupations other than agriculture and as an Indian middle class began to emerge. But even as far back as the last decade of the nineteenth century, Indians were clearly such a visible part of the population that an editorial in the *Port-of-Spain Gazette* (dated December 5, 1890) about the "Indian Spectre" said, "Are we to continue to be a West Indian island. . . . Or is the whirligig of time . . . to people the island with the East Indian population?" Tikasingh comments that the editorial found the increase in the Indian population disturbing, saying that it would lead to the displacement of "Creoles" as the majority population of Trinidad, so that "the mistake of Columbus will have been ethnologically rectified."[17] Given the extent of this visibility, it does seem somewhat surprising that the calypso did not refer to the East Indian until the 1930s, although its composers and singers had been around for three decades or more. It is possible that Indians, long after indenture had ended, were still not claimants to full citizenship in Trinidad and thus were not taken into account by those who were commenting on the social scene.

The "Indian" Calypso

Two main kinds of songs involving East Indians were sung from the 1930s until the 1980s, after which marked difference began to emerge both in the thematics and the melodic structure of what can be called calypso. The songs were usually either about East Indian women, expressing the calypsonian's desire for a relationship with an exoticized being, or about East Indian economic or political success, expressing envy at something seemingly achieved at the expense of the African. Also, cutting across both categories, there were songs that capitalized on the non-Western—and therefore seen as peculiar—customs, language, food, and dress of the East Indian, who was often held up to ridicule.

The "Indian" calypso is distinguished by its use of language, with Hindi or Bhojpuri words and phrases liberally used along with the predominantly Trinidadian English lyrics, and its use of melody and instrumentation. Some calypsos drew on Hindi film songs and others on East Indian folk music. The tassa and dholak drums, as well as the dhantal, also were frequently used along with the conventional calypso instruments. Singers like Ras Shorty I have always insisted on recognizing the mixing of Indian and African musical forms and rhythms in the history of the calypso and have contributed to further efforts in that direction (see chapter 3).

If calypso is acknowledged to be a preeminent Trinidadian popular cultural form, with an appeal that spans race, gender, and generational differences, it has to be understood as a significant site for the production of dominant notions of femininity and masculinity. In a certain type of calypso, where the Indian woman is being courted by the African man, these notions are foregrounded in such a manner as to obscure or deflect questions of race: Proper femininity is racialized as East Indian and imaged as beautiful and submissive; proper masculinity is then normed as African, embodied in the wordsmith calypsonian or the badjohn.[18] African masculinity, however, also has to be shaped alongside and against the Indian, whose masculinity is then delegitimized or becomes bad or violent masculinity. Further, I would suggest that when Indian femininity is sung into being with the desiring African male voice, from Dictator's "Moonia" to

Sparrow's "Marajhin," a kind of hypermasculinity is produced in contrast to the object of desire.

The early songs blended references to the exoticism of the Indian woman's clothing and the strangeness of Indian food; interestingly, both were seen as intensely desirable despite the Creole's unfamiliarity with them. As several studies have pointed out, calypsos about Indians were full of humor as well as sexual innuendo.[19] Desire, then, clearly did not exclude ridicule. Nor did ridicule preclude desire. Much of the suggestiveness came from a play on the "foreign"-sounding words that were part of the plantation Hindi of the Indian, which on the tongue of the calypsonian took on pervasive sexual overtones.[20]

When Atilla the Hun (Raymond Quevedo) sings of his "Dookanii" (1939) from Penal, for once a calypsonian tries to give a picture of the beauty of the Indian beloved rather than merely place her against what Rohlehr calls "the background of the Indian feast":[21]

> With her wonderful dark bewitching eyes
> I used to gaze in them hypnotized . . .
> When she smiled her face lit up rapturously
> Radiating joy, life, and vitality
> The most reserved was bound to feel
> The power and force of her sex appeal.

Another calypso from 1939, Lord Executor's (Philip Garcia) "My Indian Girl Love," also features a protagonist named Dookani, whom the singer meets while performing at a Caroni tent (in Trinidad's sugar belt) during the Hosay festival:

> It was on a night of the Hosein
> That gala Indian fete I mean to say
> . . .
> Music dancing and drum beating
> All the time her love she was repeating
> Me tell am papa
> Me love am Lord Executor.

Executor's fantasy goes as far as to envisage a wedding after Dookani proposes to him, enchanted by his performance, but ends at the point when he realizes what is happening and, as reluctant as all calypsonians to be tied down in marriage, he "run out the place."[22] While no interracial hostility is represented in this calypso, other songs by King Fighter (Shurland Wilson) or the Mighty Dictator (Kenny St. Bernard) from the '50s, while maintaining an air of humor and sometimes even self-deprecation, turned the tensions between Indians and Africans into a topic for comment in what I call the musical public sphere (see chapter 5). In King Fighter's "Indian Wedding" (1957), the protagonist gate-crashes an Indian wedding feast disguised as an Indian and singing Hindi melodies. The persona is accepted as that of an insider, and Fighter is offered the hand of an Indian girl. But the disguise is penetrated. The singer is revealed as African and is not only deprived of the food at the feast, which he had been looking forward to, but also gets a serious beating. He ends the song by requesting that he be buried next to a tray of *dhalpourie*.[23]

In Mighty Killer's (Cephas Alexander) "Indian People with Creole Names" (1950–51) we find not humor but hostility, directed especially at the Indian woman:

> What's wrong with these Indian people?
> As though their intention is for trouble
> . . .
> But I notice there is no Indian again
> Since the women and them taking Creole name
> Long ago was Sumintra, Ramnalawia,
> Bullbasia and Oosankilia
> But now is Emily, Jean and Dinah
> And Doris and Dorothy
> Long ago you hadn't a chance
> To meet an Indian girl in a dance
> But nowadays is big confusion
> Big fighting in the road for their Yankee man.[24]

It is not only urbanization of East Indians that Killer refers to in this calypso but also the alleged prostitution of Trinidadian women, including the formerly secluded East Indians, to the "Yankee man" from the American military bases established on the island during World War II. While some Creoles criticized the East Indians for remaining outside what they would call the mainstream, others worried about the Indians' "taking Creole name," disapproving of the fact that "there is no Indian again," gesturing perhaps towards the idea that the African's self-definition in Trinidad depended centrally on the existence of the Indian.

The otherness of the Indians was often represented as closely associated with their food, as in the calpyso by Fighter mentioned earlier. Dictator's "Moonia" (1955) addresses not Indian food itself but what the food is often a metaphor for in calypso—that is, sexual relations with an Indian woman.[25] Dictator is "in love with an Indian" who likes the Creole style of loving ("lika de keesing / Dat kilwal [creole] hugging and squeezing"), but the match is opposed by the girl's mother, who says her "bap [father] na likeam kilwalni [does not like Creoles]." The kilwal can't give you anything, argues the mother, and the girl cries that the kilwal is "plantin' me garden." The calypso ends with the father expressing his contempt for what he considers the animal-like "nigger breed," and the plaintive refrain, "Moonia, Moonia / Bap na likeam kilwalni," does not provide any narrative resolutions.

Dictator may not have gotten his Moonia, but by 1947 Killer was singing his famous song "Grinding Massala," about his marriage to an Indian girl. The occasion is used to satirize the rapidly urbanizing East Indians and their attempts to speak in English. Quite a few Hindi-sounding words are used in the song, more to signal the foreignness of the Indians than to refer specifically to any ritual. Raymond Quevedo, a fellow calypsonian, was of the opinion that "Grinding Massala" showed real genius, since Killer had successfully woven the "Indian rhythm" into the kaiso and, "even while singing English words, [he] simulated the speech of the average person of Indian origin who formed an integral part of our polyglot people and enriched our culture."[26] The ballad-like calypso begins with the wedding:

> This is very true
> This year ah decide to marry a Hindu
> Hundreds of Indians gather
> Yes indeed up in Marabella
> Man, Pooran get crazy
> When they start singing a sweet melody
> Sing jaago shilaam . . .
>
> *Refrain:*
> And everytime ah passin gyal yuh grindin' massala
> Everytime ah passin.

After eating a "set of dhalbaat [lentils and rice]," which burns his mouth with its pepper, Killer starts to dance with the wedding guests even as he satirizes their "Indian" accents:

> These guys are playing Amellican
> Singin, Thousand Amellican laanded in Paart ah Spain
> Some come by baatleship, some come by yaaroplane.²⁷

Even though they were caricatured, East Indian melodies, names, and words thus began to make occasional appearances in the Creole calypso. While commentators like Albert Gomes saw this phenomenon as evidence of an ethnic melting pot in Trinidad, those at the receiving end of the satire—especially East Indian leaders named in calypsos such as Killer's "Indian Politicians" (1951)—objected to the way their names were pronounced to incite laughter and mockery.²⁸

While the sociopolitical rivalry between Indians and Africans continued to grow in Trinidad throughout the 1950s, the situation never seemed as stark as in neighboring Guyana, where political parties had been reshaped along lines of race, and rivalry often had the potential to turn violent. "Apan Jaat" (1958), by Melody (Fitzroy Alexander), picks up a slogan (meaning "our race/caste/group" in Hindi) that was popular during the Guyanese elections of 1953 and later of 1957, suggesting that this was the political rallying point for East Indians in Guyana, to which Melody paid frequent visits during the '50s. The calypso features an "Indian calypsonian name Lall" who "had Georgetown like Monday Carnival." Lall's election song went this way:

> Vote Jairam—A-ha
> Vote Seeram—A-ha
> Vote Beharry A-ha
> Apan Jaat! Marsaray kay kilwili
> [our own race/caste! Beat those Creoles well!]²⁹

Melody suggests that "his people" lost the election because of laziness and high expectations (they are "too stupid") whereas the Indians turned out in high numbers and voted according to the race of the candidate.³⁰ He claims that the Indians rallied around "Apan Jaat" and even spit on the Creoles, as Lall instructed them to do (the final sound in the calypso is a spitting sound, "Twehhhhhh!").

Interestingly, a few years later—this time talking about Trinidad—Melody was able to sing in "Come Go Calcutta" (1960s) about his Indian girlfriend (referred to as "*dulahin* [bride or daughter-in-law of the family in Hindi])," who addresses him as "sweet nigger." The intergroup violence of

"Apan Jaat" here appears only in the form of the revenge that the song's Indian cuckold, Ramlal, takes on the macho calypsonian, who, however, is represented as the real victor:

> Ow nayga, sweet nayga, ow nayga
> Come go Calcutta
> . . .
> No dulahin, gyal, I cyan come back here again
> I tellin you plain, dulahin
> I cyan come back here again
> Suppose yuh man ketch we in de act
> Take a big stick and open meh back
> So yuh see somebody go dead
> . . .
> Ramlal go know de truth
> When he do gyal I afraid he shoot
> Dulahin cry when I told her dis was goodbye
> She run at me and she start to fight
> Kilwalni sleep wid me tonight.[31]

How might we read Melody's different strategies in these two calypsos? It should be noted that in the "political" calypso, the singer's opponents are all gendered male; in fact, it is never assumed otherwise. In "Come Go Calcutta," in contrast, the ethnic other is of two kinds: The first is female and sexually desirable; the second is the male of her race, who sees the African sweet man as a threat to his marriage. Interestingly, until the 1990s the political calypso did not call the names of East Indian women at all. It is as though in the public realm of politics and society, only the Indian man could appear as a rival, who won by deceit, cunning, or sheer numbers, whereas in the private realm of intimate relations, the Indian woman is sought to be integrated into the Creole imaginary through cohabitation, marriage, and her supposed desire to leave behind the patriarchal structures of the close-knit East Indian community.

The "Apan Jaat" motif was picked up by Mighty Striker (Percy Oblington), two-time winner of the Calypso Monarch competition, who sang in "The United Indian" (1959) about the defeat of the People's National Movement in the 1958 federal elections at the hands of what the party's leader, Eric Williams, notoriously called "a recalcitrant and hostile minority":[32]

> Nobody unite as the Indians
> It's hard for the Negroes to do
> . . .
> If they can't spell a-t
> They going up for election
> If they can't spell b-a-t
> Still they voting the man
> Could be a-b-c Harrylal,
> Believe what ah say
> Or never-go-to-school Ramlal
> They voting the man on election day.

Striker refers here to contentious English literacy (and property) criteria that were employed in Trinidad elections under constitutional reform, which by 1946 had been overthrown in favor of universal suffrage. The allegation was that illiterate Indians, through clannishness as well as lack of education, voted as a bloc for members of their race. Historians of modern Trinidad have pointed out that the period between 1958 and 1961 was marked by deteriorating relations between Indians and Africans, with the 1961 elections on the eve of independence fraught with violent conflict between the two groups. The Creole calypso stage dramatized these tensions, taking the side of the PNM. As D. V. Trotman says, "Afro-Trinidadian calypsonians sang in support of a ruling party identified with progress, development, nationalism, and against an Indian community which they saw as racist, monolithic and backward."[33] The calypsonian Mighty Christo (Christopher Laidlow) raged in "Election War Zone" (1962): "Whip them PNM whip them / You wearing the pants / If these people get on top is trouble / And we ain't got a chance."[34]

It is no wonder, then, that a singer of mixed Indian and African descent, Mighty Dougla (Cletus Ali), "six of one, half a dozen of the other," should want to reiterate the significance of this crucial Tinidadian racial tension at a time when PNM-driven anticolonial independence rhetoric was coding race problems as though they existed between only black and white. What if there were a policy, the singer asks, to send people back to where they came from?

> They sending Indians to India
> And the Negroes back to Africa
> Can somebody just tell me

> Where they sending poor me
> I am neither one nor the other
> Six of one, half a dozen of the other
> If they serious about sending back people for true
> They got to split me in two.[35]

A sympathetic Afro-Trinidadian, Brynner, suggests a strategy to erase what can sometimes be the only visible physical difference—texture of hair—between African and Indian in Trinidad:

> Conscientiously and constitutionally
> Forget all this lousy rumor about racial equality
> If you are an East Indian and you want to be an African
> Just shave your head clean like me
> Then they cyah prove your nationality[36]

Significantly, the pragmatics of Brynner's proposition won out in the 1962 Independence Calyspo King competition. He acquired the title. Mighty Dougla had been a close contender.

With the increased urbanization of East Indians who began to come up from the "country" to cities like San Fernando and Port of Spain, and would have been a visible presence by the 1960s, a new kind of figure emerged in the public realm: "the Indian gyul who creolise." King Fighter (1961) sings about a Hindu girl who "ignored the law of Hindustani" and dressed "like stars from the twentieth century":

> [Putting away her] orini [*odhni*, or head covering] and she sari in ah corner
> Now she wearing jeans and pedal pusher.

Unlike the creolized Indian girl who was submissive and cooked Creole food for the calypsonian, this one was

> Going out on date with she fella
> Coming in late from the cinema
> The old man was outrageous and mad
> To hear her talking with a boy in the yard
> He up with a big stick and bust she head.

Indian women were also to be found "jumping up" in Carnival, which had come to be seen as a Creole space. The response of Lord Kitchener (Aldwin

Roberts) to an "Indian lady" playing mas' in the song "Mrs. Harriman" (no date available) is grudging and resentful:

> I don't know how to tell Miz Harriman
> If she want to play mas
> We cater for one class.
>
> . . .
>
> Then she start to watch me innovate
> Like she vex because I dingolay.[37]

She didn't want her body to be touched by Kitchener's hand, saying to him: "Mister, don' wine on me." Kitchener's hand drops to her "lovely waist" and may have gone lower, he says, but Mrs. Harriman objects: "Mister, move your hand before I kick you out of de band." He calls her a "right down hypocrite," wanting to know why, then, did she "come in de band"? "Whole day she jumping shamelessly / With a little tiny bikini" and "wiggling her body," but she disapproves of Kitchener when he moves close to her. There is a suggestion here that the "class" to which Carnival caters is lower class, and Creole, while the "Indian lady" is from one of the wealthy Indian families living in Port of Spain. While there is no lack of sexual interest on the part of the calypsonian, he is enraged at the Indian woman's refusal to respond favorably.

Most calypsos, however, were not about the creolized Indian woman who might jump up in Carnival but about the exoticized foreign beauty. In "Dularie" (1966), King Fighter sings about "An Indian lady named Dularie" who "so romantically" addressed him:

> In a lovely way, this is what she say
> You must carry me a Trinidad
> Go show me one Carnaval
>
> *Chorus:*
> Yes, Dularie, come Dularie
> Well, I never lucky to go over
> But I always dream of the bacchanal.

Fighter says he will always love his "Indian gyul," whom he will bring over "in a PanAm plane." Then "she gave a farewell celebration," and the menu included *jeera* (cumin) and *dhal* (lentils), *callaloo* [Trinidadian stew], and *manicou* ("wild meat") stew.[38]

"Dularie" is about a foreign woman. Another song by Fighter addresses the rural Trinidadian Indian. In "Baytee" (1960s),[39] Fighter sings Baytee's voice in an "Indian" accent; she says that she will pray every night and day so that he will "marry to me and then carry me away . . . *jaldi jaldi* [quick quick]." He wonders if she loves him; she calls him "sugar" and gives him roti and *baigan choka* (seasoned eggplant). At the end of the song, we hear a quickly uttered phrase that sounds something like "gaana bahut chahta (liking the song/music very much)."[40] In view of the Trinidadian stereotype about Indians being from the village and Africans from the city, "Baytee" could also be expressing nostalgia for what the calypsonian represents as the lost simplicity of rural life, embodied here in the East Indian woman.

The docile Indian woman remained a significant figure in calypso into the 1970s. Even after the cultural renaissance and racial pride inspired among Afro-Trinidadians by the Black Power Movement in 1970, the calypsonian Unity could sing "My Indian Wife" (1972), which puts down African women as much as it does the "submissively feminine" Indian. The African's family objects to his wedding to an Indian, and Unity defends his choice:

> She does wake up in the morning and cook meh food
> She does give me romance when ah in the mood
> Before ah go to work she does shine meh shoes
> That is what a Negro woman wouldn't do.[41]

In the wake of the Black Power Movement's plea for interracial cultural interaction, a crucial musical development was made possible by the work of Lord Shorty (Garfield Blackman), who later renamed himself Ras Shorty I. He has often been given the credit for introducing new rhythms into the calypso, drawing on East Indian instruments and melodies. Shorty himself claims that he was the first to use the term "soca," which has subsequently become the name for calypsos that aim to function more as dance music than as political commentary, although there are remarkable exceptions like Maestro (Cecil Hume)—Shorty's less well-known contemporary—or David Rudder who straddle both arenas, often in the same song. While the terms "soca" and "calypso" are often used to differentiate between the content of the songs, many singers would see his as also marking a formal and structural difference. In a 1979 interview, Shorty asserted that he was the inventor of soca music:

> I grew up between Barrackpore and P'Town [Princes Town; both are in Indian-dominated southern Trinidad] and just hearing the names you could understand the East Indian influence. . . . I was looking for new avenues to improve the music and from "Indrani" I went to "Soul Calypso Music." . . . Calypso was dying a natural death. . . . I felt it needed something brand new to hit everybody like a thunderbolt. I knew what I was doing was incorporating soul with calypso, but I didn't want to say soul calypso or calypsoul. So I came up with the name soca. I invented soca. And I never spelt it s-o-c-a. It was S-O-K-A-H to reflect the East Indian influence in the music.[42]

In the same interview, Shorty said that he regularly used East Indian drums on his albums after the early 1970s, and even when he did not use Indian instruments, he did use Indian rhythms. He persisted in this musical innovation even when he was criticized for "playing Indian" and "doing foolishness." Although Shorty did not offer any overtly political argument for his fusion music, he showed for over thirty years — until his untimely death in 2000 — that in his music he sought to articulate, and extend, the cultural interconnections between the two major racial groups in Trinidad.

In an early song, "Indian Singers" (1960s), Shorty showed his preoccupation with "Indian" music:

> [Lines in Hindi, not clearly audible] —
> These Indian singers . . . go higher
> Day by day they getting better
> Long time hear these Indians singing
> Do-la-fa-ti
> Now they change entirely
> . . .
> with their sweet sweet melody
> [Hindi lines]
> when you hear on the radio
> Is more Indian song than calypso . . .
> And I singin, Akeyla hoon main [I am alone].[43]

Shorty's reference was almost certainly to Hindi film music, which was broadcast on Trinidadian radio for short periods during the day. Unlike the majority of his contemporaries who sang about East Indians, Shorty's "Indian" songs were not always about women. However, until his conversion to Rastafarianism, Shorty, like other calypsonians, did present the East Indian woman as an object of desire ("Kelogee Bulbul") or as an insatiable woman he was trying to escape. The unusual song "Indrani" (1973) features a wrinkled sixty-year-old woman, speaking in Hindi, who is "so bony, skinny like a whip . . . but have no fear, she's real trouble," as she "comes from the lagoon, singing an Indian tune." "Laylo bayta" [take it, boy]," says Indrani in the song. Shorty sings, "Maybe is love she want, but I feel she too old for that." However, the word "laylo" conveys "suggestivity" to Shorty, who asks:

> Woman what you want? I would like to know
> Must be important for you to behave so
> She bawl out "Baytia, baytia [boy, son]"
> "Panee, panee awaylah [bring me water]"
> Screaming off she head
> And insist ah give she panee in bed.[44]

Between asking for "panee" and telling the boy to "take it (laylo bayta)," Indrani comes across in Shorty's song as "real trouble." This song attracted criticism from some East Indian groups, and the Pawan Sajeewan Hindu Cultural Organization urged the cabinet to ban "Indrani" for denigrating East Indian womanhood.[45]

Very different from the demanding Indrani is the female protagonist of another Shorty song, "Kelogee Bulbul" (1974). Since his "boyhood days up in Lengua" Shorty has been

> a fanatic
> Of East Indian beauty
> It gives me a feeling
> Of goose pimple rising
> . . .
> Give me some roti with plenty talkari
> I feelin' to put some Indian blood in me
> Because the way I love to khelogee [play]
> . . .
> with the tassa beatin' . . .
> Bulbul khelogee, bulbul khelogee [bulbul bird, will you play
>   with me]
> Bulbul khelogee, o bulbul khelogee

Whether it's Hosay, a Muslim festival, or Ramlila, a Hindu festival, Shorty is there to make bacchanal, remarking on the "Indian woman huggin [him] up in de band."[46]

Apart from these attempts to address the racial divide between Indian and African in terms of possible erotic alliances, the popular critique of the ruling PNM and its policies offered by the Black Power Movement inspired calypsonians to explore aspects of the history of the two groups. In "Reconstruction" (c. 1971), by composer (Fred Mitchell), Trotman points out, there was an attempt at a "sober re-assessment of Trinidad and Trinidadians, and to re-think the historical development of race-relations and racial attitudes in a multi-cultural society."[47] The singer talks about the difference in relation to language and cultural practices between Indian and African and about how African names were wiped out by slavery, whereas Indian names are still prevalent.

> Why should we imitate the Englishman or copy the American
> And if your religion is not Christian why should they call you heathen
> Opportunities for every man, whether Indian, white or African
> And that's the way to the solution of Black Power demonstration.[48]

Presumably from the same time is a calypso titled "Liberation," in which Valentino (Emrold Phillip) addresses his "Indian and Afro-brothers":

> Remember one hand never clap
> So you must unite as one and come together
> [The problem is] segregation, discrimination, exploitation.

Valentino believes that only the achievement of "black people liberation" can overcome these problems. "Forget the terms nigger and coolie," he says,

> To gain liberty we must have unity
> Between the Indian and the African.[49]

Trinidadians have suggested to me in conversation that, in this period, a connection could have existed between the increased visibility of East Indian cultural forms in the media and in the public sphere more generally and the interest inspired by the National Joint Action Committee (NJAC) in cultural assertion as an antidote to a cultural neocolonialism that the PNM had done little to counter. The NJAC, a leading player in the Black Power

Movement, was known in the 1970s for emphasizing cultural exchange and interaction between Indians and Africans.[50] As Afro-Trinidadians sought to reinvent their African pasts, Indo-Trinidadians also engaged in new forms of cultural assertion. The Indian Cultural Pageant organized by the promoters of *Mastana Bahar*, which included singing, dancing, and a queen contest in "Indian costume," was hugely popular with East Indians from the 1970s on. If Shorty could say that all he heard on the radio was Indian music, Mighty Chalkdust, with characteristic wryness, sang about "Mastana Bahar (Indian Competition)" (1978), suggesting that it was becoming more popular than Carnival or calypso because of the monetary incentives it was able to offer.[51]

The same calypsonian who had paid a backhanded compliment to East Indian enterprise, as shown in the "Indian competition," or cultural pageant, hosted by the Mohammed brothers, sang another tongue-in-cheek sally in the last years before the PNM government was displaced by the National Alliance for Reconstruction. In "Ram the Magician" (1984), Mighty Chalkdust, referring to the hugely successful entrepreneur Ram Kripalani, suggested that the PNM could well learn a thing or two from him:

> Barefooted this man came
> From India seeking wealth and fame
> With a bolt of cloth he start in San Fernando
> Bought and sold anything
> He invested all his saving
> And in one year's time the empire start to grow
> [and soon Ram moves from a shack to a mansion]
>
> *Chorus:*
> If you cyaan (cannot) run the country
> Then call in Kripalani.

In the song, Chalkdust also criticizes the cabinet ministers for not knowing how to make a budget by referring to a series of financial problems in the government: "If you cyaan run the country / Then call in Kripalani."[52]

From the late 1960s on, Chalkdust was an unrelenting critic of what he and many others saw as the misguided policies of the PNM and the increased capitulation to American regimes of power and consumption. In dozens of hard-hitting calypsos through the 1970s ("Answer to Black Power," "Two Sides of a Shilling," "Trinidad Dollar," "Uncle Sam Own We"), Chalkdust and other singers, like Sparrow, Relator, and Valentino, tried to present a skeptical, satirical version of official truths. While some of the calypsonians took on the task of critiquing an "African"-dominated government they had initially supported, they did not necessarily ally themselves with the "Indian"-dominated political opposition. Instead, they often sang what Rohlehr calls "race calypsos," which "betray . . . the uncertainty with which the races have regarded each other" against a background of persistent poverty for the majority of people and endless political manipulation by elite groups.[53]

Not all calypsonians, however, represented and perpetuated racial antagonism. Singers like Shorty presented pleas for tolerance, as he does in the musically innovative "Om Shanti Om" (1979), which went on, unacknowledged, to become a major Hindi film hit in India:[54]

> Here's an Indian prayer, mmm
> From ancient times, yeh
> Created to soothe your mind
> In danger in anger remember
> Sing this mantra
> It's called a mantra
> From the master.

To help "struggle against the devil" and fight materialism, Shorty exhorts:

> Sing om shanti [peace] om, shanti shanti om
> To unite people . . .
> Sing om shanti om
> Om shanti om, shanti shanti om
> Please listen to your voice singin
> Om shanti om.[55]

In this song, one hears the distinctive soca beat credited to Shorty, accompanied by the East Indian percussion instrument, the dholak, along with shak shak, guitar, and steel band. Taking offense at the use of a holy phrase of the East Indians in a Carnival context, the Sanatan Dharma Maha Sabha (which claims to represent all Trindiadian Hindus) appealed to Pan Trinbago, the association of steelbands first formed in 1971, and the Carnival organizing committee not to allow Shorty's calypso in their programs, going on to request formally that it be banned from the streets at Carnival time.[56]

The 1980s saw other kinds of "race calypsos" that did not target East Indian men, except by implication, but instead seemed to re-eroticize the call for alliance across race barriers. Addressed to Indian women, a series of calypsos from one of the best-known singers of the century, Mighty Sparrow, invoked some critical responses from East Indian men, although the songs don't seem very different from the 1950s calypsos of King Fighter and Melody, or the earlier songs of Killer, which exoticize the Indian woman, foreground Indian cooking in their sexual imagery, and boast about the charms of the African man. Unlike in the 1950s, by the 1980s an articulate and confident East Indian middle class had emerged that periodically raised objections to how Indians were portrayed. In "Marajhin" (1982), which actually means "Brahmin's wife" but here refers more generally to an Indian woman, Sparrow sings:

> You are the genesis of my happiness
> You are the one that I have always dreamed of
> You got everything I need, everything I want
> How can I exist without your sweet love.

Sparrow is enraptured by the woman's exotic appearance:

> When I see you in your sari or your orhni [head cloth]
> I am captivated by your innovative beauty
>
> *Chorus*:
> Marajhin, marajhin, oh my sweet dulahin [bride]
> Saucy marajhin, sexy marajhin, racy marajhin, all right
> O dulahin o dulahin, hear the sweet music playing
> I want to hold you, I want to rock you
> I want to jam you, jam you, jam you, jam tonight.

Sparrow says he will do anything for his *dulahin*. He

> will work de land and give you all de paisa [money]
> And will even drink your jhoota [something she has already sipped]
> From your lota [cup]
> If you only whisper to me "aw na Baytia" [come baby]
> To the rhythm of the tassa we go soca.

In alternating Hindi and English lines, the latter glossing the former, Sparrow sings:

Mighty Sparrow. Surabhi Sharma/R. V. Ramani.

> Bolo bolo kya hamsey mohabbat kiya [say say what, you've loved me]
> Say you'll give me all your sweet loving forever
> Tum hee mera sapne sundar ki raanee [you are the queen of my beautiful dreams]
> Anyone could see you are the queen of beauty.[57]

Sparrow is willing to change many of his cultural habits for the sake of his "sweet love." He will "gladly trade [his] toilet paper for some water"; he will even "change [his] style of dress" to a typically Indian one and "wear a kapra or a dhoti" (a deliberately inappropriate reference, since few people wear these clothes anymore except on rare ritual occasions). If she wants him to, he will change his very name and start calling himself "Rooplall or Baboolall." He will learn to cook Indian food, "learn to grind massala [spices] and chonkay [to season] dhal." In a cheeky reference to a widespread Creole preconception that East Indians cannot dance to "Trinidadian music," Sparrow swears that, for the sake of his dulahin, he will "jump out of time to sweet pan soca melody."

In "Marajhin Sister" (1983), sung a year later, Sparrow courts another Indian woman at a "fiesta." She says to him:

> You try wid Marajhin and cause confusion
> Seems like yuh have ah weakness for Indian
> Like something sweeten yuh and have yuh crazy
> Well get it from somebody else not me
>
> *Chorus:*
> She sing, gori banda aadmee na mangay kam karay
> [fair one, he's a useless fellow who doesn't want to work]
> Chod dey hamaar baytee na paisa na shaadi
> [Leave our daughter alone, no money means no wedding]
> I will give you roti, I will give you dhal
> I will give you kachorie [fried savory] with pepper, that's all
> Hamar mai bola tu bada badmass [my mother says you are a big rogue]
> So if you touch me, latee mangay [want licks or blows], cutlass go
>   pass.

Sparrow proclaims that the girl is "everyting a man could ever want." But she expresses her regret, saying:

> Around me neck nana [grandfather] go break he dhantal
> Plus baap [father] no like kilwal [creole] at all, at all
> Is true yuh have honourable intention
> But nani [grandmother] go call me "neemakharaam' " [ingrate,
>   traitor].

The resistance of the family, and their invective against him, which employs derogatory names, only increases Sparrow's love for the girl:

> So when they call me kutar, bilal, chamar [dog, cat, low caste]
> Make de thing more garam and mitar [hot and sweet]
> You are mine and I am your turtledove
> Though bigotry is threatening our love.[58]

The third and last song in the series, "Marajhin Cousin" (1984) sees Sparrow wooing yet another Indian. This time, the sexualixed food imagery is central to the courtship process:

> Trying to impress Marajhin cousin ah really love her
> If you see me grind massala, grind the jeera [cumin]

> Learn to mix the flour wid ghee [clarified butter]
> And sprinkle the split peas powder
> Grease the tawa [pan], clean the chulha [stove]
> . . .
> Pound the saffron, mix with baigan [aubergine]
> Pumpkin choka [seasoned pumpkin], all for baytiya [girl child].

While the verbs (mix, sprinkle, grease, clean, pound), combined with the "Indian" names for spices and cooking vessels, suggest sexual excitement, the chorus, probably taken from an existing East Indian chutney song (mentioned in chapter 3), makes the interaction even more explicit:

> Gimme the pepper
> Be sure the sada [plain roti] have plenty choka [seasoning]
> Put ghee [clarified butter] and jeera [cumin] to make it sweeter
> Then ah want yuh leggo fire in meh kutiya [sacred place].

The woman compliments Sparrow:

> Yuh handlin your rolling pin much better than Samlal
> Oh Sparrow, chonkay [season] the dhal, don't stop at all.[59]

Other songs of this decade also employed the sexualized food imagery—for example, Sugar Aloes (Michael Osunna) in "Roti and Dhalpourie" (1989), written by Mohan Paltoo:

> I want aloo and channa, mango with paratha
> Bagailee wid kuchela
> Go fas' go and tell her.
> I'll be devoted to you faithfully
> True mih bhaiya [brother] and baitee [daughter] want for me bougie [sister-in-law]
> They go call the dulahin [bride], fix up de wedding, dance for matikor [digging dirt, a wedding ritual],
> Then I go give you the sindoor [red powder that is a sign of marriage for women]
> I'll be happy if you only marry me.

According to Louis Regis, Sparrow was attacked in 1982 by Afro-Trinidadian feminists for proposing marriage to his Marajhin, an "honourable act" that never formed part of the propositioning of Afro-Trinidadian women in his earlier songs.⁶⁰ The promise to legitimize the relationship with the Indian woman through marriage, also heard in Sparrow's "Marajhin" calypsos, seems now to have become part of the interracial courtship ritual. Shorty, who is now Rastafarian, used the rhythms of Killer's "Grinding Massala" to sing to another Indian woman in "Primattee" (1983):

> Primattee know very well I like she
> ...
> Yes I go marry the young lady
> And we go go down to Caroni.⁶¹

And in "Raja Rani (King and Queen)" (1986), also written by Mohan Paltoo, Baron (Timothy Watkins) expresses his "sincere devotion" to an Indian woman and says he will "accept [her] religion." He adds, "For you I'll do anything / I promise to be your king."⁶²

Two other developments in the calypso can be seen in the 1980s. The number of political calypsos involving East Indian political figures began to increase, along with the greater political visibility of such figures in the post-PNM scenario, when a government was formed by the NAR, a multiracial party. And more singers of East Indian origin—in particular, the hugely successful Rikki Jai and Drupatee Ramgoonai—began to appear on the calypso stage.⁶³

Increasingly heard also were voices prophesizing revolution and apocalypse, presenting their audiences with a "relentless cataloguing of social, moral and economic collapse."⁶⁴ In the context of the defeat of Black Power, Sparrow sang "Ah Diggin' Horrors" (1975), in which blacks' disillusionment with the PNM finds powerful articulation. Sparrow, who later supported the Organization for National Reconstruction, a precursor of the NAR, sang:

> Looting, shooting, rioting, and raping
> Nurses aiding mad people in escaping
> Lord, with all this resentment and hate
> Mih blood pressure in a terrible state.⁶⁵

Although the oil boom of the 1970s had benefited the economy at large, the poorest Trinidadians did not perceive any enlargement of opportunities. If anything, conditions seemed only to have gotten worse. The NAR government was sharply attacked by Sugar Aloes (a known PNM supporter), Chalkdust, Watchman (Wayne Hade), and Cro Cro (Weston Rawlins). A. N. R. Robinson, a politician from Tobago, was the main target of their attacks, although remarks about the East Indian Basdeo Panday were also made. The divided leadership of the NAR, which led to its eventual downfall, came under severe criticism from the calypsonians. Throughout the '80s, the lyrics take on corruption, social decay, and the imminent dawn of the Day of Judgment. In a host of calypsos, like Valentino's "Recession" (1983), Chalkdust's "White Man's Plan" (1985), Gypsy's (Winston Peters) "The Sinking Ship" (1986), Black Stalin's "Bun Dem" (1987), and Delamo's "Armageddon" (1985), singers pointed to a worsening economic and social situation. In all this we find very few references to "Indians," perhaps because the criticism was of a predominantly black government and its inability to look after the welfare of "its" people.

The exception to this omission is Cro Cro. In his popular "Corruption in Common Entrance" (1988), the target of criticism is the non-African (perceived as elite), particularly the East Indian. This calypso, which won Cro Cro the Calypso Monarch crown for the year, was at the center of a controversy about racism. The Common Entrance Examination is a nationwide selection test for schoolchildren that decides which school they attend after the years of primary schooling. Cro Cro's argument was that Afro-Trinidadians never made it to the best schools, not because they were not bright, but because of "corruption" that favored East Indians, Chinese, and other non-African groups:

> You doh have to be intelligent, that is ah lie
> Your father must pull a good string with complexion high.

A black child from the slums could be very bright, he contended, but would not get into a good school:

> Because they have to pick Baldeo, Boodoo, Krishna Maharaj
> Because Arjoon and Raj father have big garage
> Chaito, Bissoon, Emamali and Phoolmanie
> . . .
> Cyah get into St. Augustine Girls . . .
> You see they have to pick Baliram, Gobin, Indra and Gookool
> All ah them have to go to prestige school
> Lilwatee, Moonan, Soogrim brother, Panday
> Panday son dunce like a bat but you cyah send him dey.[66]

The litany of proper names—all East Indian—suggests that the best education in the country is reserved for the Indians, who have the financial power to send their children to the "prestige schools" while a child "bright like a bulb from Laventille," an Afro-Trinidadian slum, cannot secure admission. Criticism of this calypso was aired on several call-in radio programs, in television discussions, and in the print media. Zeno Obi Constance records that more than "one hundred and fifty . . . articles, (letters, reports, editorials) were published in the daily and weekly newspapers as the country took one side or the other."[67] While some sought a ban on the song for its overtly racist stand, others defended the freedom of expression of the calypsonian. It was suggested that it was not race that was the issue but "class and privilege," a view shared by the Calypsonians' Association.[68] Others argued that Indians formed a large part of the working class and could not automatically be assumed to be wealthy.[69] An Indo-Trinidadian woman commented that she had applied the "off switch" to calypso; she had been "totally bemused" when Cro Cro was crowned Calypso Monarch for "Corruption in Common Entrance," and since then she had never listened to calypso. She had no problems with criticism, she said, but she found objectionable the "crudity and open racism" of singers like Cro Cro and Sugar Aloes.[70]

The ominous songs of social and moral decay seemed to culminate in an incident foretold. On July 27, 1990, the Jamaat-al-Muslimeen, a group of Black Muslims led by Abu Bakr, stormed the Trinidadian Parliament, took the cabinet hostage, and tried to overthrow the government.[71] Abu Bakr and the Jamaat-al-Muslimeen were the subject of many 1991 songs, including Rudder's "Hoosay," Luta's "Think Again," Cro Cro's "Say a Prayer for Abu Bakr," Stalin's "Revolution Time," Cardinal's (Elan Baghoo) "Abu Coup," Rikki Jai's "Another Bakr Will Come." Some singers saw the attempted coup as a justifiable response to the government's "wickedness," while others—such as Shadow in "Tempo" and Sparrow in "Abu Bakr Take Over"—merely described the events without attempting to pass moral or political judgment.

The imagery of Rudder's "Hoosay" invokes the Islamic crescent moon and the tassa drums of the Hosay festival:

> Under the crescent moon
> And above the bloody asphalt
> Strange dogs were barking
> . . .

> So the roll of the tassa
> Became the rhythm of bullets
> And the thundering boom bass
> That was a bomb
> In this Muslim time
> When the Hosay is number one.[72]

Rudder goes on to remark that the Jamaat-al-Muslimeen uprising in some sense forever changed the perception of Trinidad as a Carnivalesque paradise where no serious violence ever took place. And for perhaps the first time in the history of the calypso, Hosay is mentioned in connection with African Muslims and not East Indians. The *tadjahs* and *tazias*—the elaborately constructed paper and bamboo tombs of the Muharram festival—become a metaphor for the macabre dance in which Trinidad society seems to be locked and which the calypsonian says can end only in destruction.[73]

Statistics show that the 1980s saw an 80 percent increase in rape, incest, suicide, and molestation, and the perpetrators of these crimes were not confined to any one race.[74] In 1993, Hulsie Bhaggan, then a United National Congress politician, incited her constituency in Chaguanas (Central Trinidad) to form vigilante groups to deal with African men allegedly engaged in "ethnic cleansing" through robbing East Indian homes and raping Indian women. (Bhaggan claimed that eleven Muslim virgins had been raped in her constituency.) There were newspaper reports of drug warfare between Indian dons of Central and South Trinidad and the Africans who worked for them. A series of arrests of key personnel allegedly had upset the balance of power in the gangs, and masked gunmen carried out various raids on bars and homes in the predominantly Indian communities. There were reports of rape—some confirmed, others not. Whether or not the problem was one of Africans versus Indians, Bhaggan was able to use the opportunity to question the hierarchies within her own party, which sometime later decided to disown her. Later in 1993, she caused more embarrassment to the UNC by demonstrating on the Butler Highway in protest against government's inaction regarding the floods in Central Trinidad.

Bhaggan's actions were a topic of much comment from calypsonians for nearly two years. Most of the songs referred both to Bhaggan's charge that African men were raping Indian girls and to her demonstration against the PNM government. Both Watchman ("How Low, How Low" [1993]) and Tallish ("Water" [1994]) relished the idea of Bhaggan having to go to jail and meet the rapists and robbers there, since they would be waiting to inflict a suitable punishment on her for her vigilantism (in Tallish's sexually suggestive words, to give her "plenty water").[75] Watchman suggested that the cure for Hulsie would be to "get a husband . . . / An African or Indian" to keep her quiet. Tallish proclaimed that it would be disastrous for Bhaggan to be part of the political leadership in Trinidad:

> If she ketch an Indian with a Negro Man
> She cut off she foot she two knees and hand
> And if she ketch an Indian with a Negro lady
> You could bet your life is castration for he.

Cro Cro's calypso "Respect de Law" (1994), greatly popular with Afro-Trinidadians, expressed in an exaggerated style all the violent things he would do to Bhaggan: run her down, lick her down, and so on. Cro Cro drew criticism from women's groups for the aggressive attack on Bhaggan, who wrote in the media about the matter: "The calypsonians who used vulgarity to attack me merely demonstrated their lack of imagination, creativity, artistic ability, talent and a general bankruptcy of human values and human dignity."[76] Patrick Watson, a university lecturer and occasional calypsonian, commented that in 1991 Cro Cro sang "Say a Prayer for Abu Bakr," in which he expressed sympathy for the attempted coup against the state, since "Abu did it for all of us," whereas, in "Respect the Law" (1994), he criticized Bhaggan for her protest against the government. Watson asked if Cro Cro's about-face had to do with the fact that Abu Bakr was male and African while Bhaggan was obviously female and Indian. Has an Indian woman no right to lead a protest? asked Watson. Was Cro Cro being both sexist and racist in his attack? Rohlehr, a much quoted authority on the history of the calypso, seems to agree with this characterization of Cro Cro's song, although he tries to provide a contextual explanation for the nature of the attack: "Cro Cro's raw aggressiveness was well within the spirit of the time when verbal violence and uncouth insult had become a norm [on a certain talk show]," he said. He also suggested that Bhaggan's racist characterization of the attackers could only call forth a necessarily racist counterattack.[77]

The president of the Hindu Women's Organization, Raveena Sarran Persad, issued a press release deploring the "deafening silence" of all activist groups and nongovernmental organizations to "the many degrading calypsos aimed at women." The HWO objected to what it called "dirty lyrics and vulgar expressions," especially in the songs of Crazy (Edwin Ayoung), Cro Cro, and Brother Marvin, declaring that Bhaggan's being a politician and an Indian accounted for the lack of response from feminists.[78] The HWO maintains an uneasy relationship with what it perceives as an African-dominated or Creole-dominated women's movement, and the tenuous alliances often break down on the "Hindu woman" question.

Some women, regardless of race, did see Bhaggan as an able and promising political leader and, as the calypsonian Bianca Hull did in the song "Woman to Woman" (1994), expressed their disappointment at her racially divisive arguments. Hull contended that, in speaking only " 'bout the woman in Chaguanas," Bhaggan was "defending some and not all women":

> You could be young or old, plain or pretty
> Black or white, the thief don't show mercy.

Thus, Hull concluded, Bhaggan would have to stand up for all women, not just for Indians.

Brother Marvin, who is of mixed Indian and African descent, is married to an Indian, and who later sang "Jahaji Bhai" in a significant reinscription of "Indians" into Trinidadian history, attacked Bhaggan for being against "douglarization." Marvin saw the concern with black men's sexuality as standing for a fear of racial intermixture and, perhaps, also a strong desire for what was seemingly disavowed:

> Racial harmony
> Is what we really want in this island
> But this dotish woman Hulsie Bhaggan
> Trying to destroy this lil nation.[79]

Marvin also criticizes the vigilante groups for partitioning the country into ethnic areas and asserts his right to go anywhere in Trinidad: "This nigger say we going anywhere / Without fear, they better take care! / You see, ah born here!"). Marvin's tone in addressing the "dotish" Bhaggan is very different from that of "Jahaji Bhai," which proclaimed his dougla identity and asserted his brotherhood with Indo-Trinidadian men.

The 1995 calypso "The Ballad of Hulsie X," by David Rudder—an NJAC sympathizer and a powerful social commentator since the '80s—is a satirical and humorous exposé of the incident. "Hulsie X" is hailed as the "Sugarbelt Queen" (referring to the stronghold of the UNC leader Basdeo Panday); and to the fact that Bhaggan nearly won a beauty contest some years before

David Rudder. Surabhi Sharma/R. V. Ramani.

she became a politician. According to the calypso, "If you breathe too hard in she Central [Central Trinidad] yard / She bound to be on de scene." Rudder also notes that Bhaggan's attention is being drawn to the "scourge" in the land, "an African sex machine":

> And so she rant and rave
> And she misbehave
> This girl called Hulsie X.

The Sugarbelt Queen is "vexing" the gray-haired "Manday [Basdeo Panday]," the song continues, and her "dollar wine [on the] party line" is a reference to Bhaggan's having defied her party to vote with the PNM on the issue of capital punishment, which the UNC opposed, hinting that she was trying to ally herself with moneyed interests (French Creoles and other wealthy people) and not just with rural Trinidad. Her challenge to her party puts a burden on the leader's heart (Panday has already had heart surgery, but "she bypass him three times with she own operation"). "Manday try every trick that he know / But she stick like a pepper in he tail," Rudder sings, accusing the UNC of having become a "parasite oligarchy." "The Hulsie" becomes a "party wine" (in the other sense of party—that is, a dance in a fete):

> If you want to jam with me, sit down
> Swing your bottom down to the ground
> On the highway, in the town, bring your bottom down to the ground
> Go down, go down, go down, do the Hulsie, go down.[80]

Rudder's calypso focuses not so much on Indian-African relations as on patriarchal structures within the Indian-dominated UNC, which was then in the opposition, from the point of view of a seemingly disinterested commentator who ostensibly only wants to party. "Hulsie" takes on the UNC men but is reduced to a caricature, shrieking, "Get dem out! Get dem out!"

One interesting feature of the anti-Bhaggan calypsos is that, unlike older songs that mark the racial difference of the Indian woman through her dress (orhni, sari), her language (Hindi or Bhojpuri), her food (roti, dhal, talkarie, bhaji, pholourie), or religious ritual, the songs of the 1990s cannot ridicule or describe Hulsie in this fashion or through these markers. She is a woman inhabiting the modern Trinidadian public sphere and presumably dresses and speaks like other Trinidadians, African and Indian. The "difference" of the Indian in this case is reduced to an issue of sexuality: Bhaggan, it is implied, is an insatiable Indian woman in the tradition of Shorty's Indrani and Dictator's Moonia, her activism functioning as a displacement of her sexual desire. Perhaps the concentrated violence of Cro Cro's calypso in particular can be attributed to the need to resexualize the figure of the Indian woman who is aspiring to political leadership, a figure far removed from the rural Dookanis and Baytees and Dularies to whom the calypsonian used to swear eternal love.

The HWO's criticism that no one was defending Bhaggan because she was a Hindu Indian woman did not take into account the fact that feminist groups like Working Women for Progress (WWP) often did discuss the question of how women were portrayed in calypso, and individual members such as Merle Hodge regularly wrote letters to the newspapers condemning the anti-Indian and anti-women stance of calypsonians. During the 1996 Carnival season, the WWP prepared an analysis of "commentary calypsos" by Cro Cro and Sugar Aloes, two of the finalists in the national Calypso Monarch competition. (Cro Cro won that year's contest, beating Brother Marvin and his song of racial harmony, "Jahaji Bhai"). The calypsos were Cro Cro's "All Yuh Look for Dat" (1996) and Sugar Aloes's "The Facts" (1996). The

WWP wanted to clarify that it was not asking for censorship of the calypso form, since it believed in the importance of using the medium for "social and political commentary." Although it found the two songs "dissonant," the organization realized that the calypsonians were echoing the feelings of many in the society and setting up the conditions for a public dialogue that the WWP also wanted to enter.

The WWP's main criticism was that the calypsos were "flawed" in their analysis of political performance because of their assumption that such performance was based on race. The WWP suggested that Cro Cro's position that "Indians will benefit from political patronage under the UNC-led administration as Africans will benefit from political patronage under a PNM government" indicated "the cynicism and myopia with which many view political power." The women's group challenged the notion that political power was solely about patronage and argued that the view of patronage as based on race then excluded "African supporters of the UNC and Indian supporters of the PNM." Cro Cro's song, the organization argued, was as racist toward Africans as it was toward Indians; he perpetuated "the myth that Africans are complacent, lackadaisical and preoccupied with partying" (this being the reason offered by Cro Cro for why Indians held political power in post-1995 Trinidad). If, according to Cro Cro, "lackadaisical Africans" did not go out and vote and therefore caused the PNM to lose, he was ignoring the fact that "some Africans chose not to vote while some chose to vote for the UNC," just as some Indians may have voted for the PNM. Sugar Aloes sang that "long ago dem Indians used to tell nigger / We have money and land now all we want is power." The WWP argued that this racism was "dissonant" at a time when the country was producing "some of the most liberating fusion music in [its] history."[81] The WWP also criticized Cro Cro and Sugar Aloes for their sexism. Aloes had questioned Bhaggan's contention that Indian women were being raped by African men in Central Trinidad, dismissing the rape victims as "dem gyul in Central." "Evidently," said the WWP's analysis, "he is less concerned about the women who were raped than about the race of the perpetrators," thus foregrounding race at the expense of gender. Cro Cro was also rapped for his gratuitous references to the World Conference on Women that was held in Beijing in 1995, asking where the feminists were when Basdeo Panday (then the opposition leader; he became prime minister later that year) was accused of sexual harassment. The WWP pointed out that every member of the society—not just feminists—had to worry about the abuse of women. The women's movement, the organization argued, was interested in fighting the issue at various levels—through the judiciary, the police, and unions—instead of individualizing and racializing it, as Cro Cro was doing.[82] A member of the WWP had this to say:

> Last Carnival, we took a lot of licks. It was soon after the election again, and there were two calypsonians who came out with venom on the Indian government. Working Women was the group who started the drama about them, because we went to the tent on the opening night—or very early, it might have been the second or so night—and we heard their calypsos. We all were shocked. We couldn't identify with it, and we came back and said we have to do something about it. We wrote to the newspapers, and after we wrote to the newspapers is when we hear people coming and saying, you know they agree with Working Women, they support Working Women. A lot said that, you know; Working Women was all nonsense and they don't see why it is we're defending the Indians and that kind of thing. And they singled out the Indians in the group . . . so we took a lot of licks on that. Again, like when they attack women in the calypsos and we talk about it, even politicians [when they attack]. And what we say, you attack the person not the politics, what they're not doing right for the constituency, or what they're not doing right for the country, but as a woman, leave that out of it.[83]

Another kind of criticism of Cro Cro and, even more significant, of the leading election analyst Selwyn Ryan, who claimed that "the black underclass did not go to the polls," thereby supporting the singer's contention that "all yuh [Africans] look for that" because they were complacent, came from the commentator Anil Mahabir, who argued that Cro Cro's "primordial outburst" was "divisive." How could the judges of the Calypso Monarch contest reward a lie? he wondered. He cited election figures: "In 1991 the PNM received a total of 233,950 votes and won 21 seats. In 1995 it received a total of 255,885, an increase of 21,935 votes but won four seats less." The PNM, says Mahabir, received more votes in every constituency except three. Curiously, making no distinction between a poll analyst and a calypsonian (suggestive, perhaps, of the calypsonian's status as political commentator), Mahabir asked how Ryan and Cro Cro could argue that fewer Africans voted for the PNM in 1995 than 1991? Was there no other factor except the complacency of one group of supporters? he asked. In response, he offered the explanation that the PNM had lost to the UNC not because "its supporters

Black Stalin. Surabhi Sharma/R. V. Ramani.

did not come out to vote," but because "the Opposition vote did not split," implying that Indians who earlier had voted for the PNM had not done so this time.[84]

In addition to the "race calypsos," songs occasionally appeared throughout the 1990s that thematized the Indian as friend and comrade. One example is Black Stalin's "Sundar" (1995), among the songs for which he won the Calypso Monarch crown that year.[85] The song was a tribute to the East Indian chutney singer Sundar Popo. Stalin called chutney-soca "dougla music," recognizing the Indian-African mixture in the lyrics and rhythms. In an interview, Stalin talked about his long friendship with Sundar Popo and their singing tours together: "We in the cultural business don't know nothing about them race talk created by politicians. This song would patch up that division."[86]

In late 1995, the Indian-dominated UNC came to power in Trinidad and Tobago, marking a new kind of visibility for the East Indian. Despite Cro Cro's prizewinning effort and other anti-Indian songs, the major hits of Carnival 1996 included three very different kinds of songs, all with "Indian" connections: Brother Marvin's "Jahaji Bhai," Chris Garcia's "Chutney Bacchanal," and Sonny Mann's "Lotay La." Again, in very different ways these songs brought together many of the themes of the Indian calypsos of the preceding decades. I discussed "Lotay La" in chapter 3 as part of the chutney-soca phenomenon, so I will only add here that it was the first chutney sung in Bhojpuri to function like a mainstream calypso, to be performed in uptown clubs, and to be included in calypso and soca CD anthologies of the year. "Chutney Bacchanal" was sung by the long-haired singer Chris Garcia, whose ancestry includes African on his mother's side and Indian on his father's side. The song contained nonsense words that imitated Hindi or Bhojpuri, which, Garcia claimed, was how those languages sounded to young Indo-Trinidadians whose mother tongue was Caribbean English. Rhoda Reddock writes that whenever Garcia performed the song and sang the "Hindi" lyrics, he would ask his audience (which often consisted of substantial numbers of East Indian youths), "All yuh understand what that mean?" To this the audience would roar, "No!" and Garcia would reply, "Neither me!"[87]

"Chutney Bacchanal" is about "a woman from India, loving de soca" who wants "to sing a verse in Hindi." Garcia sings, "This is what it sound like to me":

> Cha dey cur cuh chun dey
> Bur gay jar dey
> Bur gun gee
> Brick cha dey
> Bur kay jon kay lick ah
> Du ka licky nanny
> Ju ka licky nanny
> Bur gay jung gay da
> Juke ah licky nanny.

> Chutney bachchanal
> Come beti come beti
> One hand on de waist
> One hand up in the air
> Wine wine wine
> Go down go down go down
> Come up come up come up.[88]

A letter to a newspaper editor accused Garcia of singing about women's genitalia; he replied that he did not know whether the words had any meaning at all, since all he tried to do was sing "a set of stupidness" that "sound like Indian" in imitation of his "negro" grandfather who actually spoke Hindi.[89] Indeed, the song's chorus was not in any identifiable language, although it functioned to signal "Indianness."

The song that caused the most controversy in 1996 (apart from Cro Cro's "All Yuh Look for That") was "Jahaji Bhai (Brotherhood of the Boat)," by Brother Marvin, who until then had been better known as a songwriter than as a singer. Marvin begins the song with a chant in Shango-Orisha, an African-derived religion—"Kumayeh oh, dindaweh oh, ayayo"—then traces his lineage. His great-grandfather, Bahut Ajah, came from Calcutta with his "turban and he capra [cloth]," so he (Marvin) is "part seed from India." The two races, "Indian" and "African," were bound together by indentureship and slavery; the "Janam bhoomi" [motherland; literally, "birth land"] for everyone was now "Mother Trini," and there was no longer any "Mother Africa" or "Mother India." Since "Bahut Ajah" planted cane down in Caroni, "Ramlogan, Basdeo, Prakash [all East Indian men's names] and I" are "Jahaji Bhai." The reference is to the "fictive" kin groups formed on board the ships that brought the indentured workers to Trinidad. "*Jahaj*" is ship and "*bhai*" is brother in Hindi; the words refer to those who traveled together on the same ship. The notion of fictive kin is extended by metaphor to all those who traveled on ships to the Caribbean, including Indians and Africans.

Marvin claims that it is "ah great privilege" to "have such unique heritage / Fifty percent Africa, fifty percent India." Not wanting to discriminate on the basis of race or creed, Marvin goes on to say:

> Whether you're Muslim, Hindu, or Christian
> Let's walk this land hand in hand
> We could only prosper if we try
> As Jahaji Bhai.

Marvin suggests that it is only feigned ignorance that allows Afro-Trinidadians to forget that, if they could "take a trip back to [their] roots," they would see "somewhere on that journey . . . a man in ah dhoti / Saying he prayers in front of a *jhandi* [Hindu prayer flag]." It's only this vision that will allow the "African" to see "what is ah cosmopolitan nation." In a solemn, almost too sweet benediction, the calypsonian intones, "United we'll stand, divided we'll fall"; bury the past, and

> so to all races here in Trinbago
> Aapko kalyan ho dhaniaho [May you be blessed; may you prosper]
> Let us live as one under the sky
> As Jahaji Bhai—Brotherhood of the boat
> Jahaji Bhai.[90]

After initial enthusiasm for the calypso (or, as some called it, the chutney-soca) from people of all races who were impressed with its unique melodic structure and Marvin's richly resonant voice, as well as with its blending of English and Hindi lyrics, there was fierce opposition from some Africanists to Marvin's interpretation of history. One sort of criticism came from those who felt that the calypso privileged the Indian part of Marvin's heritage over the African part, a tension that was palpable in a context in which the UNC had just come to power, causing a great deal of anxiety to Afro-Trinidadians who felt they had been displaced from what they saw as their rightful place in the country's structures of political power. Marvin might be a dougla, some said, but that did not mean that every Afro-Trinidadian would find in his or her ancestry a man praying in front of a jhandi. To argue that this mixing existed everywhere in Trinidad was to take away recognition from all that was African.[91] Some listeners also complained that it was inappropriate to mix Shango religious chants with "coolie music."[92]

This particular image of the Indian man wearing a dhoti and praying aroused the scorn of others, who wrote in to complain about Marvin's inaccuracy and to argue that he could not universalize the situation of a few douglas to refer to all the people of Trinidad. Rival calypsonians wrote their own songs—as many as nine, according to Marvin—against his thesis. In his calypso "Jahaji Blues" (1997), GB (Gregory Ballantyne, the noted songwriter for the East Indian chutney-soca singers Drupatee Ramgoonai and Rikki Jai, among others), claimed that it was a fallacy that the two races were progressing side by side and "living as one." The man in a dhoti could only be an East Indian, not the ancestor of any present-day African. GB angrily contended that if Nelson Mandela heard Marvin's song, he would never welcome him to Africa.[93] In this demand for realism made on the calypso, the calypsonian's license to render a situation in metaphoric terms was disregarded. Perhaps all that Marvin was doing, as his many admirers seemed to recognize, was to signify a uniquely Trinidadian history that did not need to be the autobiography of any one person but could, at the same time, function as a symbol of a more general condition of Caribbean creolization.

When asked about the resentment generated by Marvin's calypso, Sheila Rampersad had this to say: "Let nobody fool you. Resentment about Brother Marvin's song came a long time after, and if you've been following the . . . files you will see it came late late late in Carnival and it came when questions were starting to be raised about Cro Cro and Aloes. Because they were all singing in the same tent, so they were all under the same roof, and . . . people started to resent what Aloes and Cro Cro were saying. . . . Parallel with that, people started to hold up 'Jahaji Bhai' as this is what is possible."[94]

The support for Marvin's calypso came from surprisingly different kinds of sources. There were Indians like Sat Maharaj, president of Sanatan Dharma Maha Sabha, who had spoken out for many years against what he perceived as the "douglarisation of Indian culture" but welcomed Brother Marvin to the Phagwa (Holi) celebrations on March 9, 1996, and named him the Maha Sabha calypso king. It has been suggested that an explanation for Sat Maharaj's unexpected support might be found in the centrality given to Hindi lyrics and Indian rhythms in the song.[95] Writers like Kumar Mahabir applauded Marvin for being "honest enough to condemn blacks for being prejudicial towards Indians," although the tone of "Jahaji Bhai" was far from being condemnatory. Mahabir claimed that Marvin's song was based on anthropological research and cited the many scholars who had studied the fossil primate Ramapithecus (first discovered in India but known to have existed from eastern Africa to northern India), the first precursor of the humanoid.[96] A spiritual leader of the Orishas, Molly Ahye, complimented Marvin for recognizing the links between Africa and India, "ancient civilizations" that, according to Ahye, had similar religions and spiritual practices, including the planting of prayer flags.[97] Other Afro-Trinidadians that Carnival season were dancing—sometimes at all-African house parties—to "Jahaji Bhai," remixes of Sonny Mann's "Lotay La," and Chris Garcia's "Chutney Bacchanal." A news report quoted a comment overheard in Woodford Square, a traditional Afro-Trinidadian "liming (hanging out)" area in the heart of Port of Spain: "Boy the calypsonians go bring national unity, not the politicians. You ain't see on TV how Negroes and Indians were dancing up together in the Chutney [M]onarch show."[98]

Both Marvin and Shorty were honored at the 1996 Indo-Caribbean Music

Awards ceremony, where I was privileged to see them perform their songs. In an interview, Shorty said that what was now being called chutney-soca he "simply called sokah some twenty years ago." He also expressed his happiness at being acknowledged as a pioneer "in the development of our music."⁹⁹ His bilingual duet with the acclaimed chutney singer Ramrajie Prabhoo was titled "Respect Woman (Izzat karo Aurat ki)":

> You must give her respect and honor . . .
> Like a flower you must cherish her
>
> . . .
>
> *Chorus:*
> Respect woman, Respect woman, beta [son]
> Respect woman, Respect woman bhaiyya [brother]
> Your mother is a woman
> Your sister is a woman
> Your didi [sister] is a woman
> Your bhauji [sister-in-law] is a woman
> Your mausi [aunt] is a woman
> Your chachi [aunt] is a woman
> Your nani [grandmother] is a woman
> Izzat karo aurat ki beta [give respect to woman, my child]
> (previous lines repeated in Hindi)

In a plea addressed perhaps both to Indo-Trinidadians and Afro-Trinidadians, the singers ask the "beta [boy/child]" not only to respect woman but to show her tenderness.

The year 1996 was one of possibilities. A new government was in power. New cultural questions were being posed. "This is a time that will never come again," Trinidadians said then—and, indeed, the space that was opening for discussions of racial unity soon began to shrink again. If one hadn't seen Shorty, Marvin, Terry Gajraj, Rikki Jai, Denise Belfon, General Grant, Chris Garcia, and others perform on the same stage (at the Indo-Caribbean Music Awards), one would not have registered that the possibility ever existed in Trinidad for cultural practitioners to engage generously and seriously with the musical forms of the "other race."

The remaining years of the century saw new criticism of the "Indian government." In "Tug-o-War" (2000), Chalkdust used the idea of the cabinet metaphorically—past cabinets were strong and sturdy, but Panday's cabinet was made of bamboo and would not survive. Ninja, in "Check Yourself" (2000), accused Panday of using the government's resources to "help all dem Indian." He sang, "Panday fixing all dem Indian and he eh doin one damn ting for Africans." The UNC came under sustained criticism by other singers, such as Bally and Luta, who proclaimed that they were declaring war against a corrupt and "racifee" government. In an election year, Sugar Aloes came out with a "campaign song" titled "Why ah Stay," in which he reconsidered his decision to migrate to the United States: "Next election UNC must go / Is why I stay back to ensure that with calypso." He wanted to "educate" his people and show how Indians were "racial for so." He called on Afro-Trinidadians to "come out and vote" and not "behave like a dope." Cro Cro's offering was "Dole Chadee Say," referring to a gang lord of East Indian descent who had been recently executed.[100] Cro Cro suggested that the Trinidadian attorney-general, Ramesh Lawrence Maharaj, had organized the killing of many witnesses in drug-related cases when he was the defense lawyer. It was a commonly held perception that under the UNC government, the PNM sympathizers who made up the majority in the jury for Carnival events actively encouraged singers who expressed antigovernment sentiments.

In the midst of the anti-establishment calypsos that increasingly had taken on an anti-Indian color, there were a few remarkable singers who tried to articulate the possibilities of genuinely new futures. David Rudder, for instance, suggested that dance and music would help people relate differently to each other. In "Shakedown Time" (2000), he sang:

> Young gyul body ketch afire,
> Wukking up the belly and the shoulders
> . . .
> When the rhythm of the world come down on you
> You know it's shakedown time
> See the whole world going sweetly wild
> Now that the Ganges meet the Nile.

What seems at this point to be a Trinidadian phenomenon—where Indian and African, represented by the two great rivers, have both made a mark in the public sphere—is internationalized by Rudder. Earlier known for his inclusiveness toward the "African" world—Haiti, South Africa, Jamaica—he uses the song to refer to a global phenomenon:

> The tribes are on the move
> All the world's a groove
> The Ganges and the Nile, the Danube too
> The Mississippi now, the Amazon's in flow
> The Yang Tse winds its way into the brew
> . . .
> This rhythm river runs from Rome to Birmingham
> And the world surrenders to its sweet control.[101]

Like Rudder, Machel Montano and Drupatee Ramgoonai dramatize the meeting of the Ganges and the Nile in the enormously popular "Real Unity" (2000). In this case, one could contrast Rudder's internationalism—and, perhaps, the sort of multiculturalism that might be quite unthreatening—with the resolutely "national" structure of address in "Real Unity," a song not about the world but about Trinidad. Both may be party songs—and this dance music is also *about dance*—but Machel's and Drupatee's call to "wine" may actually be seen as far more provocative in an atmosphere of increasing tension between the two major racial groups. Chapter 5, which discusses the way in which Hindi film music from India is reshaped in musical interventions in Trinidad, deals with "Real Unity" at greater length, in particular its borrowings from the Hindi film *Qurbani*, and the conclusion discusses Denise Belfon's 2004 song "I'm Looking for an Indian Man," which begins with a melodic snippet from the film *Takshak*.

Sharing the stage with Belfon in 2004 was her rival Destra, who sang one song for that Carnival season with the calypsonian Shurwayne Winchester. In a new twist, we have two Afro-Trinidadians courting each other East Indian–style:

> *Destra:*
> Aow beta . . .
> Come beta [boy], come wine on me
> I'll be your melody and you'll be my harmony
> *Shurwayne:*
> I'm a Trini beta
> Love chutney and soca
> Winin' is my culture
> Give me that Trini flavour
> *Destra:*

I'm a Trini beti [girl]
Looking for my baby
Come darling
Come beta come wine on me
Let me be your dulahin [bride].[102]

FIVE

★ "Suku Suku What Shall I Do?"

Hindi Cinema and the Politics of Music

East Indian youth: I will write a book called the *Romance of Music and Literature*. I will make this book as great as any Shakespeare play; then I will return to India to endeavour to become a genius in the film industry.
—*We Wish to Be Looked Upon*, Vera Rubin and Marisa Zavalloni, interviews with Trinidadian high-school students conducted in 1957 and 1961

I recall not being old enough or concerned enough to follow the story through but being intrigued by the obsession with shame, insult, honour. . . . I could never figure the entrapment . . . as compared to American movies. . . . As a child I used to wonder why they did not just leave town . . . or tell their family to kiss off.
—Christopher Cozier, artist, on his memories of the weekend Indian movies on TV

Ever since *Bala Joban* (Childhood, Youth [dir. Baburao Patel, 1934]), the first Indian film to be shown in Trinidad, arrived in 1935, East Indians have been fascinated by this manifestation of "Indian culture."[1] Calypso and the newer soca are important musical genres in a spectrum that includes chutney and chutney-soca, forming, as the previous chapters show, a crucial arena of cultural-political intervention. This chapter will discuss how all of these genres draw on Hindi film music, marking yet another area in which "Indians" and "Africans" are engaged in crafting Trinidadian cultural forms.[2] As Paul Gilroy and others have suggested, music is arguably the most significant cultural practice in areas of African hegemony in the New World.[3] This is so much the case, I would contend, that even in a country like Trinidad, whose population of "Indians" is more than equal to that of "Africans," Hindi film as a visual product is downplayed in favor of film music, which for decades seems to have performed a crucial role in the formation of "Indian" identities. The Hindi films themselves have aroused a host of ambivalent responses among East Indians while the songs and their many "versions" continue to circulate in diverse spaces, including Creole-dominated ones. One indicator of the popularity of film music is the existence of "camps" dedicated to the 1950s and '60s playback singers K. L. Saigal, Mohammed Rafi, and Mukesh—groups of people in localities and villages who were not formally organized but all the same were "very real."[4] This phenomenon seems to have been quite prevalent in Trinidad in contrast to what would be familiar in India—that is, fan clubs for film stars.

From all accounts, once Hindi films and their music appeared in Trinidad, older folk music, classical music, religious music, and songs from the dance dramas either slowly disappeared or became imbued with the rhythms and instrumentation of the film songs. One of the most popular Hindu bhajans in the Caribbean, for instance, was "Brindaban ke Krishna Kanhaiyaa," from the film *Miss Mary* (dir. L. V. Prasad, 1957).[5] During the "cooking night" for Hindu weddings, participants enthusiastically sang Hindi film songs alongside the chutney lyrics common to such occasions.[6] As Caldeo Sookram points out, "The era of local Indian classical music with stalwarts like Ramdhanie Sharma, James Ramsewak, Jhagroo Quawal, Ramcharitar, Taran Persad, and others soon faded into oblivion. The 'film thing' ruled the day."[7] The dance dramas popular until the 1950s were overtaken by the "cabaret dance" of Hindi movie vamps and, more generally, "film dances" performed to the film songs.

Opinions about the nature of the impact of Hindi film differ widely. One scholar argues that the "influence of Indian films played a major role in the secularisation and vulgarisation and generally, in the degradation of the purer forms of Indian dance. Such dance performances had no appeal for the more intellectual upper classes of society, as they were usually full of eroticism and were associated with a laxity of morals."[8] The musician Narsaloo Ramaya contends, however, that the coming of Indian films marked "the beginning of a cultural awakening" in Trinidad for the East Indians, and that the films "radically chang[ed] the direction of musical taste and prevailing customs." However, the old-style "*dhrupad, tilana, thumri, gazal, hori* and *bhairavi*" had disappeared by the 1940s with the death of the older generation of singers.[9] The establishment of Radio Trinidad in 1947 led to the music show *Indian Talent on Parade*, hosted by Kamaluddin Mohammed, part of the prominent Mohammed family referred to in chapter 3, known for its involvement in promoting East Indian performative traditions, who began broadcasting Hindi film songs. This is especially interesting in the light of the fact that All India Radio in post-Independence India refused to broadcast film music, considering it not properly representative of "Indian culture." Talking about her childhood, a retired East Indian schoolteacher told me that her family was "typical rural Indian." Their lifestyle "was very simple, very Indian—our food, our music. . . . In those days you had nothing but Hindi film music, . . . but we went for it in a big way. Every evening you had a half-hour of Indian music." She also mentioned that, although she still recognized some of the songs, she knew only a few words of Hindi, the script of which she had learned as a child in the 1940s but subsequently had forgotten.[10]

Hindi films were introduced into Trinidad in 1935 by Ranjit Kumar, an engineer originally from Lahore (now in Pakistan) who had studied in England.[11] In the early 1940s, Krishna Golikeri of Bombay was in Chunking, China, where he met the Trinidadian Indrajeet Bahadur, a diplomat on behalf of the British Indian government who is said to have married Rabindranath Tagore's granddaughter. Bahadur advised Golikeri to distribute Hindi films in the Caribbean. Golikeri formed a company that later merged with that of the Samtani family to form India Overseas Limited, which is still the leading film-distribution company in Trinidad.[12]

Recollecting his memories of Hindi cinema in Trinidad, the artist Christopher Cozier told me that on long drives to the beach in the 1960s his Barbadian immigrant parents and his older sisters sang "what sounded like an Indian movie song," the words of which he remembered as, "Ay yai yai Colombo cha suku suku."[13] One of my colleagues recognized the song as one that Mohammed Rafi had made famous in the film *Junglee* (Subodh Mukherjee, 1961), picturized on the wild and romantic Shammi Kapoor, although he said the words didn't seem right. I wrote back to Cozier, pointing out that the lyrics probably were, "Ai ya ya karoon mein kya suku suku," but he insisted that there was a local version (perhaps a song by Sundar Popo) in which the words must have been different—not "Karoon mein kya (What shall I do?)" but "Colombo cha (tea from Colombo)." Another Trinidadian confirmed that the song's refrain, which was popular enough to be recognized by non-East Indians, was used later in a calypso, although he couldn't remember who the singer was. It is very likely that the gaiety and brisk pace of the intonation in the original song, and the scanty knowledge of Hindi even among East Indians, helped turn the witty lament of someone suffering from *tabanca* into a nonsense rhyme that absorbed the phrase "suku suku" into the Trinidadian tradition of double entendre.[14]

"*Tabanca*" is a Spanish-derived word commonly used in Trinidad while speaking of romantic love. For Afro-Trinidadians, it refers to losing a woman's affections to another; the term is extended by Indo-Trinidadians to mean "a state of unrequited love, where a macho reputation has been prevented rather than lost." A study of East Indian village youth by Niels Sampath mentions a twenty-four year old called "Pastor" who had converted to Christianity and referred mockingly to his former religious affiliation, which was Hinduism. Pastor began to long for a young woman in the village. Not daring to speak to her, he took to walking back and forth in front of her house. Without taking his friends' advice to "make a move on de chick," Pastor watched videos of Hindi films, where "after years of separation, the hero and heroine might finally speak to each other before a painful death" and began to attend Hindu prayer meetings once again. His attempts to console himself were ridiculed by his friends: "Poor Pastor. He does want to make a move on the girl but he ain't getting nowhere. He used to mock them star-boys in Indian pictures and now he suffering just like they.... Once you does lose courage to take action, bang, *tabanca* does take hold and you back sitting and scratching, doing nothing." Sampath sees the young man's predicament as a result of his becoming a "victim of creolisation," unable to reconcile Trinidadian modernity with "Indian culture."[15] We find a similar figure, albeit presented in the comic mode, in Rikki Jai's calypso/chutney-soca "Sumintra."

Cozier, too, says that as a child he had "this sense, however ridiculous, of [the protagonists of the movies] being in an un-modern, non-liberal world."[16] For him, this contrasted strangely with how "the cities looked large and modern like in American movies." He had the feeling, shared by other Trinidadians, that "Trinidad was a small, underdeveloped place" from where Indian Prime Minister Indira Gandhi and Mao Zedong, along with Woodrow Wilson and Winston Churchill, were seen as leaders of great nations. Cozier also speaks of his childhood perception of the "puzzling stressful scenarios of the Indian films," adding that "some Trinis still feel this way." The films, unlike the songs heard constantly over the radio, perhaps present a puzzle to contemporary Trinidadians (including East Indians) precisely because they narrativize the passive revolution in India,[17] the story of the emergence of hegemonic modernities underwritten by the nation-state, making possible the construction of new kinds of urban subjectivities.

So what we have in India, broadly speaking, is one kind of national-modern, in which normative Indianness comes to be associated in part with the Hindi language films and their constructions of modern femininity and masculinity. In Trinidad, however, there seem to be competing modernities—"Indian" and "Creole"—in which the former often acquires, by contrast, the connotations of backwardness, non-rationality, and location in the private sphere while the latter appears as normative.[18] Pastor's story, then, could be read differently: not as a failure to reconcile modernity with "culture," as Sampath has it, but as the lack of fit between two kinds of national-modern formations. Pastor's difficulty lies in the fact that he perceives the erotics of Hindi film as being in opposition to notions of courtship in his Trinidadian context. Trying to formulate a sense of his cultural identity in relation to the protagonists of Hindi films takes him out of his own Caribbean history and locates him within a different, though no less modern, vocabulary of love. And Pastor, unable to separate the romantic narratives of Hindi cinema from his notion of "Indian culture," is rendered incapable of making a move on the woman because, from the perspective of his New World subjectivity, that sort of thing does not happen in the films he watches.

Another kind of response to the vexed question of modernity versus Indianness is reported by Raviji: "We looked at Hindi films for the way of being Indian, often we were copying their version of the west, re-routed through Hindi films."[19] He goes on to say that "Hindi films were offering us an India we starved for and from which we drew our idea for self." However, he claims, Trinidadian East Indians "were sensitive enough to sense that it [Hindi film] imitated blindly and resisted it." Here Raviji invokes a common trope in the subaltern diaspora: that it is the diasporic community which is concerned with preserving true Indianness while the mother country has culturally compromised itself by copying the West, the implication being, perhaps, that one has to be of the West before one can fashion a resistance to it.[20] Raviji indicates that films, comics, and even novels were "taboo" for children when he was growing up in the 1950s, although other accounts stress that going to the cinema was a family activity: "We couldn't afford it too frequently. I don't know how much it was, maybe a shilling, you went occasionally when there was a special film and when older one went more often, like all the very popular films, you never missed them."[21] In Raviji's family and others like his, "English [proper] names, eating in hotels, women wearing pants, cutting their hair, bareheadedness of women were frowned upon," and the Hindi films that broke all these rules created a stir in the community—so much so that Raviji remembers saying, as a young man, "If I see Meena Kumari [a famous female star of the '50s and '60s] in pants, I'll stop seeing Hindi films."[22] Whether or not Meena Kumari wore trousers, other Hindi film stars did and, again according to Raviji, "helped East Indians adopt Western dress."

What role, then, did Hindi cinema play in the shaping of the subaltern diaspora's modernity in Trinidad? It gave them access to glamorous worlds and people who were not of Hollywood, and it brought into their cultural practice a series of lively innovations in music and dance styles. As Sudipta Kaviraj argues in another context, modernity renders possible new types of belonging and even makes it "obligatory" for people to "[have] their earlier identities in an altogether different way,"[23] so that the meaning of being Indian in Trinidad might have changed quite dramatically due to the intervention of Hindi cinema and the spectatorial practices it initiated. But East Indians of all classes maintained a shifting and ambiguous relationship to Hindi films, either because of aspirations to high cultural forms manifested in the association of "culture," "refinement," and "Indianness," or because of cultural anxieties produced by different vocabularies of modernity that were not always in alignment. Attraction and dismissal were often coupled in the same pronouncements about Hindi cinema. This double response, I suggest, could be generated by the separation of the film songs, which were widely appreciated by East Indians and others for their melodies, from the film's narrative structure and plot devices, which invoked scorn or created embarrassment due to their alleged melodramatic excesses. The interest in Hindi film songs for most East Indians today does not derive from any understanding of the lyrics, since even singers like Drupatee Ramgoonai and Rikki Jai, who include these songs in their repertoire, assert that they do not know Hindi. By the 1950s, Hindi and Bhojpuri began to diminish in importance as a language of everyday communication, so much so that today East Indians do not watch Hindi films that are not subtitled in English. A young woman in her twenties spoke about viewing Hindi films on television when she was growing up:

> The older people love it. My nani used to sit down, my mother's mother used to sit down there, and she couldn't understand what the hell going on and sometimes she would say, "What going on, what going on?" I couldn't read when I was younger, you know [reference to the subtitles]. She'll try to understand a little Hindi that going on there and she loved it.[24]

That East Indians do not speak Hindi (sometimes referred to simply as "Indyan") any more is emphasized by a village woman in her seventies who told me:

> The chirren don' talk Indyan. But I could understan' Indyan. I used to talk wid my moder. Now we don' have no Indyan people . . . don' talk Hindi again. All o' dem only talkin' English. We moder and fader use to talk Indyan to we. But now when yuh go talk Indyan, dem chirren dey eh know what yuh sayin'.[25]

Even if Hindi became unintelligible over the years to East Indians in Trinidad, the structure of Indian films may not have been unfamiliar. East Indian forms of entertainment since at least the early twentieth century included dance dramas like *Raja Harishchandra*, *Indrasabha*, and *Krishna-leela*, based on tales from Hindu mythology. An intricate narrative with multiple songs therefore would be something the audience would expect from "Indian" amusements. As Manas Ray suggests in his work on Fijian Indian migrants to Australia, the indentureds' place of origin in India—the area including present-day Bihar, Uttar Pradesh, and Rajasthan—showed the influence of the *bhakti* tradition (forms of popular worship) in which the prominent text was the *Tulsi Ramayana*, a retelling of the Ramayana epic by the *bhakti* saint-poet Tulsidas. In such communities, the celebration of Ramlila—involving the enactment of the victory of King Rama over the demon Ravana—was common, as it is even today in Trinidad or Fiji. The eroticism of the Radha-Krishna relationship, says Ray, must also have been part of the interpretive framework with which Indians approached Hindi cinema. The fantasy scenes of Hindi films and the dazzling spectacles they provided could also be related to the diverse performative conventions in Trinidad, which included not only Ramlila but also Hosay (Muharram) and, of course, Carnival.

Popular Hindi cinema in general seldom follows what Miriam Hansen describes as the "principles of narrative dominance, linear and unobtrusive narration centering on the psychology and agency of individual characters, and continuity editing," which are the basis of Hollywood cinema.[26] Film scholars have pointed out that the genealogy of the Indian film form is somewhat different from Euro-American cinema, bearing as it does the imprint of multiple local artistic traditions, which include mythological dance dramas, devotional iconic notions of representation, and painting conventions crisscrossing the Hindu and Muslim traditions of precolonial rule. The work of Ashish Rajadhyaksha on the frontality of address in Indian cinema and politics and that of M. Madhava Prasad on the *darsanic* gaze (a spectatorial look deriving from certain Hindu devotional practices), as well as Gulammohammed Sheikh's writing on the mobility of spatial structure in Indian painting, have provided convincing arguments for the specificity of framing devices in Indian film. Since Hindi cinema partly drew on these representational practices as, in Rajadhyaksha's words, the modern came to be inscribed on the popular, early East Indian viewers in Trinidad may have related more easily to Hindi films than to those produced by Hollywood.[27]

After December 7, 1935, when *Bala Joban* appeared at the Gaiety Theater in San Fernando, all existing forms of East Indian dance, music, and devotion came to be influenced, as pointed out earlier, by Indian films.[28] According to some writers, the coming of Hindi cinema triggered "a powerful cultural revival," setting fashions in hairstyle, jewelry, and stage shows.[29] In the wake of Hindi films, the orchestra phenomenon became prominent, beginning with the establishment in 1944 of the Naya Zamana Orchestra by Nazeer Mohammed. And in 1947, when Radio Trinidad was established in pre-independence Trinidad, the immensely popular *Indian Talent on Parade* began to be aired.

The influence of Hindi film music was to be seen, as Helen Myers points out, in "the formation during the 1950s, '60s, and '70s of more than a hundred Indian combos, 'orchestras.' " Myers mentions not only Naya Zamana, but also Solo Sangeet, Satara Hind, Bean Sangeet, Mal Sangeet, Choti Sangeet Saaj, Hum Hindustani, Central Merry Makers, Sisons Naya Sansar, Acme Dil Nadan, and the BWIA National Indian Orchestra. As Myers describes them, the orchestras, comprising ten to fifteen players and found all over Trinidad, "usually include electric guitars, electric keyboards, a drum set, sometimes mandolin, congo drums, trumpet, violin, and saxophone, as well as the occasional traditional Indian instrument, for example the *bansuri* (flute), and *dholak* and tabla drums." Many of the orchestras in contemporary Trinidad are electronic, dominated by keyboards, guitar, and drums, with an occasional dholak player. The orchestras commonly play at weddings and parties and on radio and television, especially on *Mastana Bahar*, the weekly East Indian talent show established in 1970.[30] Enthusiastic singers, who usually do not know much Hindi, have taken part in the numerous contests organized around films like *Junglee* and *Sangam*, which, according to film distributors, were among the ten most popular Hindi films in the period from 1950 to 2000.[31] In a *Junglee* song contest held in 1962, for example, one of the most popular songs was "Ai ya ya suku suku." After 1963, the Junglee Merrymakers Indian Orchestra was formed, inspired by the film playback singer Mohammed Rafi. The key figure behind that orchestra was the singer Azeez Khan (d. 2001), who later won an India government scholarship to study music in Delhi and then spent a year in the film industry in Bombay, where he met his idol, Rafi, the singer of "Suku suku."[32] Azeez Khan was commended for the purity of his Hindi pronunciation by another famous Indian playback singer, Hemant Kumar, who once awarded him a prize at a competition in Trinidad. At present, the government-aided National Council of Indian Culture regularly hosts at its Divali Nagar campus in Chaguanas, Central Trinidad, a series of music competitions that include classical (Indian) singing, Memories of Rafi, Memories of Mukesh, Memories of Kishore Kumar, and the Local Song Contest on National Development.

Another Trinidadian selected for the Indian scholarship was the musician Harry Mahabir. In 1965, Mahabir and his contingent represented Trinidad and Tobago at the Commonwealth Arts Festival in London. Sharda Patasar says, "The Trinidadian Indian artists went with a repertoire of Indian film songs originally sung by the great film singers Lata Mangeshkar and the late Mohammed Rafi from India. On arrival in London the Trinidadian artistes were confronted by the contingent from India which included the very singers whom they were trying so desperately to imitate."[33] Mahabir later spoke about this as one of the greatest traumas of his life. His group changed its repertoire, adding folk songs from Trinidad. "He vowed then to work towards a unique form of musical expression that was Trinidadian."[34]

Mahabir later went to India to study music; he met film artists in Bombay and decided to study Western music after his exposure to the electronic instruments they were using.[35] Returning to Trinidad, Mahabir became the leader of the BWIA National Indian Orchestra, providing backing through *Mastana Bahar* to many East Indian singers and, according to Kim Johnson, adapting "Indian linear melodies to Western techniques of harmony."[36]

Mastana Bahar, promoted by the Mohammed brothers, who had longstanding political connections with the ruling People's National Movement, debuted on Trinidad and Tobago Television (TTT) in August 1970. The half-hour program was organized like a contest; by 1971, the contest took place over thirty-nine weeks. Auditions were held all over the island, and finalists were selected. The show was cut to twenty-six programs per series in 1981.[37] Song and dance from Hindi cinema featured prominently on *Mastana Bahar* and often became the route by which non-East Indians acquainted themselves with Hindi film. Christopher Cozier mentions that his father "watched *Mastana Bahar* avidly.... [In] those days that was how he learned about the trends in Indian movies, as most of the competitors would mime or sing songs from the movies that were popular in the local cinemas and act out dance scenes.... There was little local stuff then, much less classical Indian stuff."[38]

The popularity of *Mastana Bahar* is attested to by Mighty Chalkdust, the schoolteacher-calypsonian whose successful career has spanned four decades. He sang "Mastana Bahar, or Indian Competition" in 1978.[39] The primary addressee of the calypso is the promoter of the Calypso Monarch competition, who, Chalkdust sings, must "hang his head in shame" that an "Indian competition" is overtaking the annual calypso contests in popularity and, more important, prize money. (The first prize for the Calypso Monarch was four thousand Trinidadian dollars, whereas the *Mastana* prize was twenty thousand Trinidadian dollars. Chalkdust's reference to the prize money plays on the popular prejudice that all East Indians are wealthy.) No wonder the *Mastana* competition is able to lure all of the singers, Indian as well as African, the song says. Chalkdust then sings, "Dil deke dekho, dil deke dekho ji (Give the heart, give the heart and see) / Dil lene waalon dil dena seekho ji (Those who take the heart, you must learn to give the heart)," which comes from the Hindi film hit *Dil Deke Dekho* (1959), by Nasir Hussain. Sham Mohammed, *Mastana Bahar*'s promoter, impressed by Chalkdust's "Indian song," asks the calypsonian why he is "singing for mere chick feed / In a national competititon." Mohammed promises Chalkdust airplay on radio and television if he will "forget the calypso crown." (These lines give the impression that East Indians control a lot of space in these media.) Chalkdust warns Mohammed that this is the last time he will participate, since it is the promoter who gets "the lion's share," not the singers. Even "the fifth prize on *Mastana Bahar* / Is a trip to Barbados back!" Chalkdust then cleverly turns the lines of a romantic Hindi film song to good use, singing:

> Jo vaada kiya ho nibhaana padega
> What you have promised you must deliver
> Rokay zamana chaahe rokay khudayi
> I don't care if the world stops you, or even God
> Tumko aana padega
> You will still have to come
> Jo vaada kiya ho nibhaana padega
> What you have promised you must deliver.[40]

It was a matter of concern for some East Indians that in 1971 only five out of eighty-eight compositions in a *Mastana Bahar* audition were local, the rest being versions of Hindi film songs. It was in this context that the career of Sundar Popo began. Popo, whose first album came out in 1969, sang Trinidadian English lyrics mixed with some Hindi or Bhojpuri, innovating both musically and in terms of lyrics from a base of chutney music—the bawdy pre-wedding songs originally sung by women—as well as of Hindi film music. As I discussed in chapter 3, Kanchan and Babla, the singer-composer couple from the Indian film industry who remixed chutney songs and calypsos in the style of Hindi film music, also made an important contribution. Present-day chutney-soca, toward which singers like Sundar Popo gestured, also traces its ancestry to Ras Shorty I, who used Indian melodies, often based on film songs heard on the radio, and Hindi lyrics in his calypsos from the 1960s.

Chalkdust's reference to the growing importance of *Mastana Bahar* as representing the visibility of East Indians on the Trinidadian cultural landscape was picked up and elaborated many years later, in 1995, when the Indian-dominated United National Congress came to power in Trinidad. As Selwyn Ryan says, "The UNC was variously stigmatized as a 'Chutney,' 'Mastana Bahar,' 'Indian' or 'Hindu' government."[41] Disgruntled opposition-party supporters referred to a famous 1949 Hindi film song, "Suhani Raat

Dhal Chuki" (from *Dulari*, dir. A. R. Kardar and sung by Mohammed Rafi) when they complained that "Sohani Raat" had become the national anthem of Trinidad.[42]

Exhibition of Hindi Films

In July 1970, of fifty theaters counted in the pages of the *Express*, twelve were showing Indian films, including the famous *Kashmir ki Kali* (dir. Shakti Samanta, 1964) and *Mahal* (dir. Shankar Mukherjee, 1969); the rest were "B" movies. An advertisement for *Talash* (dir. O. P. Ralhan, 1969), "with full English subtitles," carried the tag line: "THE ANSWER TO YOUR UNENDING SEARCH for all those things that lure your mind—Possess your heart—Satisfy your soul."[43] I am told that about 40 percent of cinemas would have shown Hindi films from the 1950s to the 1980s, with some having special shows of Hindi films on certain days. Sometimes single films would be shown; sometimes there were double bills or even triples. The movies were not advertised by huge *hoardings* (billboards), as in Indian cities, although big posters appeared at the theaters. Instead, vans with loudspeakers drove through the countryside, dropping handbills and playing records from the film being advertised.[44]

Amita Basdeo's research indicates that movies were first shown monthly, and only on weekends. By the 1940s, two cinemas had weekly showings, and by the 1970s, Trinidad had thirteen full-time Indian film houses. From 1946 onward, with the establishment of the distribution company Indian Films, thirty to forty Hindi films were released each year in Trinidad, Guyana, and Surinam. Since it was difficult to get "playing time" in the theaters, which were dominated by the major Hollywood studios, Indian Films went into exhibition, leasing or purchasing cinemas in key areas in Trinidad such as Port of Spain, Tunapuna, Chaguanas, and San Fernando.[45] Public film viewing noticeably declined in the 1980s, partly because of the availability of VCRs for home use and partly because of the economic recession and the resulting increase in crimes such as mugging, which kept people at home in the evenings.[46] Television also brought down the number of Hindi-film viewers going to the cinema:

> I stopped going to the movies years ago because I recollect people would start smoking in the cinemas and I would start sneezing and we'd come out smelling of smoke and so by that time they started showing a Hindi

Theater in Chaguanas. Photo by Tejaswini Niranjana.

film on television on Saturdays or Sundays, so you looked at that instead of going [to the cinema].[47]

The general view among distributors is that audiences are not drawn to the movie theaters in large numbers anymore, whether the film is in Hindi or in English. However, journalists point to a resurgence in the 1990s in Hindi film viewing, with the popularity of a new generation of films addressing a now homogenized Indian diaspora. Such films include *Hum Aapke Hain Kaun* (dir. Sooraj Barjatya, 1994), *Dilwale Dulhaniya Le Jayenge* (dir. Aditya Chopra, 1995), *Pardes* (dir. Subhash Ghai, 1999), and *Kuch Kuch Hota Hai* (dir. Karan Johar, 1998). The normative diasporic here is the immigrant to the First World, as the settings of many of these films indicate. The structure of address includes the cosmopolitanizing middle class in India as well as the non-resident Indian. The category of NRI (which now also extends to the PIO, or person of Indian origin) is being invoked in both India and the diaspora as one that also encompasses the older migrations, where a newly culturalized India is made available for global consumption. As I suggested in chapter 1, the promise of equality on new terms (which may no longer appear as those set solely by the homeland) is being extended to subaltern diasporic people who live in the West. In a somewhat different manner, contemporary Hindi films also hold out this promise, with the West no longer

181

vilified but, instead, becoming the location in which a pure Indian nationalism, unsullied by the irritations of daily life in the Third World, can be practiced.⁴⁸

Although it was not until 1976 that a Hindi film was shown on TTT, a long-standing demand existed for such films, as expressed in newspaper columns and readers' forums. A letter writer calling himself or herself the "Non-European God Soul," for instance, wrote to the *Daily Express* in 1975 complaining about TTT: "All normal people hold the view that television and radio must of necessity reflect the good taste and culture of all the peoples of Trinidad and Tobago [even if TTT doesn't think so]. A tally of films shown in this country place[s] films of India in modern Hindi as the most popular group of films in Trinidad and Tobago. [People who watch these would like to see them on TV at home.] But instead we are having American and British films rammed down our throats. And most of these films are alien to our taste and way of life." The writer calls for intervention by Prime Minister Eric Williams, who had once called East Indians a recalcitrant minority. "I hereby issue warning: [S]how films of India on Television, or face a campaign of action until the same is achieved." The demand by "God Soul" produces a curious metaphor suggesting that major cultural differences exist between Africans and East Indians. The writer says that not showing Hindi films on TV is like denying entry of Jamaican potatoes when Trinidadian shops have none and getting plantains and beef, which East Indians apparently do not need, from Guyana instead.⁴⁹

Even if Hindi films did not appear on television until the 1970s, in the oil-boom years from the early 1970s to the mid-1980s many Indian singers were invited to perform in the Caribbean. There is a reference to one such entertainer in the calypso "Sumintra" (1989), written by Gregory Ballantyne and sung by Rikki Jai in his solo debut on the calypso stage.⁵⁰ "Sumintra" begins with an imitation of an India Indian (and not Trinidad East Indian) man's voice saying, "It gives me great pleasure this evening to welcome to the Caribbean . . . Lata Mangeshkar, Lata Mangeshkar, Lata Mangeshkar" (reverb). Then we hear Jai's voice singing a phrase from an old Lata song, "Bindiya chamkegi" (from the film *Do Raaste*, dir. Raj Khosla, 1969), while the chorus chants, "Give me soca ah ha / Boy give me soca, ah ha."⁵¹ The song then quickly warms to its main theme: the "Indian gyul that creolize," to use the words of a 1939 calypso by Lord Invader. The calypsonian is courting an East Indian village girl—"born in a shack in Debe . . . / Her parents from Indian Walk"—called Sumintra.⁵² When she refuses to answer his letters, he "hit the record shops" and buys up "Indian records" to give her, in the firm belief that "music is the food of love." But when he "reach by the gyul she say stop, Rikki, stop," for he has got it completely wrong. As the refrain goes:

> Hold de Lata Mangeshkar
> Give me soca ah ha ah ha
> Tickle me with a lavway
> Soca me till I sesay
> Hold de Lata Mangeshkar
> Give me soca ah ha ah ha.[53]

Sumintra cautions her suitor:

> Doh let mih catch you in dat foolishness
> Trying to reach de Indian in me
> . . .
> Boy I'm Trinbagonian
> I like soca action
> Take your Mohammed Rafi [the Indian playback singer]
> Bring me Scrunter or Bally [calypsonians]
> Only then you be talkin' to me.[54]

As the song goes on to indicate, Sumintra has drawn a line between "roots and culture": Her roots may be in the land of Lata Mangeshkar, but her "culture" lies in the land of calypso and soca. Once again, a musical metaphor points to modes of self-fashioning; here, an Indo-Creole person differentiates between ethnic identity and cultural identity. When asked why Sumintra needs to choose between the two, Rikki Jai insisted that she was not choosing soca over Indian music: "She is very accustomed to Indian music, but now she wants calypso. She's saying that at this particular stage she wants soca, when she's being courted."[55] Interestingly, while Rikki Jai himself started out in calypso and also sings reggae, parang, chutney, and Hindi film songs, he is best known as a chutney-soca singer, having won numerous awards, including the recently instituted Chutney Soca Monarch title. This musical form does not claim a solely "Indian" or "African" origin, as I elaborated in chapter 3. In the words of Drupatee's song "Hotter Than a Chulha (Indian Soca)," in chutney-soca, "Rhythm from Africa and from India / Blend together in a perfect mixture." Here Drupatee presents a musical option that is very different from preferring soca to Hindi film

"Hold de Lata Mangeshkar": Rikki Jai in Debe. Surabhi Sharma/R. V. Ramani.

music, or the other way around, as the crowds thronging her shows and those of other chutney-soca performers indicate.

There are East Indians, however, who reject chutney-soca as well as calypso in favor of Hindi film music and Hindi films. Among them is Rajnie Ramlakhan, who articulates a peculiarly Trinidadian connection between the films and Hinduism. In a *Daily Express* column titled, "Hinduism Here to Stay Forever," Ramlakhan applauded the importance of the joint family as shown in the film *Hum Saath Saath Hain* (dir. Sooraj Barjatya, 1999, which incidentally did not do well in India) and talked about the Sanatan Dharma Maha Sabha's recent executive meetings in which the joint family, seen by Ramlakhan as a key feature of Hinduism, came up for discussion. She called *Hum Saath Saath Hain* brilliant because it is "a re-affirmation in Hinduism done through an exciting medium. It is a strong declaration of faith in Hindu dharma, taking us into the new millennium." Ramlakhan goes on to say that, "just when you think Hindi movies couldn't get any better, especially after last year's mega hit *Kuch Kuch Hota Hai* [dir. Karan Johar, 1998], comes [*Hum Saath Saath Hain*] to surpass it. There are also many other very good movies around for the year like *Taal* [dir. Subhash Ghai, 1999] and

Dillagi [dir. Sunny Deol, 1999]."[56] These are very diverse kinds of romantic films, although they share the new production values that make up the globalized "Bollywood" film (as opposed to the "Hindi" film, which addresses a more local audience in India), and a good deal of ingenuity would be required to read them as promoting "Hindu values." What might be interesting to investigate here is the possibility that, while earlier Hindi films circulated in Trinidad as markers of cultural difference, they might now be read as representations of idyllic East–West synthesis in which, unlike the situation in Trinidad, the strains do not show.

Ramlakhan's insistence on the "Hinduness" of Hindi cinema is perhaps not new in the Caribbean context. As far back as the 1940s, the bulletin of the Sanatan Dharma Maha Sabha, which became the umbrella organization of Hindu groups in Trinidad, carried advertisements for Hindi films, which the organization considered part of the revival of Indian culture.[57] The main aim of the bulletin, according to Patricia Mohammed, was to disseminate information about the organization to "hold and build its membership."[58] Another example of the close association of Hinduism and cinema can be found in a brief biographical account of the family of Kavita Maharaj, who works for Radio 90.5 FM, which is dedicated to "East Indian music" (chutney and Hindi film music). Maharaj's great-grandfather was Pandit Vyakaran Bhushan Ramjatan, the "leader of the Hindu masses" according to the station's website, who was responsible for government recognition of Hinduism. Kavita is also granddaughter of Bajnath and Cecilia Maharaj, pioneers of Indian film distribution in the Caribbean.

Some East Indians and their African counterparts today support the political and cultural polarization of the two racial groups, with the shrillest voices accusing each other of fundamentalisms that may not mean much to most Trinidadians in the context of mounting criticism from all sides of an Indian-dominated government that was finally brought down by infighting in its second five-year term. Some of those in what the calypsonian Black Stalin calls "the cultural business" are now sidestepping the race talk common in the public sphere and are presenting messages of integration in hugely popular songs like Machel Montano's and Drupatee Ramgoonai's "Real Unity" (2000).

The song intertwines parts of the Hindi film song "Aap Jaise Koi" (from the film *Qurbani* [dir. Feroz Khan, 1980], sung in Hindi by Drupatee with Montano singing, "Unite de nation." His words ostensibly refer to "jumping up" ("Cause yuh know we love de jumpin' jumpin' / And that is real

Drupatee and Machel: *Real Unity* CD cover.

unity") during Carnival, playing mas' ("Pretty in we costume with plenty sequin"), and "wining" to the music ("Everybody looking at we / How we wining in ah unity / Is Mr. Machel with Drupatee / Movin like ah big family / And that is real unity"). The chorus is woven around the incantatory chant, "Unite de nation / unite de nation / unite de nation." For Machel and Drupatee, dancing and singing together stands for the larger project of living in harmony: "Why we fuss and fight? / Tonight we come to unite." Not since the Black Power Movement of the 1970s, perhaps, has there been such a direct call for unity between Indian and African. However, unlike the initiatives of that time, "Real Unity" touches on the most difficult question between the races, and one that is seldom articulated as political: douglarization, or cohabitation between Indian and African.[59]

The message of unity in "Real Unity" is clearly sexualized, and to anyone who has seen or participated in Carnival-style dancing, the reference seems also to be to cohabitation between the races:

> Noting wrong with wining on ah Indian gyul
> Noting wrong with wining on ah Chinee gyul

> Noting wrong with wining on ah African gyul
> Noting wrong with wining on ah Syrian gyul
> Is real unity.[60]

In contrast, the Hindi lyrics run:

> Aap jaisa koyee meri [Someone like you]
> zindagi mein aaye [comes into my life]
> To baat ban jaaye [then that will be something / things will happen]
> Ah ha to baat ban jaaye.

The language is that of a highly romantic and erotically charged love song, a feature common to many Hindi films of the period. But the juxtaposition of the words about what the Indian woman wants and Machel's celebration of wining suggests that the desire to unite physically is related to the desire for the unification of the body politic. More strongly put, "Every creed and race . . . jumpin' as one" and loving "one another" is what, according to the calypsonians, will make possible "unification . . . 'pon de plan" of the nation itself:

> Har kisi ko chaahiye [Everyone desires]
> Tan man ka milan [meeting of body and mind]
> Kaash kucch pal aisaa [I wish for some minutes thus]
> Dil aap ka ho jaaye [My heart would be yours].

In an interview, Drupatee pointed out that the tassa drums "did it for people" in her earlier hit "Mr. Bissessar." In "Real Unity," however, it was "the Hindi song together with the music, . . . the blend of Machel's voice and my voice, the film tune mix with Machel soca."[61] Asked how she came to record the song with Machel, Drupatee said that she had been asked to go to Machel's studio for some work. When she got there, Machel started to hum "Aap jaise koi," she said. "As soon as he started to hum it, I recognized the tune, 'cause I knew the movie long time."[62] Obviously, the Hindi film song was part of the cultural memory of both the African singer and the East Indian one. The newspaper article that carried this interview with Drupatee began with the comment that she was "weathering [a] storm of protest from people . . . opposed to the unity message in her current hit."[63] It concluded with Drupatee saying that "Africans and Indians should give themselves a chance . . . to come together." The first statement was a reference to a rumor that some East Indian radio stations had refused to play

"Real Unity" because of objections to its line, "Noting wrong with wining on ah Indian gyul." This sort of controversy is not new for Drupatee, many of whose songs since the 1980s have attracted similar criticism from East Indian men concerned about her exuberant sexual explicitness. Interestingly, Trinidadian media do not carry criticism of the raunchy dances in present-day Hindi films or of the skimpy clothes worn by female stars in, for example, the movies commended earlier for upholding Hindu values. The attacks on chutney-soca, and on Drupatee's music in particular, have little to do with "Indian" films. They are part of a debate in the musical public sphere of Trinidad. Chutney-soca may borrow from Hindi film music, but it has created a uniquely Trinidadian expressive space that attracts both appreciation and criticism on its own terms, though often in contrast with Creole modernity.

As I argued in chapter 4, Drupatee's chutney-soca performances draw attention to a certain "grain of the voice" that could seem far more threatening to notions of female sexual propriety than the lyrics by themselves could convey. In fact, Drupatee's voice is far less robust in "Real Unity" than it is in her earlier hit songs "Mr. Bissessar" or "Lick Down Mih Nani," and with good reason: In "Real Unity," she has to counterpoint Machel's guttural, rough voice with lyrics that almost float on the surface of the song. Again, more significant than the lyrics is the interleaving of Drupatee's voice with Machel's and the sensual effect produced by the juxtaposition. Writing about the significance of Machel's band, Xtatik, performing a party song rather than a sociopolitical-commentary calypso, Sheila Rampersad points out that "the song's title . . . subverts the national unity slogan of the [then] ruling United National Congress (UNC) and suggests itself as a representation of real unity."[64] Beyond the platitudes of politicians about racial unity, and beyond the race talk of some calypsonians, Machel and Drupatee strive to create a space for a "soca chutney jam" in which "everybody hug up together as one." The complex task of unification—to be sought in the music because it perhaps cannot be accomplished anywhere else—is underscored by the sweet sounds of Xtatik as it performs with Dil-E-Nadaan and JMC Triveni, two of the leading East Indian orchestras, who play their version of the Hindi film song "Aap Jaise Koi."[65]

The use of Hindi film lyrics and melody in "Real Unity" represents a departure from the older calypsos that used them predominantly for humorous effect, as in "Sumintra" or "Mastana Bahar." It is also new for an East Indian *woman* to be singing the Hindi film lyrics. Far from turning this into a gesture that simply essentializes racial and cultural identities by mapping feminine onto "Indian" and masculine onto "African," the Hindi film melody—and the sound of the lyrics—in "Real Unity" create a space from which the East Indian woman can articulate the distinctiveness of her cultural location.

If the East Indian woman in the calypso tradition is usually courted by the African man, the Indian man seems to be finding a new suitor. In the 2004 Soca Monarch competition, a crowd favorite was the Afro-Trinidadian Denise Belfon (a.k.a. Saucy Wow). Belfon, a former beauty queen who grew up watching *Mastana Bahar* and Indian films on television, claims to be fascinated by Hindi cinema and picked up Indian melodies and dance styles, including intricate head movements from classical Indian dance. Clad in a glittering blue sari that she drapes herself, and surrounded by chutney dancers, Belfon, who sang a popular English and Bhojpuri remix of Sonny Mann's "Lotay La" in 1996 and who, singing in Hindi and Bhojpuri, has also been a contestant in the Chutney Monarch competition, comes onstage to the beat of a musical phrase from the Hindi film *Takshak* (dir. Govind Nihalani, 1999). The beat heralds Belfon's hit song "I Am Looking for an Indian Man."[66] In her high-energy performance, Belfon casts off her sari and emerges in orange tights as she wines down the house. While for decades male calypsonians sang about the exotic Indian woman, representing her as the normative feminine, this was the very first time that an African woman represented in music a desire for the Indian man. In doing so, she performed an implicit critique of normative Creole Trinidadian masculinity.

There is a postscript to the Belfon story. In early 2004, I took the Indian rock-pop star Remo Fernandes to the Caribbean for a series of collaborations with local singers. One of the events we managed to set up after many hours of telephoning was a recording session with Belfon. Over a long day in May in Kenny Phillips's studio in San Fernando, in southern Trinidad, Remo (who is also well known for his hit songs in the Hindi film industry) and Saucy Wow recorded a reply to "Looking for an Indian Man." What can happen when an academic initiative extends into musical practice is the subject of the last part of this book. My Afterword deals with how a group of India Indians became involved with narratives of Trinidadian femininity and masculinity.

AFTERWORD

★ A Semi-Lime

Chutney-soca, chutney-soca / Chutney-soca from Trinidad to Goa
I drop in from India / From far far away
I hear this new rhythm / Making Trinidad sway.
The beat drive me crazy / The beat drive me wild
The beat give me fever / I wanna take it home.
—Remo Fernandes (lyrics for collaborative song with Rikki Jai)

A rhythm from the islands / A rhythm from my soul
A rhythm filled with fire / To warm up your soul.
The spirit of a people who came from India
With African vibrations call it chutney-soca.
—Rikki Jai (lyrics for collaborative song with Remo Fernandes)

> I am lookin' for an Indian man / I callin' for an Indian man
>
> I hungry for an Indian man / I yearnin' for an Indian man.
>
> —Denise Belfon (Saucy Wow), "Looking for an Indian Man"
>
> Saucy baby I'm your Indian man / I ain't come from Port of Spain
>
> Neither Penal / I'm your Indian man from India.
>
> —Remo Fernandes (lyrics for collaborative song with Denise Belfon)

Just when I thought I had finished writing this book and said my goodbyes in Trinidad, something unexpected happened: I became acquainted with a well-known Indian popular singer who admired Caribbean music and got into a discussion about musical practice. The account that follows tells the story of a musical adventure inspired by my research.

If I was looking for confirmations and conclusions, a way to tie things up tidily and achieve closure, I did not find them in this project. What did happen, however, was that new areas of investigation—and possible intervention—opened up, making it imperative for me to continue to hold the door open. At the end of this afterword, I reflect on how the musical project brought together the concerns of my research and, just as important, contributed to the re-texturing of the book itself.

★

On May 11, 2004, India's premier rock-pop star Remo Fernandes was performing on the St. Augustine campus of the University of the West Indies with several Trinidadian musicians. The organizer, the Department of the Creative and Festival Arts at the university, had billed the event as a "semi-lime." "Semi" was short for "seminar" (also, of course, meaning "partly"); "lime" means "to party, to hang out with friends, to relax, chill out."[1] The idea was that we would have a discussion with students, faculty, and guests before and after the jamming session with Remo about the conceptualization of the popular-music project that had brought our crew to Trinidad. It

The Semi-Lime. Surabhi Sharma/R. V. Ramani.

seemed the perfect name for a conversation which would attempt to characterize something that came out of an academic project but had moved into the realm of musical practice and pleasures of an order different from purely scholarly ones.

Signifying Serendipity

As the American Airlines flight from Miami circled around Kingston Harbor in preparation for landing at Norman Manley Airport in Jamaica, I, half asleep from the fatigue of a journey that had taken us in twenty-four hours from Bombay to Dubai to London to Miami and now to Kingston, wondered what foolhardy impulse had prompted me to lead a crew of seven people, including a temperamental rock star, to the Caribbean for a monthlong stay. Waiting for us was a customs broker we had contacted from India on her cell phone. She would see our film equipment and luggage through Jamaican Immigration. Having for a decade traveled in and out of the Caribbean with only one comfortable suitcase of books and clothes, I groaned at the prospect of many hours of cross-checking serial numbers of microphones and mixers. My thoughts went back to a time many months earlier when I had first listened carefully to the music of Remo Fernandes.

Anyone familiar with popular Hindi films of the 1980s and 1990s would recognize Remo's voice. He has composed or sung several major hits over a fifteen-year period, including "Jalwa" (from the film *Jalwa*, dir. Pankaj Parashar, 1987), "Humma Humma" (from *Bombay*, dir. Maniratnam, 1995), "Pyar to hona hi tha" (from *Pyar to hona hi tha*, dir. Anees Bazmee, 1998), and "Huiya Ho" (from *Khamoshi: The Musical*, dir. Sanjay Leela Bhansali, 1996). Some would also know Remo as one of the most interesting independent musicians singing mainly in English since the 1980s. A series of best-selling albums, comprising witty sociopolitical criticism as well as party music, dot his long and still flourishing career, which began even before the idea of an Indian pop music as distinct from film music was more or less unthinkable.[2] Although his voice is familiar to the enormous audience for Hindi films, Remo has acquired the reputation of a somewhat avant-garde pop musician, his considerable talent appreciated in its diversity (Remo sings, composes music, and plays the electric and acoustic guitar, bamboo flute, and drums) only by the small number of people who follow independent contemporary music in India.

On a visit to Goa, I had picked up a few cassettes of Remo's music. When I listened to them, I remarked with surprise on their resonances with Trinidadian calypso. One song in particular, "Ocean Queen," put me in mind of David Rudder, one of my favorite Trinidadian singers. I set to wondering idly whether Remo was familiar with Caribbean music. Almost as a joke, I wrote to the address on the back of the cassette, sending Remo my compliments and introducing myself as someone who worked on music in Trinidad and who would be happy to send him Rudder's music if he wasn't already familiar with it. Soon I received a friendly e-mail from Remo saying that he would love to hear Rudder and other Trinidadian singers. That is how our correspondence began. I sent Remo my favorite compilations of soca and chutney, and he wrote back saying how fantastic he found the music. Some exchanges later, we met in Goa in the village of Siolim, where he lived. I had brought him more music, and he had made compilations of sega music from Mauritius for me, since he said it sounded a little like Trinidadian music. Remo asked with curiosity about my interest in the Caribbean and said he was envious that I went so often to that part of the world. I asked him if he would like to visit the Caribbean, and he answered that he would drop everything to go if he got the chance. Before I left Goa, I phoned Remo to ask if he was serious about wanting to go to the Caribbean and whether he would work on a project with me that might make the trip possible.

On my return home, I wrote up a proposal that, with Remo's approval, I started circulating to funding agencies. Drawing on my preoccupation with conversations across the South, I called the project "Outside the Metropolis: Music and Alternative Globalizations." I proposed to help initiate a musical collaboration that involved the making of new music out of the interaction of artists from India and the Caribbean. I suggested that Remo Fernandes could enter into a series of conversations with musicians from Trinidad and Tobago (such as David Rudder, Drupatee Ramgoonai, Ataklan [Mark Jiminez], Rikki Jai, Mighty Chalkdust, and Mungal Patasar) and from Jamaica (such as Anthony B, Mutabaruka, and Beres Hammond). The initial conversations were envisaged as taking place in the Caribbean, with follow-up visits planned in India at a later date.

The project was presented as arising directly from my work on popular music in Trinidad. I argued that much of the interaction between musics of the world was mediated by metropolitan capitals; that historically, London, Paris, and New York were the places where musicians from different countries came together to create beats that more often than not ended up in the homogenized performance spaces provided by MTV and similar companies. Given the distribution networks and international reach of such companies, this homogenized "world music," unmoored from its original production contexts, floats into homes across the globe. (The problem obviously has to do not with the fact that these musics are internationally accessible but with the frames of their accessibility.) Popular music in particular is all the more amenable to the smorgasbord effect, where the hugely complex sociocultural-political production locations of the songs are completely obliterated in favor of flashy jump-cut visuals and a standardized booming bass rhythm, no matter what the country of the singer's origin. This phenomenon, I contended, was acquiring a relentless, monotonously repetitive quality in the unipolar post–Cold War world of the late twentieth century and early twenty-first century.[3] One way to counter this, I suggested, was to rearticulate histories and interconnections that had become invisible in the present, as I had been trying to do in my academic research. Here, I said, was an attempt to take South-South collaboration into the realm of musical composition and performance, proposing that Remo Fernandes of

Goa, India's foremost rock-pop artist, was eminently qualified to pioneer this process.

This would be practically the first time that a popular singer from India would be collaborating with Caribbean musicians by consciously contextualizing the music in terms of the cultural politics of the two spaces. There was one earlier instance in the late 1960s, discussed in chapter 3, when the Hindi film singer-composer duo Kanchan and Babla performed in Trinidad and remixes of some local popular songs. That engagement did not extend into any sustained interaction with the histories of the different kinds of music involved, although Kanchan and Babla developed a career as "Caribbean" musicians. The Indian government's cultural initiatives in the area have consisted of taking "classical" dance and music practitioners to the West Indies, as they would to other foreign countries, the "classical" being the register in which discussions about the composition of "Indian culture" are conventionally undertaken. This has often had the effect of freezing Indian artistic forms in an eternalist frame and presenting them as "ancient Indian culture," a notion to which some Caribbean people of African origin have reacted negatively because it can be mobilized in a patronizing and negative mode. (I refer to the "claiming culture" problem in the introduction to this book, where I mention some of the pedagogical issues related to teaching Caribbean texts in India.) Interaction between popular musicians, however—especially those who are known for their thoughtful commentary on contemporary events—could open up new possibilities for intercultural dialogue, not just between South Asia and the Caribbean, but also, for example, between different racial groups in Trinidad.

The musical achievement of the project, I thought, would be to bring together different sets of influences and reorganize them to produce new music. While Jamaican reggae and dancehall draw on West African drumming, colonial brass bands, and some forms of African American music, Trinidadian calypso, soca, and chutney-soca draw on French, Scottish, English, and Spanish lyrical traditions; Hindi film music; and folk music from West Africa and northern India. Remo's influences range from Konkani folk songs, chants, and *mando* (ballad) to Latin American music, Indian classical music, and Euro-American rock. In addition to English, Konkani, and Hindi, Remo sings in Portuguese and French. As a Goan, he was brought up against a backdrop of music from Spain, Portugal, Brazil, and even the Caribbean, making him different from the conventional Indian classical/traditional musician who normally represents India abroad.[4]

The project would also be unique in bringing an academic researcher together with a popular musician to collaborate in creating a new kind of music. I saw myself as providing the analytical frameworks through which Remo would process Caribbean music and its historical locations. To this end, I planned the project in two stages. In the first stage, Remo would familiarize himself with the music and the cultural context of the West Indies, especially that of Trinidad and Jamaica. He would work with me to get acquainted with the music of the singers, instrumentalists, and composers he would meet in the Caribbean. During this time, Remo would, I thought, listen to and analyze different kinds of Caribbean music, watch videotapes of musical performances, look through books and journals about the Caribbean, be exposed to visual material such as photographs, and familiarize himself with the Caribbean historical context. In the second stage, Remo would spend four to five weeks in Jamaica and Trinidad, conversing and playing with a range of music makers; talking to scholars of reggae, dancehall, chutney, calypso, and soca; and working on a new piece of music. I planned to go along with him to establish the network and facilitate conversations and to guide the film crew (director, camera person, and sound recordist), all first-time visitors to the Caribbean, while documenting the experience. Although the film was initially visualized only as a documentation of the musical collaboration, it eventually acquired a life of its own, with its director, Surabhi Sharma, deciding to treat the story of Remo in the Caribbean as the main strand in a narrative that would weave together the journeys from India with the everyday experience of music in Trinidad and Jamaica.

Why Remo?

In the light of my research over the past decade, I asked myself again what sort of project this might turn out to be. What did I hope to achieve, and how would it further my own critical objectives? What would be the part played by the film in opening the issues I was trying to raise? As we made the frustrating rounds of funding organizations, TV channels, the government-supported Indian Council for Cultural Relations, and the Indian Ministry of External Affairs (which has a section that funds the production of Indian films to be shown abroad), we were confronted with questions that swirled around a key set of issues: What was the connection between the intellectual and creative aspects of the project? Why was Remo selected rather than one of India's leading classical musicians? Why were we taking only one musician? Would not this run the risk of "essentializing" Remo as "the Indian"? What was the relationship of the film to the larger project?

I replied that this musical collaboration was different from one that might be conceptualized as a purely creative process, since it was my research into Trinidadian (and, broadly speaking, Caribbean) music and cultural politics that anchored the project. As the intellectual mentor of the project, which was admittedly a creative one, I was providing the conceptual basis for thinking about new kinds of music, and this conceptual basis had to be understood as *an integral part of the musical conversations*. Thus, I emphasized, I did not want to see the musical outcome as a practical working out of an already established (non-musical) agenda. Rather, I wanted to see the project's musical agenda as itself being shaped in the context of the larger framework of engagement between Southern societies.

Answering the question as to why Remo, I contended that the main reason to choose him was precisely that he worked with popular idioms and was not a classical Indian musician. This was important for several reasons: (1) popular music being a traveling form, there were innumerable examples of the fascinating cross-fertilizations of such music in different contexts; (2) in popular music, there was a flexibility and a willingness to experiment with forms and ideas that were not easy to come by in exponents of the Indian classical traditions; (3) if one were to be sensitive to cultural politics in the Caribbean, it was extremely important to make the kind of intervention that my project proposed—that is, to take an Indian *popular musician* there rather than a classical or traditional musician. I explained that Indian classical performers tended to be seen as representing ancient traditions, an idea that sometimes comes to be mobilized against people of African origin, who in turn are seen as having no culture or history at all. This clearly had the potential to cause resentment of all kinds. My project sought to circumvent the problem by avoiding the high culture–low or popular culture (or even Indian–non-Indian) divide and arguing for an engagement entirely located in the popular realm. The project, I stressed, was committed to popular music because of what it meant in the Caribbean and for what it would enable in general. The Caribbean musicians with whom I was in touch had readily agreed to collaborate on the project after hearing Remo's music, I would venture to argue, *because* he was a popular musician. I did not think it appropriate to select self-professed avant-garde musicians, either, though they might be in the forefront of fusion experiments, because the

Caribbean popular musicians would have found it difficult to discover common ground in terms of the idioms employed. To reiterate the framework from which the music project had emerged, it was popular music that was the terrain for cultural-political interventions in the Caribbean.

Other reasons to select Remo, I argued, were his accessibility and enthusiasm for the project and the fact that he actively reflected on his own practice, unlike many other popular singers. Crucially, Remo is a multitalented musician who composes, sings, and plays a variety of instruments, including the easily portable electric guitar and the flute. His ability to handle many instruments in addition to his singing, I felt, would be a great asset in working with the Caribbean musicians. In one of his latest albums, *India Beyond*, Remo had even experimented with Hindustani (North Indian) classical music. Very few popular singer-composers in India, let alone classical musicians, have his sort of range.

Remo's has been a particularly difficult journey in India. Belonging to a minority community (Roman Catholic with a Portuguese inflection) and hailing from Goa, with its own blend of diverse cultural influences, he cannot be classified by the industry as either "traditional" or "modern." Any simple distinctions between these terms would be confounded by Remo's style of working with elements of old and new musical resources. Because he does not belong to any conventional genre or school of music, he is open to producing music that draws on unusual stylistic combinations. I thought it would be fascinating to introduce a figure like Remo *as Indian musician* into a context such as Trinidad, with its own imaginary of India. Trinidadians were used to Roman Catholic East Indians and to East Indians with Western names. But an Indian from India called Remo Fernandes? (Fernandes—not an "Indian"—is one of the biggest manufacturers of rum and spirits in Trinidad.)

Although Trinidadian East Indians are unlikely to have heard of Goa, Goan musicians trained in Western musical styles have made an important contribution to Hindi film music since the 1950s in terms of instrumentation and the arrangement of compositions. Remo's involvement in singing and composing for Hindi films can be seen as part of this circuit, which involves the migration of melodies to other places where these films were exhibited, such as the Caribbean. As I discussed in chapter 5, Hindi film music's assimilation of Western instruments and harmonies inspired similar experiments in Trinidad, such as those of the arranger Harry Mahabir.

In response to the question about why we were taking only one musician on our journey, I insisted that there would be a certain necessary simplicity in taking just one singer from India and documenting his interaction with a small number of Caribbean musicians. We didn't need to see Remo as having a representative status in relation to contemporary Indian musicians to emphasize the importance of taking him to the Caribbean. The aim of the project was to affect the way in which he produces popular music in India, just as we hoped to influence the Caribbean musicians he would work with. It might be important to focus on one singer-composer both in terms of the cultural aspects of the project and in terms of its production aspects.[5] There was, I felt, little danger of essentializing the "Indian" component because of our focus on one musician. As the earlier chapters of this book made evident, there is also an India in the Caribbean that is imagined and deployed in a multitude of ways. Thus, there is no clearly bounded space called "India" from which Remo travels; instead, he would be interacting with genres and singers also known by the name "Indian" in the Caribbean, and with musicians of African origin who might use "Indian" elements in their music. Remo's collaborations with the calypsonian and chutney-soca singer Rikki Jai (who is East Indian) and with the soca and chutney singer Denise Belfon (who is of African descent) proved to be hugely productive not only in musical terms but also in interrogating further what "Indian" could mean in both Trinidad and India.

My point was that it was not as if clearly defined cultures were entering into a first-time interaction with each other. This historical process had been going on for centuries. We needed to emphasize that the space of musical practice was already extremely complicated in terms of influences and sources and that it might be both difficult and unnecessary to separate out the specific cultural components. Indeed, the agenda of the project would be not to initiate the mixing, since that process has been under way for a long time, but to create a context in which the musical practice could be articulated, and advanced, in relation to the cultural politics of India and of Trinidad and Jamaica. In elaborating this context, I expected the film to play a major part. When I drafted the proposal, I had included the film documentation as only one part of a larger project. Through subsequent conversations with the director, I came to realize that the film would be a crucial outcome of the project, on par with whatever musical outcomes might be produced. Far from being a mechanical documentation of the musical interactions, the film had taken on other dimensions, grappling in its own way with the history of migration and music. We now saw the film as showcasing the unique framework within which the project was being undertaken, laying out in visual terms the rich sociopolitical contexts of the different locations. What I did not anticipate was how the camera, and a "production budget," would open up the space of my own research in a way difficult for a lone Third World academic to envisage.

How did I conceptualize the encounters between the musicians? What did I expect would happen when they first met? There had to be a difference, I thought, between a chance meeting and one that we had prepared for by establishing contact in advance, playing the music of the singers to each other. When I attempted to discuss this aspect of the project with Remo, he was reluctant to comment on what he saw as a creative process. I have no idea what will happen, he said. We might do some spontaneous jamming. Something may come of it, or we may utterly fail to communicate. I certainly won't know in advance. I struggled to explain to him that it wasn't a matter of wanting to know in advance what would happen, but wanting to know what to hope for.

In compliance with Remo's demand for materials, I obtained for him several "riddim tracks" from a Jamaican music producer I had recently met, and he set to fashioning a vocal response to the challenge of the drum machine's electronic beats.[6] This was also a way of introducing Remo to the dominant mode of music production in the contemporary Caribbean, where the "riddim track" pioneered by Jamaicans is fast becoming one of the key determinants of the musical scene. The track is composed through a process of electronic sampling by a music producer–sound engineer, and several singers and DJs are invited to vocalize over the same "riddim." An album is then prepared foregrounding the riddim track and presented as a compilation of the various performers doing their own versions. Two significant compilations to come out of Jamaica in recent years have an "Indian" edge: *Coolie Skank* and *Diwali Riddim*.[7]

The Journey

To prepare Remo and the film crew for the Caribbean trip, I arranged a series of meetings over a three-month period during which I made presentations to them on the music project and on Caribbean history and politics in relation to the music. This "audience" required a different kind of pedagogy from what I had used in my graduate classes on Caribbean "literature and culture" in a university English department. I pulled out the lecture notes from my Caribbean classes and piled up the CDs and books I wanted my team to hear and see. The crew's questions were very different from graduate students', and it was nearly impossible for me to juggle them as I tried to find answers. They ranged from the singer's questions (Can I take my own band with me? What sorts of microphones will I have? Where are we recording? What software do they use? What about copyrights?) and the film director's (When will we have a script? How will we get characters? Can you find me Drupatee's dressmaker, an oil worker who goes to calypso tents, an old woman who sings chutney . . . ?) to the sound recordist's (Can I hear the different kinds of sounds I might encounter? Are we filming indoors or outdoors? How many lapel mikes should I take? What about ambient sound?) and the cinematographer's (What kind of lighting can I expect? Can I see some still photos of Trinidad? What might be the advantages of the Betacam video format over the Mini-DV format? What is our shooting ratio going to be?). Although they were not "students" in any traditional sense of the word, they were newcomers to the Caribbean. I played them hours of music, showed them DVDs of the Chutney-Soca Monarch competitions, pointed to grainy images of Drupatee and Rikki Jai and chutney dancers, skirted around concepts like modernity, subjectivity, sexuality.

Once we had obtained initial funding, we started discussing the itinerary. After much debate about where we would go first, I planned the trip to start from Kingston and end in Port of Spain, mirroring my own journey from Jamaica to Trinidad all those years ago. My fear was that if I took Remo to Trinidad first, the East Indian presence and the Latin strains in the music might make Trinidad appear to him too much like "back home in Goa." I decided instead to confront him with the totally unfamiliar by taking him straight to Kingston. As I did when I first went to Jamaica, Remo knew Bob Marley's music and imagined the Caribbean as an "African" or black space. But while in my case Jamaica had been friendly and hospitable and comforting *because* it was exotic, for a musician who was a major star in his own country, Kingston was inhospitable to the point of being dismissive. Although I had made contact with a music producer and some DJs on an earlier visit, given the informal nature of the music industry and the amount of traveling Jamaican musicians did, it became impossible during our ten-day stay to have Remo work with well-known performers. In the end, he jammed with several young musicians and bands and collected a dozen "riddim tracks" from different music producers to work with when he returned home. But the problem was not just one of logistics. The "internationalization" of

Jamaican music in the 1970s with the intervention of the Euro-American music industry and Marley's rise to fame meant that the circuits were already formed. The popularity of reggae, and now dancehall, in metropolitan music markets had helped to "fix" the distinctive sound of Jamaican music. Remo's eclectic blending and mixing may not have made for a commercially viable collaboration with the ruling dancehall beat (although producers like Mikie Bennett commented appreciatively on his "Eastern" handling of the notes). The self-contained nature of the Jamaican space of music production could make it culturally intimidating for the outsider.

The encounters we had hoped for did not materialize. The ones that did were unplanned. On our first day in Jamaica, we were invited to attend a "Living Legends" concert in preparation for Jamaica Carnival (a fairly recent import from Trinidad supported by the uptown middle classes and generally frowned on by the "massive"), where Remo was introduced to Mighty Sparrow and David Rudder backstage. Despite a lively impromptu jam between Remo and Sparrow, since the latter as well as Rudder were now living for the most part in New York or Toronto, we couldn't make arrangements to meet and work together in Trinidad. And although we briefly encountered Jamaican stars like Lady Saw, Beenie Man, and Bounti Killa when they were performing, the soundscape of those situations was completely geared to the dancehall performers, both DJs and dancers, leaving no space for the kind of musical intervention Remo could make.

It was almost a relief finally to reach Port of Spain. In chapter 1, I dealt with my intellectual journey from Jamaica to Trinidad and the racial equations in which I found myself in both places. The trauma of being claimed by different groups as though, being "Indian," I had a stake in Trinidadian cultural politics was, after all these years, no longer the defining feature of my engagement with Trinidad, since I had begun to understand what the interests of such claims might be. Because of my Trinidadian contacts in the media, or because of the different self-perceptions of Trinidadian musicians—who, unlike Jamaican musicians, do not usually think of themselves as having the potential to be the next big "international" star—Remo was welcomed warmly, and his presence was marked on television and radio. Within a day of our arrival, we had met four of the best-known singers in Trinidad and had begun collaborations with two of them, Rikki Jai and Ataklan. Because of the "Indian" radio stations that constantly played Hindi film music, and Radio Masala, which played "world music," Remo's voice had been heard by quite a few Trinidadians, who connected the name with his songs when they saw him being interviewed on television. Remo got repeated requests while on TV shows in Trinidad to sing the romantic "Pyar to hona hi tha (Love Had to Happen)," from the Hindi film *Pyar to hona hi tha* (dir. Anees Bazmee, 1998), which was a popular song in Trinidad. Another factor that worked in Remo's favor was that, compared with Jamaica, which is already connected to an international music circuit driven by the United States and the United Kingdom, the Trinidadian music industry is much more provincial. Only now is it looking to gain visibility in places where there is no Trinidadian diaspora to ensure album or concert-ticket sales. There appeared to be a general Trinidadian concern, expressed by singers and music producers, that Trinidadian music does not travel. They seemed to view the collaboration with Remo as helping open another market—or "selling units," as Denise Belfon's producer KMC (Ken Marlon Charles) put it—and bringing them international visibility.

After Jamaica, no one in our team was prepared to take anything Caribbean at face value. What I refer to here is the estranging effect of Jamaican popular-culture practice on the Indian film crew, who had no familiarity with Caribbean contexts. The electrifying dancehall performative space and the aggressive sexuality of the representative style of a musician like Lady Saw jolted the crew members into an awareness of spaces that were neither simply the "West" (with which most Southern urban people have a superficial familiarity) nor unproblematically similar to their own. The perception of dancehall, or even of the Revival church we visited, as being distinctly Afro-Jamaican had a role to play in how eventually Trinidad, too, was rendered unfamiliar even though a large percentage of its population is "Indian." In the introduction, I discuss how the Southern investigator aware of the hegemonic systems of knowledge production informing the representations of her own context does not automatically become aware of similar representative structures in another Southern location. While my initial Caribbean encounters, which were in Jamaica, had made me wary of Indo-Trinidadian claims on "India" as jeopardizing an imagined South-South solidarity, I had subsequently begun to see what the claims signified. My own understanding of Indo-Trinidadian difference from India had been mediated through the intervention of the "African." More precisely, I had come to appreciate how the subaltern diaspora's intersection with Caribbean African histories had contributed to the specific formations of Indo-Trinidadian modernity described in chapters 3–5. I hoped that Remo and the crew would also intuit this by reaching Trinidad via the Jamaican detour.

Jamaica had indeed taught the crew to treat the familiar with suspicion, so East Indians were appropriately marked as "Trinidadians" and not mistaken for "Indians." Despite the Hindi film music blaring from maxi-taxis and loudspeakers in Tunapuna and Chaguanas, East Indian music was heard as part of the spectrum of Trinidadian music (including calypso, soca, chutney, and so on) rather than being constantly compared to music from India. And the crew tackled the Trinidadian roti with the respect due to a formidable Caribbean dish rather than treating it as "Indian" food. Coming to Trinidad via Jamaica and encountering the Indian in the Caribbean as I had done seemed to enable the members of the music and film crew to recognize in their own way the distinctiveness of that figure in its difference from India Indians.

The event that decisively established this difference for our group was the cooking night of an East Indian Hindu wedding that we attended on our first Saturday in Trinidad. The previous night we had filmed the matikor ceremony and heard the bride's great-aunt, wearing a Western dress and odhni, singing chutney while other female relatives and neighbors danced to the beat of the tassa drums. For the cooking night, the bride's family had hired an Indian orchestra called Winston Sound, with three singers—two women and one man, who also played the keyboards while another man drummed the dholak. One of the female singers, her ample body clad in a black, sequinned trouser suit, admonished the not yet lively crowd, "Go home and get your waists and come back!" At the side of the wedding hall (an area outside the house covered by a canvas tent), the bride's mother and her relatives started parching the rice (*laawa*) over an earthen stove (*chulha*). The orchestra launched into laawa songs in Bhojpuri. Although the occasional word was intelligible to our film crew, the wining of the women around the fire took them by surprise. The songs began to be sung faster and faster, moving from Bhojpuri and Hindi to Trinidadian English and back again. "Bacchanal fuh so, Wine your bottom low," exhorted the male singer. At the back of the house, a vegetarian dinner was being served: buss-up shut, pumpkin chokha, curry mango, channa, rice. The only drink on offer was lemonade. But outside on the street from the trunks of cars, rum and coke was being dispensed liberally. Around midnight, with the pundit long gone, even this feeble effort to maintain the sanctity of the wedding hall was given up, as coolers were hauled in from the street, and the women sitting sedately in the white plastic chairs picked up their drinks. Even the members of the film crew who were familiar with North Indian wedding *sangeet* (singing and dancing) were stunned into silence by the chutney-wine and spent the rest of their time in Trinidad trying to figure out what impossible combination of pelvic movements wining consisted of.

The musical collaboration and its film component enabled me to revisit the sites of my research and reopen once again the question of mobilizing India in Trinidad. Ensconced in a bus loaned by the Tourism and Industrial Development Corporation of Trinidad and Tobago, surrounded by mounds of film equipment, I undertook for one last time journeys across the length and breadth of Trinidad. The two-and-a-half-hour drive from northern Port of Spain to San Fernando, in the south, became integrated into our daily routine as we gained entry to people's homes, direct access to singers, and front rows at music performances. "Making a film" and "crew from India" became the passwords that allowed us to interview chutney-singing grandmothers, custodians of temples, bandleaders, maxi-taxi drivers, and calypsonians. With the lens of the camera trained on them, people seemed to talk more generously than they would across the table to an academic with a notebook.

Remo's collaborations in Trinidad exceeded all our expectations. In the original project proposal, I had said that he would work on one new piece of music while in the Caribbean. As it turned out, apart from the three riddim tracks he worked on in Jamaica, Remo managed to compose or contribute to six more songs in Trinidad, five of which exist in recorded form.[8]

Remo composed a song and melody with the upcoming rapso performer Ataklan. (Rapso is a speaking-singing form that dates to the 1970s, with legendary practitioners such as Brother Resistance. It has found a contemporary voice in the dynamic trio 3Canal, a group to which Ataklan used to be very close.) However, due to lack of time and studio space, it could not be recorded. Ataklan, who is in his twenties, lives in Laventille with his grandmother, who brought him up. He was trained by Ras Shorty I and Andre Tanker, two innovative musicians who have since passed away. Ras Shorty liked his writing, Ataklan told us, and taught him to carry a melody and to sing. He explained to Remo that Shorty had taken the Indian dholak and the African drum to create soca, which was, he said, a music meant to bring the "two races" together. (Ataklan also has both African and Indian ancestry, although so far this is not thematized in his musical practice, and he comes across as "Creole" in his performative style.) In contrast to Ras Shorty's music, Ataklan's music is more like rapso, a genre that Remo had not yet encountered. To him, Trinidad brought memories of calypso, and when he

Ataklan and Remo. Surabhi Sharma/R. V. Ramani.

proposed to Ataklan that they write a song "about harmony," he asked if they would use a "calypso rhythm." At that point in the conversation, Ataklan suddenly coughed and choked. In deference to an older man, perhaps, he could not point out that he did not really "do calypso," that his music was far more experimental than that. The previous night we had gone to a rehearsal of the Amoco (now BP) Renegades, a famous steel band, and Remo had taken video footage of the performance. While talking to Ataklan, he checked his video monitor and played back some of the music to himself, listening for a "typical calypso beat." He had the first few lines of a song and began to improvise as he strummed his guitar: "I might have been you / And you might have been me / I am you and you are me / And we are all together." Ataklan joined in, "In another place, in another time / What could the difference be?" He informed Remo that a "feel-good" song had to be three to four minutes long. Although Remo wanted to sing about race relations in Trinidad, Ataklan felt that "people in the outside world" did not understand the detailed political scenarios of Trinidad, which is why the music does not travel easily. But he appeared to want to do this "I might have been you" song with Remo, which was unlike anything he had done and seemingly

Rikki Jai and Remo at Morton House, Tunapuna. Photo by Ashish Rajadhyaksha.

in a genre for which he had no great enthusiasm, in the hope of an international release. His interest in the collaboration, consequently, seemed to go through alternating phases of engagement and disengagement. When it looked as if he and Remo had worked out the lyrics and the melody, he said they were ready to go into the studio, but then he was unavailable over the phone or otherwise elusive for days. Finally, a couple of days before we were to leave Trinidad, Ataklan resurfaced, but by that time it was too late to record. In hindsight, I wonder if our attempt to work with popular musicians had not mistakenly interpellated Ataklan, who was struggling to be a different kind of musician in that small industry.

In contrast, when we worked with singers or bands in a spontaneous mood, with no ultimate goal of recording, it did not seem to matter what kind of musicians they were. One exhilarating jam session took place with a well-known percussionist (Sean Thomas), keyboardist (Chantal Esdelle), and bassist (Russell Duity) on the weekly show *Taal* (which means "beat" in Hindi) on Gayelle TV, a new, all-Trinidadian channel launched by the renowned producer Christopher Laird, who had once made a film about a Trinidadian singer traveling in Ghana. On this show, Remo played the electric guitar and bamboo flute and both sang (in three languages) and scatted. The crew gained an unexpected insight into Trinidadian cultural politics when Remo asked for something on a 6/8 beat, and Sean Thomas remarked that that was "a sort of African-type rhythm." A surprised Remo said that it was "an Indian type of rhythm, too, and it existed in India long before..." Thomas cut in with a laugh: "Welcome to Trinidad, brother."[9]

Of the collaborations, from the perspective of my *Mobilizing India* project, two of the most significant were with Rikki Jai and Denise Belfon.[10] In the sections that follow, I provide an account of Remo's work with these two singers. What should be of interest is the continuous play on what is or comes to be seen as "Indian."

"From Trinidad to Goa"

Remo and Rikki had four encounters—at Morton House in Tunapuna, near the university where the crew was staying, and at the Gayatones studio in Ste. Madeleine near the city of San Fernando in southern Trinidad. The first meeting was to introduce the two singers to each other; the second session began with songwriting in Tunapuna and moved south to start working out the melody. The third and fourth sessions were for laying the tracks in the studio. The final versions of the vocals were recorded separately by the singers at the same studio and then mixed by Rishi Gayadeen.

When Remo and Rikki were introduced, Rikki invited Remo to rehearse with his band, the Gayatones. Enthusiastic about the prospect of playing with other musicians, Remo agreed readily, only to be taken aback when the journey to the studio in southern Trinidad ended in a converted garage filled with computers and electronic equipment. Here, as we were soon to find out, the synthesizer ruled. Although live guitar and drums were used in performances, when it came to the recording studio, electronic music and the technology of sampling became the basis for the distinctive beats of soca and chutney. Remo, who in India prided himself on using live instruments, took a while to reconcile himself to the Trinidadian mode of music production, where it was not uncommon for "bands" like the Gayatones to own and practice in recording studios.

At their first meeting, Rikki gave Remo a picture of musical tastes in Trinidad, telling him, "Hindi film songs are really big here." When asked why he thought Indo-Trinidadians liked listening to film songs even though Hindi was rarely spoken, Rikki claimed that "the loss of language is only in my generation." He further explained that this was due to Westernization, cultural pressures on Indians, jobs that needed only English, and so on.

Taal on Gayelle TV. Photo by Ashish Rajadhyaksha.

He also said that although they didn't speak the language, they still loved it: "It's part of us. It's part of our music." I wondered what sense Remo made of this nostalgia for Hindi as that which was "Indian," Hindi not being a language that was part of Remo's linguistic upbringing. But while speaking of chutney, Rikki offered a different kind of insight into Trinidad Indian music: "Chutney uses the beats we have here. There are more Afro-Trinidadians doing calypso and soca than Indians, but we live on the same island. We're influenced by each other's music. What's working for 'them' will also work for 'us.'"[11] The language question also arose when the singers were discussing whether they should do their collaborative song in English or in Hindi or Bhojpuri. The reason for the language issue to come up at all could have been that, while Rikki is famous for calypso and chutney-soca, he often sings Hindi film songs and Bhojpuri chutney, while Remo, although he sees himself primarily as an English-language singer, is more famous in India for his Hindi film songs. Rikki's desire to break into the market in India also must have prompted this discussion about which language to use. There is a tension between this desire and wanting to sing, as Rikki declared, for a "world audience." Eventually, both singers—the Indian as well as the Indo-Trinidadian—settled for English, the language they were most comfortable with. Curiously, as it turned out, there are many more Hindi words in the Denise Belfon song to which Remo responded than in the song he composed with the Indo-Trinidadian Rikki Jai. The Rikki-Remo song, tentatively titled "Chutney-Soca," is a playful comment on the genre that has enchanted the visitor from India who sees everyone—"man, woman and child"—wining to the chutney beat. Rikki's verse narrativizes the location and kinetic effects of chutney-soca; it is a Trinidadian invention that the Indo-Trinidadian offers to the India Indian who wants to "take it home."

"The Indian Man"

In 2003, the latest crossover chutney singers were the East Indian men who sang "Dhalbelly Indian" (Vedesh Sookoo) and "Rum till I Die" (Adesh Samaroo). Both play with the stereotype of the East Indian plantation worker, the man who will eat just dhal and rice to save money, and who drinks a lot of rum. While "Rum till I Die" was adopted as the anthem of male East Indians ("Rum till I die, oh, rum till I die / Becos' she go leave me / And that's the reason why"), it is "Dhalbelly Indian" ("Wine up on me, she say, wine up on me / She say she want a dhalbelly Indian to wine up on she") that presents, in ironic contrast to the supposedly muscular African man, the new Trinidadian sex symbol: the Indian man with the big dhalbelly. There were several replies to these songs, some by women who rejected the advances of the dhalbelly Indian. Denise Belfon's 2004 song "Looking for an Indian Man" joins this conversation, declaring that if her Indian man should have a dhalbelly, "then better still for me." But Remo Fernandes, answering Denise's call, adds the lack of a dhalbelly ("I don't have a dhalbelly / Shaking like a big jelly") to the list of qualifications that, in addition to not knowing how to wine, make him her "Indian man from India." As his lyrics indicate, he is "One hundred percent . . . genuine" and "unadulterated," with "no additional flavor." The cultural risks of entering a conversation about Trinidadian masculinity with descriptions such as these can be immense. In proclaiming the Indian from India as the answer to Denise's prayers, Remo's lyrics almost verge on a disavowal of the specific history of Trinidadian Indians. But the humor of his lines lie in how they gesture to his own, often challenged, claim to Indianness in India. Nowhere else in our journey did he capture so profoundly his sense of connection with East Indians in the Caribbean, both joint heirs to the formations of modernity rendered illegitimate by the narratives of nationalism in India.

When we met Denise Belfon at the KMP Music Lab in San Fernando, she turned out to be a short, plump woman with a pleasant smile, belying the deep and powerful voice we had heard on the CD of "Looking for an Indian Man" and her reputation as the most dexterous winer in the Americas.[12] She spoke about the early reactions to her song by some East Indians, who protested that she was "disrespecting the sari, disrespecting the Indian man and the Indian woman." They also said she was being "raunchy and degraded." The criticisms, reminiscent of the 1990s attacks on chutney-soca discussed in chapter 3, came from a group called Women against Discrimination and Racism, who, according to Denise, "made the fuss, everyday, no lie, in all the months leading up to Carnival." It was, she added, "just controversy, controversy, controversy."

Denise Belfon said she couldn't see what the fuss was about: "It was a song about unity. I don't know why no one realize what it is I was tryin' to say. Negro guys always sayin' they want a Indian woman, so I decided Negro gyul cyan say she want an Indian man!"[13]

Living up to her reputation as a winer woman, Denise demonstrated two movements involving pelvis and buttocks ("Now move your waist like a snake!"). Then we watched the DVD of the 2004 Soca Monarch competition on a small video monitor in the cramped studio, placed on the right wall away from the console. We were riveted by Denise's performance from the Soca Monarch competition. She was wearing a blue sari sparkling with sequins and what looked like an orange blouse. After a few head movements typical of Indian classical dance, Denise pulled off the sari, and the blouse turned out to be the top part of a leotard-like outfit. Her voice boomed out as she began to wine, surrounded by chutney dancers in bright pink and silver "Indian" costumes: "I am lookin' for an Indian man / Yes, I'm lookin' for an Indian man / To hold on me and jam."

Denise told us, "The Indian man never show up. He was too frightened!" She then asked someone from the audience to come up and dance with her. So in the video it is an African Trinidadian—bare torso, wearing diaphanous, pink "Eastern" trousers and a tight-fitting cap on his head—who wines with Denise. At some point, he drops the pink trousers and is seen to be wearing boxer shorts. We see only his back while we catch the scornful expression on Denise's face as she stands with hands on her hips and watches him dance. Then she tells him to "go down" and "rides" him triumphantly across the stage.

"Looking for an Indian Man," International Soca Monarch competition, 2004.

Inspired by the video, Remo rewrote his reply so Denise could intervene with ad libs and the refrain, which uses a food-sex metaphor (as calypso often does). The original song used the Hindi word "*chonkha*" (tempering food, usually with hot oil and spices) as "*chunkay*," but Denise changed it to "*chonkhay*" for the version with Remo on the suggestion of the Hindi-speaking film director. In "Looking for an Indian Man," Denise demands: "Chunkay meh curry, chunkay meh dhal." Now she issues instructions to Remo, telling the Indian Man how she wants it: "Do it like this: 'I want to chonkhay your *aloo* [potato], and your *baingan* [aubergine].' " She explains, "You're putting it to me, and do it aggressive!" The Indian Man replies somewhat plaintively, "I don't know how to wine / Only to drink it / You be my guru / And I'll be your pupil." Once Remo has done his verse, Denise comes back with:

> I'll teach yuh, I'll bite yuh
> Chonkay meh aloo
> Are yuh the Indian man for me to chonkay me in de party
> When your pepper meet mih sauce, we goin' a [biting sound]
> I wan' a Indian dhoti
> To join mih sexy sari
> Waitin' for he
> To chunkay Saucy.

Finally, Denise records ad libs to be inserted after Remo's verses: "I understan' that yuh come from India? Authentic? Hear? One hundred percent? Yeh, come, come, come. Real real Trini woman meet up one hundred percent Indian man. Yuh reach? Wheh yuh from? Come, show me, show me!"

★

What if, I have wondered on occasion, Rikki and Remo had to have a conversation about who is the answer to "Looking for an Indian Man"? What kind of Indian does Saucy Wow want? A true-true East Indian Trinidadian from Penal or an Indian man from India? After all, Rikki was the singer of "Sumintra," that iconic portrayal of East Indian–Creole women's subjectivity from the perspective of a non-threatened East Indian man willing to go along with her tastes, as long as music remained "the food of love," whether it was Mohammed Rafi or Scrunter, Lata Mangeshkar or Bally.

The collaboration between Remo and Rikki focused, however, on cultural exchange of a classical kind, a sort of upbeat multiculturalism that

Remo and Denise recording. Surabhi Sharma/R. V. Ramani.

included the "African" bongo drum as well as the "Indian" dholak. The woman question did not feature here at all. (See the discussion in chapter 4 of Brother Marvin's "Jahaji Bhai," in which the relationship between African and East Indian men is one of brotherhood, so long as the issue of female sexuality does not emerge.) Interestingly, Rikki—who is often the East Indian "other" in Creole-dominated Trinidad—is also the Other in relation to the singer from India, but in this othering, Rikki stands in for the Caribbean. In India, Remo is seen as having a "Western" touch; in Trinidad, Rikki is marked as "East Indian." But in their collaboration, Rikki was the person from the West, bringing the Trinidadian tune, the soca beat, and Trinidadian mixing styles.[14] Remo was the Indian, with abundant musical dexterity but also with the inflexibilities of Indian English, a class-bound phenomenon unlike Trinidadian English. The unfamiliarity for Remo of Rikki's background and his setup comes through time after time in the conversation.

Unlike in the song with Denise Belfon, in the song with Rikki Jai, Remo is not "playing the Indian," either musically or in the song's content. In India, he punctuates his Indian English songs with Konkani ("Merry Mary") or Hindi ("O Meri Munni") or sometimes just plays with regional accents. Clearly, this set of references will not work in the Trinidad song, so Remo sticks to a more standardized English. Perhaps he is envisioning the audience as being located not only in India but also in the Indian and Trinidadian diasporas. Remo is the stranger here, and "Chutney-Soca" is his song about his encounter with Trinidad, with Rikki the calypsonian providing the counterpointing "local color." Throughout the recording sessions, Rikki kept deferring to Remo as the more senior singer and as the "international star," asking him what special Trinidadian touches he wanted and emphasizing that the song would be for a market different from that for Rikki's usual compositions.

In contrast, "Looking for an Indian Man" is Denise Belfon's song, and Remo comes in to provide the exotic touch. He "plays the Indian" (with his *alaap*, flute solo, ad libs like *jhatka matka de* [do a twist and a turn]) and plays with his "Indianness" (producing an "Indian" accent for the crucial line, "I'm an Indian man from India," and declaring that he does not know how to wine). Denise's song marks a disruption in the conventional Trinidadian narrative of the African calypsonian wooing the East Indian woman, representing the "Indian" man for the first time as the desired object. As more and more female calypsonians and soca singers come onto the African-dominated Carnival stage, what might this do to the traditional representation of the female East Indian in these musical genres? How might the discourses of "Indian" nationalism in Trinidad accommodate the newly sexed Indian man? What could happen to the demand, as expressed in the chutney-soca controversy, for the culturalized femininity of East Indian women if the Indian man were to take center stage? And what would the East Indian man have to say to an India Indian stepping in to answer Denise's call? What, by contrast, would be the reactions in India to Denise "Saucy Wow" Belfon's wining in her "sexy sari"? As Rikki Jai whispers, "Chutney . . . soca . . . , chutney . . . soca . . . ," and as Denise imperiously calls on the Indian to "chunkay," the unlikely "Indian" Remo Fernandes brings the beat "home."

Conclusion

I will end by briefly revisiting some of the methodological issues and theoretical questions raised by the project, speculating about their implications for how we think about contexts that are different from our own but have similar geopolitical locations.

My main efforts in this book have been to conceptualize frameworks for comparative research across Southern contexts and to contribute to developing alternative frames of reference. The method has been broadly interdisciplinary, drawing on literary studies, feminist theory, anthropology, musicology, and film studies, all of which I bring to the analysis of cultural practice.

The tensions of the project have lain in my ambiguous relationship with (1) a region—the Caribbean—that initially came before me as an object of ethnographic inquiry, with all its attendant anxieties, and on which I had to learn to bring to bear the sorts of critical post-Orientalism questions that I was asking in my own postcolonial context; and with (2) a subject—"the Indian in the Caribbean"—whose history and even future, as I mentioned in the introduction, may not have much in common with my own. Yet, I have argued, thinking about this region and this subject may well alter the ways in which India Indians conceptualize issues of their cultural identity. Given the historical linkages between India and the Caribbean, the comparative research project described in this book has had to take on the challenge of not merely pointing out similarities and differences but also investigating how each location is marked by the other.

What this book has tried to do primarily is to displace Western modernity as the singular legitimating pole of comparison for analyses of Southern societies. Noting that all scholarship is comparative by definition, and that the implicit point of reference is bound to be the West (although imagined differently in each context), the book began by making an argument for alternative frameworks of analysis that might strain against the inherent asymmetries of the comparativist project.

The specific undertaking of the book has been to look at the invocations of Indianness in the Caribbean. The perspective from which these invocations were examined was one of an Indian from the subcontinent in South Asia, halfway across the world, an inhabitant of the region that was Columbus's original destination on the journey that "discovered," and mistakenly named, the (West) Indies. The historical connections between India and the Caribbean are often consigned to the marginal notes in the story of empire. A central argument in the book was that focusing on these obscure connections would produce a very different narrative from the conventional one about the formations of modernity in both India and Trinidad. While the invocation or mobilization of "India" in these two Southern locations clearly has divergent histories, I have argued that, in looking at the histories together, we have been able to throw new light on the meanings and resonances of that imagined cultural space.

The focus of the book's comparative endeavor has been the question of women, concentrating on the representations and deployment of that category rather than simply talking about empirical women. The book has approached "Indian women" in many diverse ways: in rethinking the history of indentureship in relation to the campaigns of early-twentieth-century Indian nationalism and, consequently, arguing for a new perspective on the making of normative Indian femininity; in looking at women of Indian origin as producers and performers of an exciting new kind of Caribbean music; in working through the historical deployment of the exotic Indian female in calypso and soca, or in reexamining that figure in contemporary Trinidadian cultural politics; and in exploring how Trinidadian music of all genres draws on the Hindi film industry in India, dealing with Rikki Jai's Sumintra, Real Unity's Drupatee, and Denise Belfon in her blue sari as different sorts of engagement with films and film music. These chapters also establish implicit connections between the disavowal of the subaltern Indian diaspora by India and the mobilization of India in the Caribbean, emphasizing once again the centrality of notions of the "Indian woman" to both sets of processes.

The other thread running through the book has, of course, been the emphasis on popular music as a key site of cultural politics. While retaining the focus on the shaping of "Indian women" and the fashioning of "Indian" identities, I have sought to explore a range of musical practices in Trinidad—from chutney, calypso, and soca to chutney-soca, Hindi film songs, and rapso—with a view to analyzing how they demarcate the musical arena where these identities are socially performed.

The general argument of the book is that the discourses and practices of nationalist modernity, and the formation of modern subjectivities, in India and Trinidad can be understood differently by repositioning the frame of analysis. Such a repositioning, I have suggested, can be achieved by using a double strategy: investigating the multiple processes by which "subaltern" migrants from India are *disavowed* in past and present in their country of origin, dealt with especially in chapters 1 and 2, and an inquiry into the contemporary cultural practices implicating the descendants of these migrants in their current home, which I pursued in chapters 3, 4, and 5.

The aims of the musical-collaboration project discussed in this afterword were inspired by my research concerns, even as they sought to take my questions in directions dictated by musical practice and practitioners. At the end of our collaborations, we saw a new spin on the questions animating my research, which had to do with South-South conversations, sexuality, and femininity-masculinity; "Indianness" in the Caribbean; and popular music.

While the musical project drew on the conceptualizations of the book project, the book project has in turn been reilluminated by the musical project. Earlier in this chapter, I spoke about how the presence of the film camera while revisiting the sites of my research helped open up new conversational situations. Snatches of these conversations have found their way into the rest of the book, tweaking historical arguments, supplementing newspaper discussions, and adding information and interpretation to the elaboration of musical contexts.

Importantly, the music project underscored for me the centrality of popular cultural forms in the Caribbean in providing spaces of signification. The rearticulation of histories and interconnections that the research sought to emphasize happened constantly—often in the most trivial situations—throughout the musical journey, whether in Remo's conversation with the calypsonian Black Stalin about the basic rhythms of Trinidadian music and Goan folk song, or in his hilarious exchange with the percussionist Sean Thomas about the "ancient" 6/8 beat being Indian or African.

On a host of occasions where Remo engaged in musical composition and performance, the South-South encounters yielded new opportunities for me to reflect on their difficulties and attractions. Frustrating moments when the film crew's discussions with Remo broke down, or when he and Rikki Jai—failing to understand the complexities of each other's market— were not able to agree on the modalities of contracts, made me regret the day I decided to embark on the musical project. Counterpointing these were the exhilarating ad libbing sessions for "Looking for an Indian Man" with Denise Belfon and the semi-lime at the University of the West Indies, where Remo's voice soared as it feinted with the steel pan, the saxophone, the electric guitar, the dholak, and the jazz piano.

Remo's collaborations with Rikki and Denise in particular helped me to push further the question of what "Indian" could mean in both India and Trinidad. Remo (with the atypical Indian last name Fernandes and singing Western-style music), introduced into the Trinidadian scene *as Indian musician*, did complicate the picture of the "authentic, genuine Indian man" who responded to Denise's call. There were fascinating moments when Rikki and his band played film songs from India that Remo did not recognize but that were foundationally important for the Indo-Trinidadian sense of cultural identity.

The music project also clarified for me the process by which I had come to understand that the Indian subaltern diaspora's modernity was fashioned in the intersection with African histories in the Caribbean. It was, as I discussed earlier in this chapter, the Jamaican detour and the responses of the film crew and Remo to their Caribbean experiences—in particular, their perception of what was "Indian"—that confirmed my hypothesis about Indo-Caribbean modernity as having taken shape outside of the narratives of nationalism in India, thereby rendering the formation unintelligible to India Indians.

What happens, then, when India Indians encounter Trinidad Indians, as in the musical-collaboration project? My struggle as a researcher to produce a set of analytical frames through which to view Trinidad Indians takes on other shapes in the musical conversations. The "Indian man" created by Remo's reply to Denise Belfon claims representative as well as parodic authority in relation to India even as he positions himself as a daring caricature in Trinidad.

What happens when non-Indian Trinidadians meet India Indians? I feel compelled to end with a story. Although India in the early twenty-first century is participating in new forms of globalization, when the book research started in the early 1990s that process was not yet fully under way. As we anticipated the formation of new hegemonies and wondered what sort of critical interventions might be shaped, we looked back to an earlier phase of globalization—that inspired by empire—to track the migration and transformation of bodies and cultural practices and to speculate on what kind of subject formation the un-housing and re-housing might enable. Geographic and historical displacements, as this book has tried to show, have formed uniquely local identities in the Caribbean. A few years ago, I was returning home from Trinidad, and had boarded a British West Indies Airways plane to New York en route to Bombay. I fell into conversation with an elderly Afro-Trinidadian woman who asked where I was headed. India, I said. And why are you going there? she wanted to know. I live there, I replied. And how is it, she asked, that you come to be living so far away from home?

NOTES

Introduction

Epigraph: Lamming, "The House of Reconciliation," 189.

1 I use the term "Third World" with some reservations, aware that it no longer carries either the (negative) critique of neocolonialist underdevelopment or the (positive) nationalist burden of forging solidarities based on our common experience of colonialism and our common struggles for self-determination and sovereignty. For my purposes, "Third World" refers to a location formed by the Non-Aligned Movement and the Bandung project, along with its subsequent failures, and to describe a postcolonial political subject—formed by Marxisms and nationalisms of various kinds—who has had to address herself or himself in recent years to questions of caste, race, community, and gender that had not (indeed, could not have) figured centrally in the decolonization debates and that today throw seriously into question the modernizing projects of elite nationalism. For a stimulating discussion of the politics of using Western and Third World, Northern and Southern, and now One-Third World and Two-Third World, see Mohanty, *Feminism without Borders*, 221–51.

2 For discussions and background of the anti-Mandal agitation, see, for example, Sonpar, "Caste and Affirmative Action in an Indian College." See also entries in the electronic media archive of the Centre for the Study of Culture and Society at http://www.cscsarchive.org.

3 I postpone a detailed discussion of these changes to a later occasion, only indicating, for example, that I have had to find ways to introduce students—at least, aurally—to the popular culture of the West Indies while simultaneously attempting to initiate a discussion on the politics of language in the Caribbean.
4 This paper, titled "'History, Really Beginning': Compulsions of Postcolonial Pedagogy," has been subsequently published under Sunder Rajan, *The Lie of the Land*, 246–59.
5 Niranjana, "History, Really Beginning," 249.
6 Ibid., 249.
7 Ibid., 250.
8 Ibid., 250.
9 The Walcott, Brathwaite, and Lamming texts often become assimilated into literature courses in such a way that their links to popular culture—both formal and thematic—are obscured, leading to their being read like any other modernist text.
10 Interestingly, it is not just the reading of the cultural artifacts of the South that is seen as an anthropological activity. The ethnographic question "sticks" to the production of the artifacts, too. For example, a standard critical literary dismissal of African writers like Chinua Achebe is that they are "too anthropological." The same question might sometimes stick to minority literatures in the First World (African American writing immediately comes to mind) or to Indian dalit writing or women's writing.
11 But in the years after decolonization, anthropology has come under a sustained interrogation of its originating impulses and procedures from several different quarters, noteworthy among them—for our purposes—the postcolonial-turned-anthropologist. See, among others, Asad, *Anthropology and the Colonial Encounter*. See also Scott, "Locating the Anthropological Subject," 75–84.
12 See Said, *Orientalism*, for the now classic argument about the formation of modern disciplines in nineteenth-century Europe and their imbrication with the project of Western imperial expansion. See also Asad, *Anthropology and the Colonial Encounter*.
13 Clifford, "On Ethnographic Authority," 118–46.
14 See Asad, "The Concept of Cultural Translation in British Social Anthropology"; and Niranjana, *Siting Translation*, especially chapter 2.
15 Asad, "The Concept of Cultural Translation in British Social Anthropology"; Fabian, *Language and Colonial Power*.
16 Mbembe, "Prosaics of Servitude and Authoritarian Civilities," 142–43. This is further elaborated in Mbembe, *On the Postcolony*.
17 Niranjana, *Siting Translation*, 69–70.
18 Appiah, "Ethnophilosophy and Its Critics," 148.
19 Ibid., 151.

20 For accounts of this kind of engagement, see Niranjana et al., *Interrogating Modernity*, introduction; Niranjana, *Siting Translation*, chapter 1.
21 Writing about the African context and using the term "colonial library" coined by V. Y. Mudimbe, Achille Mbembe contends that, prior to any contemporary discourse on Africa, there is a " 'library,' an inaugural prejudice that destroys all foundations for valid comparison. One can perhaps never repeat it enough: Colonization was not only an 'assemblage' of institutions. It was also a 'paradigm,' a network of axioms, concepts, discourses by which one aspired to invent (cf. Mudimbe) Africa as an object of knowledge; categorize it, and compare it to other units of civilization": Mbembe, "Prosaics of Servitude and Authoritarian Civilities," 141.
22 As David Scott has remarked, "The issue, of course, is not to erase the West as though to restore to its others some ancient precolonial unity, as though, indeed, the West were erasable. The issue . . . is rather to establish a reflexively marked practice of dialogical exchange that might enable the postcolonial intellectual to speak to postcolonials elsewhere. . . . through these shared-but-different histories and shared-but-different identities": Scott, "Locating the Anthropological Subject," 83–84. See also Scott, *Refashioning Futures*. The stimulating discussions with participants in the 1996 Rethinking the Third World conference, organized in Kingston, Jamaica, by David Scott and myself, have contributed significantly to the development of the ideas presented in this introduction.
23 Mukherjee, "The Caribbean and Us."
24 Rodney, *The Groundings with My Brothers*, 33–34.
25 Mudimbe, as cited in Mbembe, "Prosaics of Servitude and Authoritarian Civilities," 142.

ONE "The Indian in Me"

Epigraphs: Naipaul, *The Overcrowded Barracoon*, 33; Selvon, "Three into One Can't Go," 21; Lamming, "The Indian Presence as a Caribbean Reality," 47.

1 Anderson, "Exodus," 314–27.
2 We may well wonder if long-distance nationalism is a feature only of the newer migrant communities. When Anderson says that "the true total for Indians living overseas is between 11 and 12 million" (ibid., 327, n. 23), he blurs the distinction between the NRI and the "Indians" (do they necessarily see themselves as "overseas Indians"?) of the older diaspora.
3 Das, "Long-Distance Nationalism."
4 Remark made in a poem-pamphlet by J. Ravindranath. Needless to say, the words "for Indians" must be read into his sentence.
5 Discussed in James's appendix to *The Black Jacobins*, 392.
6 Filmed interview, May 7, 2004.

7 See Rodney, *A History of the Guyanese Working People*, and Laurence, *A Question of Labour*, for influential accounts of the effects of indentureship.

8 Filmed interview, May 7, 2004.

9 In *Women, Labour and Politics in Trinidad and Tobago*, Rhoda Reddock argues that the question of the number of "Indian women" was "a major point of contention and policy" from the very beginning of indenture. As she points out, between 1857 and 1879 the prescribed ratio of women to men changed about six times, "ranging from one woman to every three men in 1857 to one to two in 1868 and one to four in 1878–79. These changes reflected the difficulties and contradictions in recruiting *more* women at the same time as recruiting 'the right kind of women'" (ibid., 27–36). See also Laurence, *A Question of Labour*, especially chapter 4.

10 Laurence, *A Question of Labour*, 104. During years of labor shortage, however, there were a few attempts to recruit workers from southern India and even, in 1884 and once again in 1905, to reopen the Madras agency. These attempts, however, were soon abandoned as unsuccessful. See, however, Brinsley Samaroo's comment on p. 25.

11 Filmed interview, May 9, 2004.

12 Reddock draws our attention to the fact that even as late as 1915, when Commissioners McNeill and Chimman Lal came to the Caribbean to prepare their report on indenture, they found that only about a third of the women came from India as married women. The rest were either widows or runaway wives, and a small number had been prostitutes: Reddock, *Women, Labour and Politics in Trinidad and Tobago*, 30. For an extended discussion of the implications of the disparate sex ratio and the marital status of women migrants, see chapter 2.

13 Among others, see Tinker, *A New System of Slavery*.

14 Rodney, *A History of the Guyanese Working People*, 39. Although Rodney writes about British Guiana, his analysis is applicable to Trinidad.

15 Mahabir, *The Still Cry*, 87–88.

16 Ibid., 108.

17 Ibid., 132.

18 Nevadomsky, "Economic Organization, Social Mobility, and Changing Social Status among East Indians in Rural Trinidad," 63.

19 Klass, *East Indians in Trinidad*, 231.

20 Nevadomsky, "Economic Organization, Social Mobility, and Changing Social Status among East Indians in Rural Trinidad." See also Nevadomsky, "Changing Conceptions of Family Regulation among Hindu East Indians in Rural Trinidad"; and "Wedding Rituals and Changing Women's Rights among the East Indians in Rural Trinidad."

21 La Guerre, *From Calcutta to Caroni*, xiii.

22 Brereton, *Race Relations in Colonial Trinidad, 1870–1900*, 180. See also Brereton, "The Experience of Indentureship."

23 Nevadomsky, "Economic Organization, Social Mobility, and Changing Social Status among East Indians in Rural Trinidad," 65.
24 Ibid., 77. See also Reddock, "Social Mobility in Trinidad and Tobago 1960–1980." Reddock's study was commissioned by the Institute for Social and Economic Research (ISER) at the University of the West Indies, St. Augustine campus. It examines factors such as occupation and education to come to the conclusion that overall social mobility in the period was greater for Indian men and, to a lesser extent, for Indian women than for any other group.
25 Vertovec, "Oil boom and Recession in Trinidad Indian Villages," 103. The reference is to Hindu religious rituals.
26 Ibid., 107.
27 Two major institutions, the cricket team and the university, are shared and supported by all of the West Indian or Anglophone Caribbean countries.
28 There is also a "mixed" population that is said to be as high as 15 percent of the total.
29 See Rodney, *A History of the Guyanese Working People, 1881–1905*, and Cross, "East Indian–Creole Relations in Trinidad and Guiana in the Late Nineteenth Century."
30 For illuminating discussions of the formation of such stereotypes, see, among others, Espinet, "Representation and the Indo-Caribbean Woman in Trinidad and Tobago," and Rohlehr, *Calypso and Society in Pre-Independence Trinidad*.
31 Kingsley, *At Last, a Christmas in the West Indies*, 101.
32 Gilroy, *There Ain't No Black in the Union Jack*.
33 I use the term "homogenizing" to suggest that these stories of NRIS' success posit, in some sense, a unified world in which racial and economic inequalities are erased, with "Indian" merit finding its just reward in America or Europe.
34 Sheila Rampersad, interview, April 30, 1996.
35 Parvati, interview, August 31; 1998.
36 Cross, "Colonialism and Ethnicity."
37 Samaroo, "Politics and Afro-Indian Relations in Trinidad," 88.
38 La Guerre, *The Politics of Communalism*, 23.
39 Gosine, "East Indians in Trinidad and Their Inter-ethnic Relations," 77.
40 "*Dougla*" is a Hindi-origin word for bastard. It is commonly used in Trinidad to refer to a person of mixed African and Indian parentage.
41 Clarke, *East Indians in a West Indian Town*, 131. More current data is provided by the 1991 ISER study on national social mobility, which indicated that Indians' attitudes toward interracial marriage varied with gender (Indian men were more favorably disposed to it than Indian women) and religion (Christians other than Presbyterians were most favorably disposed to it; Hindus were less favorably disposed): See St. Bernard, "Ethnicity and Attitudes towards Interracial Marriages in a Multiracial Society."
42 Ali, "A Social History of East Indian Women in Trinidad since 1870," 85.

43 As cited in Aziz, "Indian Culture as Portrayed in Calypso," 9.
44 Sahidan, interview, May 4, 1997.
45 Naipaul, *The Middle Passage*, 44.
46 Parekh, "Some Reflections on the Indian Diaspora."
47 See the essays in Sangari and Vaid, *Recasting Women*, and in Niranjana et al., *Interrogating Modernity*.
48 Walcott, "The Caribbean," 7.
49 Ibid., 8.
50 Walcott, *The Antilles*, unpaginated.
51 The figures are from Brereton, "The Experience of Indentureship, 1845–1917," 22. Brereton cautions against possible errors in these figures due to confusions in recordkeeping.
52 See the articles in Schwartz, *Caste in Overseas Indian Communities*.
53 Kusha Haraksingh, filmed interview, May 7, 2004.
54 Citing the work of R. S. Chauhan, Baptiste raises this question in "The African Presence in India," 22–23.
55 Klass, *Singing with Sai Baba*.
56 Schwartz, "The Failure of Caste in Trinidad," 122.
57 Ibid., 119.
58 Ibid., 121.
59 Clarke, "Caste among Hindus in a Town in Trinidad."
60 Brinsley Samaroo, filmed interview, May 9, 2004.
61 "*Varna*" is the term used to describe the broad, fourfold characterization of castes in India. "*Jati*" is used to describe specific and highly differentiated caste groups that analysts attempt to fit, sometimes unsuccessfully, into the *varna* categories.
62 Schwartz, "The Failure of Caste in Trinidad," 133.
63 Niehoff, "The Function of Caste among the Indians of the Oropuche Lagoon, Trinidad."
64 Vertovec, *Hindu Trinidad*, 28.
65 Ibid., 34.
66 See Jha, "The Indian Heritage in Trinidad," 11.
67 Vertovec, *Hindu Trinidad*, 40–42.
68 Jain, "Overseas Indians in Malaysia and the Caribbean."
69 Hosay or Hosein is a Shia Muslim commemoration of the death of the martyr Hussain. In Trinidad, it came to be celebrated also by Sunni Muslims; Hindus and Christians (among the East Indians) and Africans also joined in.
70 Mohapatra, "The Hosay Massacre of 1884," 3.
71 Petition from Muslim youths dated July 22, 1929, no.152/1929, in General Letters to the Protector of Immigrants Office, 1929 vol., Trinidad National Archives, as cited in Mohapatra, "The Hosay Massacre of 1884," 30.
72 Jha, "Hinduism in Trinidad."

73 Brereton, "Race Relations in Colonial Trinidad, 1870–1900," 183.
74 Korom, "Memory, Innovation, and Emergent Ethnicity."
75 As cited in Aziz, "Indian Culture as Portrayed in Calypso," 32.
76 Campbell, "The East Indian Revolt against Missionary Education 1928–1939," 119.
77 Vertovec, Hindu Trinidad, 112. See ibid., chapter 2 for a detailed discussion of Hindu religious practices in Trinidad.
78 Campbell, "The East Indian Revolt against Missionary Education 1928–1939," 121.
79 Samaroo, "The Indian Connection," 55.
80 Vertovec, Hindu Trinidad, 123.
81 For analyses of Indians and Black Power, see the contributions of Kenneth Parmasad, John La Guerre, and Khafra Kambon in Ryan and Stewart, The Black Power Revolution 1970.
82 Regis, The Political Calypso, 69–73.
83 Vertovec, Hindu Trinidad, 139.
84 Ibid., 229, n. 26. The discussion of Hindi films in chapter 5 of this volume shows that many of them do not deal with "religious" themes at all.
85 Ramlakhan, "Call to Close Ranks in Defence of Dharma," 17; emphases added. Ramlakhan goes on to say that Hindus in Trinidad must write their own history; that so far it has been written by Muslims and Christians; and that there was Hindu resistance to Christianity that has not been highlighted: "The story of the Hindu experience of indentureship and colonialism is yet to be told. . . . The holding of the World Hindu Conference 2000 here could also serve as a catalyst for local Hindus to take charge of their destiny and chart the course of their existence [seen as crucial in the face of intensifying Christian attacks, from Evangelicals and Pentecostals in particular]. It is now a matter of urgency that Hindus close ranks and unite in the defence of dharma."
86 Another East Indian, Ramlakhan's political ally Kamal Persad, wrote, "Shri Singhal's speech is undoubtedly the most powerful given in Trinidad to Hindus. . . . [He] has called for Hindu unity, an invitation for Hindu organisations of the Caribbean to become part of the [Vishwa Hindu Parishad (World Hindu Forum)]. . . . For the first time a resurgent Hindutva in Bharata is reaching out to Hindus in the Caribbean . . . and [is] establishing links and brotherhood": Persad, "The Hindu Agenda."
87 Jha, "The Platform of Hate," 8.
88 Shah, "Darkness Descends on India, Pakistan."
89 Sanghvi, "Isle of Hope for Parivar Hawks."
90 I am indebted to the work of scholars like Bridget Brereton, Kusha Haraksingh, Patricia Mohammed, Marianne Ramesar, Rhoda Reddock, Brinsley Samaroo, Verene Shepherd, and many others who have helped me begin to understand what it might mean to claim India in the Caribbean. Seen together, their

work helps create a picture of (1) relationships between East Indian men and women; (2) the caste, class, and gender composition of the indentured laborers; and (3) the relationships between the two main racial groups, "African" and "Indian."

91 Initial work in this regard has been done, among others, by Espinet, "Representation and the Indo-Caribbean Woman in Trinidad and Tobago," and Rohlehr, *Calypso and Society in Pre-Independence Trinidad*. See also Kanhai, Matikor, and Puri, *The Caribbean Postcolonial*.

TWO *"Left to the Imagination"*

Epigraph: Gandhi, "Indentured Labour," Collected Works, Vol. 13, 249.

1 The term "constitutive outside" is used in Judith Butler's sense, as referring to that "domain of abject beings" who are not subjects but nevertheless are necessary to the process of formation of the subject: see Butler, *Bodies that Matter*, 3.
2 M. G. Ranade, "Indian Foreign Emigration," Sarvajanik Sabha Quarterly (October 1893). See Nanda, *Gokhale*, especially chapter 37.
3 At the Calcutta meeting of the Congress, Gandhi had Gokhale's assurance that a resolution on South Africa would be passed, and when his name was called, Gandhi read the resolution. As Gandhi wrote about that moment: "Someone had printed and distributed amongst the delegates copies of a poem he had written in praise of foreign emigration. I read the poem and referred to the grievances of the settlers in South Africa." Since all resolutions passed unanimously, Gandhi's also passed, but that did not mean that the delegates had read and understood it. "And yet the very fact that it was passed by the Congress was enough to delight my heart. The knowledge that the *imprimatur* of the Congress meant that of the whole country was enough to delight anyone": Gandhi, *My Experiments with Truth*, 341.
4 Some of the famous biographies of Gandhi include Erikson, *Gandhi's Truth*; Fischer, *The Life of Mahatma Gandhi*; and Rolland, *Mahatma Gandhi*.
5 Gandhi, *Satyagraha in South Africa*, 428.
6 Morton, *John Morton of Trinidad*, 185.
7 Reddock, *Women, Labour and Politics in Trinidad and Tobago*, 27–29.
8 Laurence, *A Question of Labour*, 119.
9 Ibid., 123.
10 Tikasingh, "The Establishment of the Indians in Trinidad, 1870–1900," 262.
11 Sahidan, interview, May 4, 1997.
12 Yasmin, interview, May 4, 1997.
13 CO 571/5, 27680, 1917, as cited in Reddock, *Women, Labour and Politics in Trinidad and Tobago*, 30.
14 Laurence, *A Question of Labour*, 124.

15 Mangru, "The Sex Ratio Disparity and Its Consequences under the Indenture in British Guiana." Longden to Carnarvon, no. 218, October 20, 1875, CO 384/106, is cited ibid., 223–24.
16 Emmer, "The Meek Hindu," 192–94.
17 McNeill and Lal, "Report to the Government of India on the Conditions of Indian Immigrants in Four British Colonies and Surinam," 313.
18 Mahabir, *The Still Cry*, 79; the words in brackets are my glosses.
19 Weller, *The East Indian Indenture in Trinidad*, 63.
20 An investigator in 1891 wrote about one estate where women earned from 10 cents to 25 cents, and men earned 25 cents to 40 cents. On another estate, men earned between 50 cents and 70 cents per day, and all women earned 25 cents. In 1913, when the last two commissioners, McNeill and Lal, visited Trinidad, and women were indentured technically for three years, they earned half to two thirds of the men's wage—that is, half a crown to three shillings weekly: Reddock, *Women, Labour and Politics in Trinidad and Tobago*, 36–38.
21 Mahabir, *The Still Cry*, 84–85.
22 Around 1914, just a few years before indentureship was abolished, it was noted that the Canadian Presbyterian schools accounted for about 90 percent of school-going Indian children: see McNeill and Lal, "Report to the Government of India," 44.
23 Morton, *John Morton of Trinidad*, 349.
24 All of the excerpts are from Morton, *John Morton of Trinidad*, 187–88, 342. The text in square brackets is in the original; S. E. M. is Sarah E. Morton, editor of the volume.
25 Kingsley, *At Last, a Christmas in the West Indies*, 192.
26 CCCB (1878–79), 158–59; *Mungaree v. Nageeroo*, 13 July 1878, as cited in Tikasingh, "The Establishment of the Indians in Trinidad, 1870–1900," 270.
27 *Daily Argosy*, March 23, 1913, and April 24, 1913, as cited in Mangru, "The Sex Ratio Disparity and Its Consequences under the Indenture in British Guiana," 227.
28 Scott to Kimberley, no.100, Aug 15, 1870, CO 111/376, as cited ibid., 227.
29 Laurence, *A Question of Labour*, 236–39.
30 See Andrews and Pearson, "Report on Indentured Labour in Fiji," 34–35, and Meer, *Documents of Indentured Labour*.
31 Discussed in Laurence, *A Question of Labour*, 126.
32 PIR for 1897, CP 76/1898, 5, as cited in Tikasingh, "The Establishment of the Indians in Trinidad, 1870–1900," 272.
33 Webber, *Those That Be in Bondage*.
34 Longden to Kimberley, no.161, August 21, 1873, CO 295/269, as cited in Trotman, "Women and Crime in Late Nineteenth Century Trinidad," 253.
35 Comins, "Note"; Minutes of the Legislative Council, October 21, 1890, as cited in Tikasingh, "The Establishment of the Indians in Trinidad, 1870–1900," 272.

36 Ibid.
37 Laurence, *A Question of Labour*, 239.
38 TRG, LV, no. 23, June 9, 1886, CP 47, Prison Report for 1885, 618, as cited in Weller, *The East Indian Indenture in Trinidad*, 66.
39 Kingsley, *At Last, a Christmas in the West Indies*, 192.
40 Mahabir, *The Still Cry*, 56.
41 Weller, *The East Indian Indenture in Trinidad*, 66.
42 TRG, L, no. 6, February 2, 1881, Minutes of the Legislative Council Meeting of January 28, 1881, as cited ibid., 74.
43 Ibid., 69.
44 Tikasingh, "The Establishment of the Indians in Trinidad, 1870–1900," 266; emphasis added.
45 Young, letter to M. Hicks Beach, 24 May 1879, cited in Mangru, "The Sex-Ratio Disparity," 224–25.
46 According to Reddock, in 1891 only 6.2 percent of the female population of Indians were officially "housewives" (not estate workers). The later years of indenture saw women's withdrawal into the domestic economy. Depressed wages for Indian laborers were accompanied by permission to produce cane and food crops on a piece of land that would be looked after by wives and children. Women who worked for the family thus received no wages, although they were involved in "cane farming, market gardening, rice production and animal husbandry": Reddock, *Women, Labour and Politics in Trinidad and Tobago*, 36–39.
47 Mangru, "The Sex Ratio Disparity and Its Consequences under the Indenture in British Guiana," 224–25.
48 CO 571/4 W.I.22518, 1916, as cited in Reddock, *Women, Labour and Politics in Trinidad and Tobago*, 44.
49 For insights into the process by which the representation of women by colonial officials and nationalist critics converged, see Kale, *Fragments of Empire*, especially chapter 7.
50 Tinker, *A New System of Slavery*, 334.
51 Ibid., 334–47.
52 Reddock, *Women, Labour and Politics in Trinidad and Tobago*, 45.
53 Tinker, *A New System of Slavery*, 288.
54 Chatterjee, *The Nation and Its Fragments*, 121.
55 Banerjee, *The Parlour and the Streets*, 76.
56 Chatterjee, *The Nation and Its Fragments*, 127.
57 *Tattwabodhini Patrika*, 1880, as cited in Banerjee, *The Parlour and the Streets*, 56.
58 Ibid., 71–72.
59 Ibid., 172.
60 Kusha Haraksingh, filmed interview, May 7, 2004.
61 Cited in Banerjee, *The Parlour and the Streets*, 171.

62 Tharu and Lalita, "Empire, Nation and the Literary Text," 208.
63 Tharu and Lalita, *Women Writing in India, 600 B.C. to the Present*, 13.
64 Ibid., 12–13.
65 Sarkar, *Hindu Wife, Hindu Nation*, 41.
66 *Hindur Achar Vyavahar*, 60, as cited in Sarkar, *Hindu Wife, Hindu Nation*, 42.
67 Ibid., 42.
68 Gandhi, "Speech on Indentured Indian Labour," 133.
69 Gandhi, *Collected Works*, Vol. 13, 249.
70 Gandhi, "Indenture or Slavery?" ibid., 1467.
71 Kelly, *A Politics of Virtue*, 48.
72 Note that after the end of indenture, the women's question in India became a social issue to be resolved through legislation, not political mobilization.
73 Gandhi, *Collected Works*, Vol. 22, 349.
74 Kelly (*A Politics of Virtue*, 30), for instance, points out that in the case of Fiji, the critics of indenture stressed the sexual abuse of Indian women.
75 C. F. Andrews, Gandhi's emissary on the indenture issue, wrote in 1915, "Vice has become so ingrained that they have not been able to recover their self-respect. . . . The women of India are very chaste; but these women, well, you know how they are, and how it can be different, situated as they are, living the lives they do, brought up in this atmosphere of vice and degradation?" as cited ibid., 33–34.
76 Bayly, *Caste, Society and Politics in India from the 18th Century to the Modern Age*, 196.
77 Laurence, *A Question of Labour*, 432–34.
78 Ibid., 448–54.
79 Ibid., 465.
80 Ibid., 465.
81 Ibid., 476.
82 Gandhi, "Abolition of Indentured Emigration," in *My Experiments with Truth*, Vol. 2, chapter 11.
83 Laurence, *A Question of Labour*, 477–78.
84 Tinker, *A New System of Slavery*, 350–52.
85 Ibid., 267–68.
86 Ibid., 340–41.
87 Recent unpublished work by Rhoda Reddock and Patricia Mohammed makes interesting beginnings in this direction.
88 Rohlehr, *Calypso and Society in Pre-Independence Trinidad*, especially chapter 1.
89 Kingsley, *At Last, a Christmas in the West Indies*, 72.
90 Sinha, "Gender in the Critiques of Colonialism and Nationalism," 477–504.
91 Ibid., 483.
92 Ibid., 494.

THREE "Take a Little Chutney"

1. The Road March refers to the music played by the bands on the floats at Carnival, consisting of the hit songs of the season. Mas' is short for masquerade, referring to the Carnival convention of processionists' dressing up in various elaborate costumes, depending on the band they are playing with. Wining refers to dancing that emphasizes pelvic movements, perhaps from "winding."
2. Ottley, *Women in Calypso*.
3. *Port-of-Spain Gazette*, September 19, 1874, as cited in Tikasingh, "The Establishment of the Indians in Trinidad, 1870–1900," 215–16.
4. An extended discussion of the representation of East Indians in the calypso can be found in chapter 4.
5. Lord Shorty, "Indrani" (Shorty s-002, 1973, LP), also on the album *Shorty's Gone, Gone, Gone* (Island Series FP-1006, 1973); Lord Shorty, "Kelogee Bulbul" (1974), on *The Love Man, Carnival '74 Hits* (Shorty SLP-1000, LP).
6. Mungal Patasar, interview, June 19, 2003.
7. As with other musical terms in the Caribbean, however, there is some controversy as to the exact distinction between calypso and soca, although there are separate annual competitions for National Soca Monarch and National Calypso Monarch during the Carnival season.
8. While singers like Rikki Jai insist it is the melody that distinguishes chutney from calypso (filmed interview, May 4, 2004), some performers, according to Tina Ramnarine, insist that chutney refers to music made by a group with voice, dholak, dhantal, and harmonium. The addition of any other instruments, brass or electronic, makes it a different branch of chutney: Ramnarine, *Creating Their Own Space*, 15.
9. Maharaj, "Some Aspects of Hindu Folk Songs in Trinidad," 64.
10. Ribeiro, "The Phenomenon of Chutney Singing in Trinidad and Tobago," 15.
11. Khempatie Rampersad, interview, May 3, 1997.
12. Ribeiro, "The Phenomenon of Chutney Singing in Trinidad and Tobago," 7.
13. Miriam Gajadhar, filmed interview, May 4, 2004.
14. " 'Kutiya' is a Hindi word meaning temple. There is no connotation whatever to sexuality or the sexual organs. The use of 'kutiya' in [the] context [of Sparrow's songs], taken literally, is ludicrous and highly irreverent, but its use as an element of calypso's famous double-entendre is effective": Espinet, "Representation and the Indo-Caribbean Woman in Trinidad and Tobago," 52. However, in contemporary Hindi, "*kutiya*" means "hut."
15. Patasar, interview, June 19, 2003.
16. Ramaya, "Evolution of Indian Music," 22–23.
17. Myers, *Music of Hindu Trinidad*, 109.
18. Ibid., 155–56.
19. The ethnographic present tense also underwrites the argument about "cultural

persistence" advanced by Myers's mentor, Morton Klass, in his well-known *East Indians in Trinidad*. Those who find Klass's description of that community politically pernicious, as well as insufficiently historicized, have taken issue with that work. Klass defends his use of the term "persistence" as opposed to "retention" in the 1988 preface to his book: see Klass, *East Indians in Trinidad*, xxx.

20 Curiously, Myers's book on music in "Hindu" Trinidad has on its cover page a Bhojpuri woman in a village in *India*, clad in a sari, listening to a cassette player. In the other pictures inside the book, the women of Felicity are seen wearing Western dress but singing *bhajans* (Hindu religious songs). It might be worth asking what the academic stakes are in the mobilization of notions of Indian authenticity in relation to Trinidad.

21 Calypso and steel band were dominated by Afro-Trinidadians, with few exceptions. One of them is Mohan Paltoo, a major calypso songwriter. Another is Jit Samaroo, celebrated arranger of pan (steel band) music, whose arranging for the Amoco, (now BP) Renegades steel orchestra won the group the top prize in the Panorama Championships throughout the 1980s and '90s. There have been others—singers and musicians of East Indian descent—from as early as the 1940s, like Jap Beharry and Selwyn Mohammed and the calypsonians Rajah, Hindu Prince, and Mighty Dougla. For a full account, see Constance, *Tassa, Chutney and Soca*.

22 Ali, "A Social History of East Indian Women in Trinidad since 1870," 154.

23 Saywack, "From Caroni Gyal to Calcutta Woman." Bassant and Orie ("Understanding the Chutney Phenomenon," 27) indicate a different date for the release of the Surinamese album from Saywack: "[Twenty] years ago . . . [the] Surinamese singer, Drupatee, launched her first record of breakaway songs. This marked the opening of what was formerly a very closed-door affair."

24 Manuel, "Chutney and Indo-Trinidadian Cultural Identity," 26.

25 No good discography is available for Sundar Popo or for chutney music in general. A selection of Popo's songs can be found in the following albums: *The Ultimate Sundar Popo* (Masala Records, 2004, CD); *Classic: Sundar Popo and JMC Triveni* (JMCCT 1082, 1994, audio cassette); Babla and Kanchan and Sundar Popo, *Musical Voyage: East Meets West* (JMCCD 1185, 1988, CD).

26 BWIA (British West Indian Airways), the Trinidadian national airline, is affectionately known as BeeWee but also as "But Will It Arrive?"

27 Johnson, "The Beat of a Different Drum."

28 Patasar, "The Evolution of Indian Musical Forms in Trinidad from 1845 to the Present," 29.

29 In an interview, Babla said: "That music is very raw. Their singing is in their own style. They don't speak Hindi, and their accent is more Trinidadian accent." When I asked him what sort of changes he and Kanchan had made in the original compositions, he replied that the melody remained more or less the same, but "the singing style" became different. Kanchan and Babla also changed some of

the words, because "they [Indo-Trinidadians] have no grammar, and the words have no meaning sometimes": interview with Tejaswini Niranjana and Naresh Fernandes, Mumbai, October 27, 2003.

30 Kanchan's and Babla's albums *Kaise Bani* and *Kuch Gadbad Hai* are popular in Bihar and Uttar Pradesh, in northern India, but are not known elsewhere. Babla claims that some of those chutney songs are now sung at weddings in Bihar.

31 Mohammed, "Women Who Sang Calypso," 27. My research in the West Indiana collection of the University of the West Indies, St. Augustine campus, yielded a couple of brief news items that mentioned East Indian female performers: The *Daily Express*, June 6, 1975, had on its front page an article about the Guyanese singer Mark Holder, who was detained at the airport for debt on his way to Grenada, "where he was to have performed along with popular Trinidadian singer Hazel Rambaransingh [an East Indian name] who sings at the Chaconia Inn hotel." Another item was a front-page photograph from the *Express* on August 22, 1977, showing "A Songbird from Penal"—Gangadaye Latchuram—in the Indian song competition in San Fernando's Skinner Park. The photograph shows Gangadaye as a young woman in conventional India-style sari and puffed open-sleeve blouse, with bangles on her wrists—an appearance very different from that of Drupatee in the late 1980s. There is a tabla player on a chair next to her, and no other accompaniment is visible.

32 Constance, *Tassa, Chutney and Soca*, 66.

33 Myers, *Music of Hindu Trinidad*, 377.

34 Much of this information comes from conversations with Patricia Mohammed and Hubert Devonish in Jamaica and Rhoda Reddock in Trinidad, February–March 1994. I also thank Rikki Jai for his insights into the Trinidadian music and performance scene. For access to newspaper accounts of the chutney controversy, I am indebted to Rawwida Baksh-Soodeen and the Caribbean Association for Feminist Research and Action (CAFRA) archives in Trinidad. See also Baksh-Soodeen, "Power, Gender and Chutney," 7.

35 Ramsingh, *The History of Felicity Village (1838–1996)*, 104–5.

36 When asked if there was no dancing earlier, Gajadhar clarified that it was a different kind of dancing ("They could dance good," and it was not "vulgar dance an' ting"). Also, that dancing took place in the "private" space of the wedding: Miriam Gajadhar, filmed interview, May 4, 2004.

37 All quotations in this section of the chapter are from the filmed interview with Drupatee, May 10, 2004.

38 Drupatee Ramgoonai, "Mr. Bissessar, or Roll up de Tassa" on *Chutney/Soca* (JMCCD 1228, 2000).

39 Constance, *Tassa, Chutney and Soca*, 70.

40 Drupatee accounts for her stage success by saying that her "presentation" was good, "plus what I wore and the movement, the dancing, I give them the works!" When asked what she wore, she said it was something "Indianish."

41 Drupatee Ramgoonai, "Lick Down Mih Nani, or Careless Driver," on *Chutney/Soca* (JMCCD 1228, 2000).

42 In a reading of the same song, Shalini Puri points out that the "cultural nationalist" outcry displaced the "narrative of rape and violence," which is another aspect of the lyrics. She suggests that this other meaning is "glossed over in that nationalist discourse which subordinates class, feminist, and formal and aesthetic considerations to a racial-cultural nationalist agenda": Puri, *The Caribbean Postcolonial*, 197–204. Without intending to make any apology for Indo-Trinidadian cultural nationalism, I will stress (1) that the song as it is *sung* as well as its performance are saucy, playful, and mischievous, like other Drupatee songs; and (2) that it was the song's suggestion of interracial sex that caused the outcry—a suggestion that is implicit in the form and performance but not necessarily in the lyrics. A less textual focus, and a contextualization of the song as part of Drupatee's larger body of work, would, I believe, yield a different interpretive frame from the one Puri offers. I would also be hesitant to accept that the violence narrative is self-evidently more "feminist" than the playfulness narrative.

43 "Mr. Bissessar" was also unique because it included for the first time the recording of live tassa drums, which are very difficult to capture mechanically. According to Drupatee, tassa drummers were taken on stage for song performances, creating the sound one hears both at Matikor and Muharram (Hosay).

44 Drupatee Ramgoonai, "Hotter Than a Chulha," on *Chutney/Soca* (JMCCD 1228, 2000). Selections of Drupatee's chutney songs are on *Drupatee in Style* (JMCCD 1224, 2000) and *Explosive Moods* (Masala Records, MAS-1202, 2002, CD).

45 Interestingly, the Bhojpuri and Hindi lyrics indicate that it is a bhajan, a popular religious song. To translate, "All of us should sit together in a group / And sing Sita Ram / Who will play the dholak and the dhantal?" Cecil Funrose, "Khirki Na Din," on *Chutney Party Mix* (MC Records, MC-0015, 1995, CD).

46 Saywack, "From Caroni Gyal to Calcutta Woman."

47 Manuel, "Chutney and Indo-Trinidadian Cultural Identity," 40.

48 Johnson, "The Beat of a Different Drum," http://209.94.197.2/jan99/jan17/features.htm.

49 As quoted in Aziz, "Indian Culture as Portrayed in Calypso," 30.

50 As quoted in Smith, "Chutney Soca," 12.

51 Myers, *Music of Hindu Trinidad*, 107.

52 Manuel, *Caribbean Currents*, 217–18.

53 Rikki Jai, who performs chutney, chutney-soca, and calypso, asserts that the melodic line in these forms is quite distinct. Chutney and Hindi film songs have an "Indian *gamak*," he says, a different vocal style from that of soca or calypso: Rikki Jai, filmed interview, May 4, 2004. He would perhaps argue that chutney-soca is more like soca than like chutney.

54 Rikki Jai was one of the first singers to hire a dance troupe and a drama troupe

to perform the background narrative for his chutney and chutney-soca performances. He felt that the chutney industry was "too dormant" compared with the more interactive performances in the "soca industry." Before he introduced soca performative elements, he said, there were "no hands in the air, no rags, no towels [being waved]": ibid.

55 Kusha Haraksingh, personal conversation, April 25, 1996.
56 Syriac, "The Chutney Phenomenon," 44.
57 Ibid., 28–29.
58 Ribeiro, "The Phenomenon of Chutney Singing in Trinidad and Tobago," 29.
59 Miller, who is professor of anthropology at University College, Oxford, writes that "chutney" is "a syncretic form, based on Indian film and classic [sic] music but with elements that emulate black dancing, including its lasciviousness." This statement is both factually incorrect and sweeping in its cultural generalizations. As the preceding discussion and the music show, chutney does not derive primarily from either Indian film music or "classic" music. And why "lasciviousness" should be a peculiar Afro-Trinidadian trait remains unexplained: see Miller, *Capitalism*, 298.
60 Balkaransingh, "Chutney Crosses over into Chutney-Soca," 48–49.
61 Cuffy, "Soca Song with a Little Chutney," 7.
62 The English translation from the Bhojpuri is by Anita Sharma. Sonny Mann, "Lotay La," on *Chutney Party Mix* (MC Records, MC0015, 1995, CD).
63 Although Sonny Mann reached the Soca Monarch finals, he was booed off the stage by a predominantly Creole audience without being allowed to sing.
64 It is a measure of racial polarization in Trinidadian political life that the two major parties, the PNM and the UNC, have come to be identified as the "African" and "Indian" parties, respectively, although both have candidates as well as voters from the other race.
65 Saywack, "From Caroni Gyal to Calcutta Woman."
66 Manuel, *Caribbean Currents*, 218.
67 Manuel, "Chutney and Indo-Trinidadian Cultural Identity," 30.
68 Author's fieldnotes.
69 According to colonial writers such as J. A. Froude, the bejeweled Indian woman presented "quite a contrast to the ordinary coarse negro woman:" as quoted in Tikasingh, "The Establishment of the Indians in Trinidad, 1870–1900," 369. In chapter 2, I discussed how the "African" jamette woman of Carnival is contrasted with the Indian woman, whose femininity is shaped in contrast to that of the former.
70 I owe this insight to Kirk Meighoo, with whom I have had many useful discussions on the topic of Afrocentrism in the Caribbean. The term "Indo-Saxon" is employed to refer to "Westernized" Indians, but it does not seem to be used as frequently as "Afro-Saxon."
71 While a whole spectrum of ethnic identities is subsumed under the term "Cre-

ole," in common usage it seems to refer to all that is not Indian—in particular, the African.

72 Gordon Rohlehr, personal conversation, February 1994.

73 A 1993–94 controversy surrounds East Indian Member of Parliament Hulsie Bhaggan, who became the target of political satire in the calypsos of the 1994 Carnival in Trinidad (see chapter 4). In 1996, Occah Seapaul, an East Indian woman who was then speaker of Parliament, was the subject of calypsos.

74 Female East Indian singers and dancers, however, are not necessarily a new phenomenon. As mentioned in the earlier sections of this chapter, there appears to have been a tradition of women who took part in public performances, such as Alice Jan in the early twentieth century and Champa Devi in the 1940s. But for the reasons addressed partially in this section, their performances clearly did not evoke the kind of response that chutney-soca did in the 1990s.

75 "Indian chutney is breaking up homes and bringing disgrace.... Quarrels break out in the home when the wife or children are not allowed to go. Some run away, not caring if they are not allowed back into the home. Their only concern is to be at the show.... I see young girls drinking and some of them are not dressed properly. I see respectable married women, women separated from their husbands and widows bringing down shame on their families and themselves": Michael Ramkissoon (Wizard Drummer), letter to the editor, *Sunday Express*, December 16, 1990, 46.

76 The musician Narsaloo Ramaya, as quoted in "Critics Rage over Chutney Wine," *Sunday Express*, December 9, 1990, 17.

77 Kamal Persad, Indian Review Committee, Viewpoint column, *Sunday Express*, December 16, 1990, 43. See also L. Siddhartha Orie, letter to the editor, *Trinidad Guardian*, January 8, 1991, 8.

78 Jagdeo Maharaj, letter to the editor, *Trinidad Guardian*, July 30, 1990, 9.

79 Kelvin Ramkissoon, "A Brand of Dancing Not Associated with Hinduism," *Express*, July 14, 1992.

80 Danny, "Chutney Chulha Still Hot, but Sandra Cool."

81 The quotes are from unnamed informants in Danny, "No Culture Barrier for Drupatee," 10.

82 Mahabir Maharaj, "Drupatee—Queen of Local Crossover," *Sandesh*, February 19, 1988.

83 Persad studied Bharatanatyam with Rukmini Devi Arundale in India in 1965–67 and in 1967 founded the Krishna Dance Group, later renamed Trinidad School of Indian Dance: as quoted in Mayers, "Rajkumar Krishna Persad," 61.

84 Baksh-Soodeen, "Power, Gender and Chutney," 7.

85 Indrani Rampersad, Hindu Women's Organization, "The Hindu Voice in Chutney," *Trinidad Guardian*, December 25, 1990, 10. In this chapter, I draw mainly on textual sources for East Indian views on chutney. These probably represent a range from lower middle class to upper middle class. Most of my conversations

with women and men from this class background indicate that these views are representative. My 1997 fieldwork, however, suggested radically different attitudes toward chutney on the part of working-class women, who frequently went to chutney fetes.

86 The government of India funds two professorships at the University of the West Indies, one in sociology and the other in Hindi. The sociology position was converted a few years ago into a history position, with its first occupant being a historian of medieval India. The Indian High Commission also has a Hindi professor to conduct language classes for Trinidadians. In addition, the High Commission helps bring exponents of classical "Indian culture" to Trinidad.
87 Rampersad, "The Hindu Voice in Chutney."
88 John, "Controversy Reigns."
89 See Baksh-Soodeen, "Power, Gender and Chutney," 7.
90 Baksh-Soodeen, "Why Do Our Hindu Women Break Out and Break Away," 24.
91 Khan, "Purity, Piety and Power: Culture and Identity among Hindus and Muslims in Trinidad," 170.
92 *Trinidad Guardian*, January 15, 1991.
93 Ibid.
94 *Sunday Guardian*, February 16, 1997, 21.
95 Mahabir Marajh, Barataria, opinion column, *Express*, March 21, 1972, 15.
96 Mahabir Marajh, *Express*, September 29, 1972, 23.
97 "'Backless' dress won't do": H. M., Point Fortin, *Express*, July 19, 1976.
98 Interview, August 29, 1998.
99 Interview, April 30, 1997.
100 *Sunday Express*, March 5, 2000, 16.
101 See Robin Balliger's discussion of her fieldwork in "Popular Music and the Cultural Politics of Globalisation among the Post-Oil Boom Generation in Trinidad."
102 *Express*, February 11, 2000, 17.
103 Indira Maharaj, *Express*, March 10, 2000, 17.
104 Interview, April 30, 1996.
105 Interview, August 20, 2000.
106 Barthes, "The Grain of the Voice."
107 They also talk about its *newness*. See, for example, some of the songs by Drupatee Ramgoonai and Rikki Jai—in particular, Drupatee's "Hotter than a Chulha" and Jai's "Jump Like an Indian."
108 Barthes, "The Grain of the Voice," 181.
109 Ibid., 182.
110 Ibid.
111 Ibid.
112 Ibid., 183.
113 "The song must speak, must *write*—for what is produced at the level of the geno-

song is finally writing" ibid., 185. Perhaps writing is another word for signification?

114 Ibid., 188. In the famous essay "From Work to Text," in the anthology *Image—Music—Text*, Barthes suggests that the transformation of "[literary] work" into "text" involves the movement beyond seeking the equivalence of meaning to understanding its ungraspability.

115 This is not to downplay the large populations of working-class Indians who are part of the new migrations to the United Kingdom and the United States, but only to make a point about the specific Indo-African cultural forms in the Caribbean. Musical genres are emerging in the United Kingdom that bring together the Punjabi bhangra rhythms of working-class Indian migrants with Jamaican dancehall, which are beginning to have an impact on film music in India. However, an engagement with British Asian music is beyond the scope of this study.

FOUR Jumping out of Time

1 Hundreds of calypsos are composed and sung every year. There is no authoritative account of how many of them deal with East Indians, but more than one hundred songs explicitly referring to them are listed in Constance, *Tassa, Chutney and Soca*. In the 1990s, songs about East Indians increased in number along with their cultural and political visibility. I am indebted to Gordon Rohlehr for his informal compilation of "Indian calypsos" (hereafter, cited as GRIC), which I have drawn on extensively for this chapter. Every attempt has been made to trace the original release date of songs quoted in this chapter. This is an effort that has met with only some success. A valuable but still incomplete discography for calypso and soca is www.calypsoarchives.co.uk. See also www.calypsoworld.org for pre–World War II recordings.

2 Rohlehr, *Calypso and Society in Pre-Independence Trinidad*, 3–4.

3 Hosay is the Muslim festival of Muharram; obeah is a form of African worship often castigated as "black magic"; Shango is an Afro-Caribbean religion that combines the worship of several Yoruba deities; the Shouter Baptists represent a form of Afro-Caribbean Christianity.

4 According to the calypsonian and academic Hollis "Mighty Chalkdust" Liverpool, Africans celebrated the end of slavery by "applying Carnival traditions and rituals to their victory celebrations": see Liverpool, *Rituals of Power and Rebellion*, 127.

5 Rohlehr, *Calypso and Society in Pre-Independence Trinidad*, 8.

6 On February 27, 1881, in the early hours of the first day of the Carnival celebration, Jouvert morning, the inspector-commandant of the police, the Englishman Arthur Baker, and his Barbadian policemen clashed with revelers carrying sticks, stones, and bottles, causing injuries to both sides. The governor of the colony had to intervene before ruffled feelings subsided.

7 The gloss is provided by various authorities cited in Campbell, "Carnival, Calypso, and Class Struggle in Nineteenth Century Trinidad," n. 54.
8 Brereton, *A History of Modern Trinidad*, 132.
9 The female chorus is still a feature of contemporary calypso and soca.
10 R. C. G. Hamilton, as cited in Rohlehr, *Calypso and Society in Pre-Independence Trinidad*, 19.
11 Warner-Lewis, *Guinea's Other Suns*, 142. Warner-Lewis also remarks on the delight in verbal contest and the aesthetic display of language, which she says is characteristic of African communities.
12 Sankeralli, "Carnival, the Trinidadian Folk and the Indian Presence," 10. Contrary to widely held perceptions that East Indians do not commonly play mas', Sankeralli notes that Indians actually participate in large numbers. In addition, there are a few very prominent band leaders, like Ivan Kallicharan in San Fernando and Raul Garib in Port of Spain, whose bands have a high proportion of Indo-Trinidadians.
13 Rohlehr, *Calypso and Society in Pre-Independence Trinidad*, 18–24. See also Liverpool, *Rituals of Power and Rebellion*.
14 Kim Johnson points out that groups of Indians participated in steel-band drumming in Port of Spain in the 1950s. There was an early East Indian attempt to play South Indian music on the steel drum, but at the time the instrument was not complex enough for the microtones: Kim Johnson, filmed interview, May 7, 2004. Stephen Stuempfle contends that four kinds of bands influenced the early steel drum: the tamboo-bamboo band, the Orisha drums, military marching bands, and Indian tassa ensembles. Especially in St. James (in Port of Spain), both Africans and Indians play tassa as well as steel band, and there is enough basis to claim that the two percussive traditions have had an impact on each other: see Stuempfle, *The Steelband Movement*, 40.
15 Raymond Quevedo, the famous calypsonian otherwise known as Atilla the Hun, is one of several writers who argues that the word "calypso" is derived from the African (language not specified) word "Kaiso," meaning "bravo" or "well done." Atilla claims that in fifty years' association with kaiso and Carnival tents, this was the only word he heard, suggesting that the perpetuation of the term "calypso" was "the result of irresponsible journalese": Quevedo, *Atilla's Kaiso*, 4.
16 Liverpool, *Rituals of Power and Rebellion*, 376–83.
17 Tikasingh, "The Establishment of the Indians in Trinidad, 1870–1900," 374. Tikasingh also writes that by 1901, East Indians were one third of the total population and that 44.8 percent of this third had been born in Trinidad: ibid., 213.
18 The badjohn figure is a young, unemployed man represented as one who is proud of his frequent skirmishes with the law.
19 Rohlehr, *Calypso and Society in Pre-Independence Trinidad*, 499; see also Aziz, "Indian Culture as Portrayed in Calypso."
20 An early calypso by Duke of Normandy (1930) refers to his affair with an East

Indian, saying, in the only lines that remain in popular memory, "After she give me parata / She had me cooraja" (parata is a kind of bread, whereas cooraja is a nonsense word employed for its suggestiveness). In the mid-1930s, Roaring Lion (Raphael de Leon) sang "Bhagi Pholourie" in praise of Indian food, his familiarity with it coming from the fact that he had at some point lived with an Indian family in San Fernando (the refrain goes, "Bhaji pholourie, dal bhat and dhalpourie / Channa paratha, and the aloo talkarie"): *Calypsos from Trinidad: Politics, Intrigue and Violence in the 1930s* (Arhoolie Productions, CD7004, 2004). In contrast, Lord Invader (Rupert Grant), in "Maharaj Daughter" (1939), rejected Indian food altogether, demanding instead a rich and attractive Indian girl who would maintain him in style, singing, "I want every body to realize / I want a nice Indian girl that is creolize / I don't want no parata or dhal water / I want my potato and cassava": as quoted in Rohlehr, *Calypso and Society in Pre-Independence Trinidad*, 257). Bhaji is cooked vegetable; pholourie is a small, deep-fried flour casing; dal bhat is lentils and rice; dhalpourie is Indian unleavened bread made with crushed lentil mixed into the dough, channa is chickpea, paratha a kind of layered bread, aloo is potato, and talkarie is a generic term for vegetable.

21 Rohlehr, *Calypso and Society in Pre-Independence Trinidad*, 251.
22 However invisible interracial unions were, they did exist, even decades before this song, as shown by a report in the *San Fernando Gazette*, 20 June 1893, that "in June 1893 three Indians assaulted an African whom they suspected of harbouring an Indian wife": see Tikasingh, "The Establishment of the Indians in Trinidad, 1870–1900," 363.
23 Rohlehr, *Calypso and Society in Pre-Independence Trinidad*, 253–54.
24 As quoted in Trotman, "The Image of Indians in Calypso," 388.
25 Mighty Dictator, *Moonia* (VITA 1002, Kay TC 102, 1955, 78 rpm).
26 Quevedo, *Atilla's Kaiso*, 87.
27 Unless noted otherwise, I transcribed all of the quotations from the "Indian calypsos" from GRIC.
28 Rohlehr, *Calypso and Society in Pre-Independence Trinidad*, 495.
29 Lord Melody, "Apan Jaat," on *Calypso Carnival* (Balisier Records, Balisier HDF 1003, 1958, LP).
30 Compare this with Cro Cro's 1990s calypso "All Yuh Look for Dat" (Kaiso Gems 1996, Carotte CD 21C), which produces a similar explanation for an "Indian" election victory in Trinidad.
31 Lord Melody, "Come Go Calcutta," on *Calypso Awakening* (Smithsonian Folkways 40353, 2002).
32 The PNM was opposed by the Democratic Legislature Party, dominated by (mostly Hindu) East Indians, as discussed in chapter 1.
33 Trotman, "The Image of Indians in Calypso," 302.
34 For an interesting discussion of the violent sexual metaphors in anti-Indian calypsos by Striker, Superior, and Killer, see Puri, *The Caribbean Postcolonial*, 185.

35 Mighty Dougla, *Split me in Two* (Telco TW 3070, 1961, 7").
36 Brynner (Kade Simon), 1961, as quoted in Constance, *Tassa, Chutney and Soca*, 30.
37 Lord Kitchener, "Mrs. Harriman," on *Hot Pants* (Trinidad TRSC-0002, 1972, LP).
38 King Fighter, "Dularie," (Telco TW 3312, 1966, 7").
39 "*Baytee*" or "*beti*" is Hindi for daughter. It is used in Trinidad as a generic term for a young East Indian woman.
40 King Fighter, "Baytee," on *Me Go Tell Granny/Baytee* (Tropico T7-1061, 1968, 7").
41 Constance, *Tassa, Chutney and Soca*, 18.
42 Interview with Roy Boyke, *Trinidad Carnival* magazine, 1974, as cited ibid., 63–64.
43 Lord Shorty, "Indian Singers," on *Indian Singers/Comic Strip* (Telco TW 3302, 1966, 7").
44 Lord Shorty, "Indrani," on *Indrani/Calypso Is Ours* (Shorty S-002, 1973, 7"); also on *Shorty's Gone, Gone, Gone* (Island Series FP-1006, 1973, LP).
45 Regis, *The Political Calypso*, 196.
46 Lord Shorty, "Kelogee Bulbul," on *The Love Man, Carnival '74 Hits* (Shorty SLP 1000, 1974, LP).
47 Trotman, "The Image of Indians in Calypso," 395.
48 Composer, "Reconstruction," on *Trinidad: Land of Calypso* (Antillana LPS 1001, 1971, LP).
49 Valentino, "Liberation," on *Liberation/Mad Mad World* (Strakers S-0099, 1973, 7").
50 For an account of these initiatives, see Parmasad, "Ancestral Impulse, Community Formation and 1970," 309–18.
51 See chapter 5 for a longer discussion.
52 Mighty Chalkdust, "Ram the Magician," on *Chalkdust: Kaiso with Dignity* (Hot Vinyl HVLP 001, 1984, LP).
53 For a detailed discussion of social-confrontation calypsos of this period, see Rohlehr, "Man Talking to Man," in Rohlehr, *My Strangled City and Other Essays*, 324–41.
54 A quarter century later, Shorty's legacy endures. Rikki Jai's "Song of Unity" (on *Calypso Music* [Samraj Jaimungal, 2003, CD]) passes on a message the singer is supposed to have had in a dream from Ras Shorty: "You got to sing about unity / You got to do it musically / He said: Sing a song for the African / Sing a song for the East Indian / Sing a song for your own nation."
55 Lord Shorty, "Om Shanti Om," on *Soca Explosion* (Shorty SCR 1004, 1979, LP); also on *Greatest Hits* (Charlie's Records, SCR 107, 1999, CD).
56 Regis, *The Political Calypso*, 197.
57 Mighty Sparrow, "Marajhin" (1982), on *Sparrow's Dance Party* (Lorne Dawson, BLS Records, 1992, audio cassette).
58 Mighty Sparrow, "Marajhin Sister" (1983), on *Soca Lingo* (BLS/RIAA, BLSCD1032, 2000, CD).
59 Mighty Sparrow, "Marajhin Cousin" (1984), on *Soca Lingo* (BLS/RIAA, BLSCD1032, 2000, CD).

60 Regis, *The Political Calypso*, 197.
61 The reference is to the sugar belt dominated by East Indians: as quoted in Constance, *Tassa, Chutney and Soca*, 20.
62 Baron, "Raja Rani" (1986), on *Sweeter Than Ever* (BSBSR-BA-044, 1986, LP).
63 For a discussion of "Sumintra," see chapter 5. Drupatee's career is discussed in chapter 3.
64 Rohlehr, "Apocalypso and the Soca Fires of 1990," in Rohlehr, *The Shape of That Hurt and Other Essays*, 308.
65 Mighty Sparrow, "Ah Diggin' Horrors" (1975), on *Calypso Maestro* (RARA 5050, 1975, LP).
66 As quoted in Constance, *Tassa, Chutney and Soca*, 53.
67 For a more complete discussion of the controversy, see ibid., 53–56.
68 McLeod, in *Trinidad Guardian*, March 1988, as cited in Constance, *Tassa, Chutney, and Soca*, 54.
69 After the discussions about Black Stalin's "Caribbean Man" (1979) (as well as about "Caribbean Unity" [1979], on *To the Caribbean Man* [Wizards MCR-147, Makossa 2342, 1979], LP), which sang about the Caribbean man as though he were African, omitting all reference to Indians in Trinidad, this was perhaps the first concerted criticism of the portrayal of Indians in calypso. See Deosaran, "The 'Caribbean Man,'" 81–117.
70 Parvati, interview, August 31, 1998.
71 Although Islam is often seen as an "Indian" religion in Trinidad, there is a long history of "African Islam" that is not so visible. In the early nineteenth century, Muslim Africans from West Africa were brought as slaves to the Caribbean, and many of them lived later in communities of freedmen. One such was the Mandingo community, whose members retained Muslim names in addition to their Creole ones and expressed their determination to go back to Africa one day. There were also many Mandingo and Muslims among the free Africans who emigrated to Trinidad in the 1840s and '50s. See Brereton, *A History of Modern Trinidad, 1783–1962*, 67–68.
72 Rudder, "Hoosay" (1991), on *No Restriction: The Concert* (Lypsoland, CR 027, 1997, CD).
73 Rohlehr, "Apocalypso and the Soca Fires of 1990," in Rohlehr, *The Shape of That Hurt and Other Essays*, 368. Abu Bakr's Jamaat party supported the PNM to return to power in the midterm elections of October 2002, leading to UNC leader and former Prime Minister Basdeo Panday criticizing it as an unholy and opportunistic alliance.
74 Boodan, "Figures Show Steady Rise in Assault on Women," *Sunday Guardian*, July 4, 1993, as cited in Rohlehr, "Working Towards Then Beyond a Balance of Terror," 9. I am grateful to Gordon Rohlehr for allowing me to read his manuscript and quote from the songs about Hulsie Bhaggan that he discusses.
75 Tallish, "Water" (1994), on *Water* (Tallish Sheet Metal 1013, 1994, 12″).

76 Hulsie Bhaggan, "Calypso Must Respect Our Women," letter to the editor, *Trinidad Guardian*, February 5, 1994.
77 Rohlehr, "Working Towards Then Beyond a Balance of Terror," 32.
78 "Hindu Women See Kaiso All-Time Low," *Express*, February 13, 1994, 4.
79 Brother Marvin, "Miss Bhaggan" (1994).
80 David Rudder, "The Ballad of Hulsie X" (1995), in *No Restriction: The Concert* (Lypsoland, CR 027, 1997, CD).
81 Presumably the reference is to chutney-soca, and to Mungal Patasar's sitar and steel-pan fusion music. See Mungal Patasar and Pantar, *Nirvana* (Rituals Records, CO2597, 1997, CD).
82 Working Women for Progress, "Why Race Calypsoes Flawed," 9.
83 Jacquie Burgess, interview, May 1, 1997.
84 "Cro Cro and Ryan Dead Wrong," *Newsday*, March 4, 1996, 8.
85 Black Stalin, "Sundar," on *Carnival Special Volume 2* (ICE 950201, 1995, LP); also on *Message to Sundar* (ICE 951402, 1995, CD).
86 Stalin, as quoted in Sandra Chouthi, "Take a Little Chutney, Add a Little Laiso, and You Get Dougla Music," *Sunday Express*, January 8, 1995, 17. After Sundar's death, Stalin did a song with Rikki Jai in which both singers complained about "all de people wid de race talk" and talking about the necessity for changing "our habit" if we don't want to "seal our fate." The chorus goes: "Mere dosti mera yaar [my friend, my dearest friend], Yuh is my brother / Yuh is my friend / We go love dis country / Right to de end." At the end of the song, Black Stalin goes off to look for doubles, an East Indian snack, and Rikki Jai looks for bake and saltfish, a Creole dish: on *Calypso Music* (Samraj Jaimungal, 2003, CD).
87 Reddock, "Jahaji Bhai," 579.
88 Chris Garcia, "Chutney Bachhanal" (1996), on *Chutney Bachhanal* (JMC 1120, 1996, CD).
89 As quoted in Reddock, "Jahaji Bhai," 580.
90 Brother Marvin, "Jahaji Bhai (Brotherhood of the Boat)" (1995–96), on *Just D'Beginning* (C. B. Henderson and Edwin Ayoung, 1996, CD).
91 See Pearl Eintou Springer, "Some Balance Please, Brother Marvin," letter to the editor, *Trinidad Guardian*, February 16, 1996.
92 As reported by Hubert Devonish in personal communication, 1996.
93 As cited in Richards, "A Racial Calypso, Ent?" 9.
94 Interview, April 30, 1996.
95 Reddock, "Jahaji Bhai," 584.
96 Mahabir, "Brother Marvin's Bone of Contention," letter to the editor, *Newsday*, April 7, 1996, 22.
97 Ahye, "Brother Marvin Knows Africa and India Linked," *Daily Express*, February 24, 1996, 10.
98 Small, "Call It the Alla Padma If You Want to Know the Real Thing," 1.
99 Joseph, "The Dynamic Duet," 3.

100 Cro Cro, "Dole Chadee Say," on *Kaiso Gems 2000 Volume 2* (Banga Seed BSCD 103, 2000, CD).
101 Rudder, "Shakedown Time" (2000), on *Zero* (Lypsoland, CR 032CD, 2000, CD).
102 Destra and Shurwayne Winchester, "Come Beta," on *The Soca Switch The Perfect Ten* (KMC, JWCL267, 2004, CD).

FIVE "Suku Suku What Shall I Do?"

Epigraphs: Vera Rubin and Marisa Zavalloni, *We Wish to Be Looked Upon*; Christopher Cozier, personal communication, February 17, 2002.

1 I thank Christopher Cozier, Raviji, and Anita Samtani for detailed responses to my queries.
2 The Indian film industry produces films in many languages, but Hindi is the one that claims widespread distribution territories in India and abroad. Although Tamil films are popular in some parts of the Indian subaltern diaspora, in Trinidad it is only Hindi films that are shown.
3 Gilroy, *The Black Atlantic*, especially chapter 3.
4 Raviji, personal communication, March 20, 2002.
5 Ibid., March 19, 2002. A bhajan is a Hindu prayer song, as described in chapter 3.
6 For East Indians, the community "cooking night" is the Saturday night before the Sunday wedding, as described in chapter 3.
7 Sookram, "Evolution of Indian Music," 31.
8 Ramjas-Maharaj, "Indian Dance in Trinidad," 2.
9 Ramaya, *Hindi Film Songs*, 45. The musical forms mentioned here span both classical and popular idioms in India.
10 Parvati, interview, August 31, 1998.
11 Samaroo, "The Indian Connection," 44.
12 Basdeo, "Indian Cinema in Trinidad," 2.
13 Christopher Cozier, personal communication, February 17, 2002.
14 The double meanings in calypso usually have to do with the sex act or with men's and women's sex organs, as shown by the discussions in chapters 3 and 4. Remo Fernandes says that the original "Junglee" song was inspired by an American pop number that used the phrase "suku suku."
15 Sampath, "An Evaluation of the 'Creolisation' of Trinidad East Indian Adolescent Masculinity," 248.
16 Cozier, personal communication, February 17, 2002.
17 For an influential discussion of "passive revolution" as a useful term for understanding twentieth-century Indian history, see Chatterjee, *Nationalist Thought and the Colonial World*.
18 To complicate matters further, one should note that these characteristics are also associated with vernacular languages in India, as opposed to English, al-

though in the internal linguistic and cultural hierarchies, languages like Bangla or Hindi appear more "modern" than some of the South Indian languages.
19 Raviji, personal communication, March 17, 2002.
20 See, for instance, the Fijian Indian who looks to Indian music for a sense of her cultural identity and is disappointed that young women in Bombay dance to heavy metal and hard rock: see Ray, "Bollywood Down Under," 174. A similar idea can be found in Manuel ("Music, Identity, and Images of India in the Indo-Caribbean Diaspora," 25), which discusses the way in which an Indo-Guyanese *tan* singer decried the "Westernizing influence of Indian films."
21 Parvati, interview, August 31, 1998.
22 Raviji, personal communication, March 17, 2002.
23 Kaviraj, "Religion, Politics and Modernity," 296.
24 Yasmin, interview, May 4, 1997.
25 Ibid.
26 Hansen, "The Mass-Production of the Cinema," 63.
27 See Rajadhyaksha, "The Phalke Era," 47–82; Sheikh, "The Viewer's View," 143–54; Madhava Prasad, *The Ideology of the Hindi Film*.
28 Earlier Indian films shown in Trinidad were all in English—for example, during 1930–33 *Shiraz*, *Light of Asia*, and *Karma*. According to Patricia Mohammed, *Bala Joban* was still being screened as late as 1944, drawing large crowds at the Palace Cinema in San Fernando: Mohammed, "From Myth to Symbolism."
29 Mohammed, *Mastana Bahar and Indian Culture in Trinidad and Tobago*, 43, note 5.
30 Myers, *Music of Hindu Trinidad*, 126.
31 Anita Samtani, personal communication, April 19, 2002.
32 It is not clear whether this year in Bombay was part of the India government scholarship, given the ambivalent attitude of government-owned institutions like All India Radio to Hindi film music.
33 Patasar, "The Evolution of Indian Musical Forms in Trinidad from 1845 to the Present," 35.
34 Ibid., 35.
35 Ibid., 34–35.
36 Johnson, "The beat of a different drum, Unity of dougla music," *Express*, available at http://209.94.197.2/jan99/jan17/features.htm.
37 From 1962 on, Moean Mohammed, the 1950s radio presenter who is from the same family that later promoted *Mastana Bahar*, put on an Indian variety show on TTT.
38 Cozier, personal communication, March 14, 2002.
39 Mighty Chalkdust, "Mastana Bahar" (1978), on *Calypso vs. Soca* (Strakers GS 2224, 1979).
40 The lyrics are from a song that appeared in the Hindi film *Taj Mahal* (dir. M. Sadiq, 1963). In 1975, according to Shamoon Mohammed, African competitors won the majority of special prizes—best singer, best musician, best group, and

so on, on *Mastana Bahar*. He does not, however, mention the names of the singers: Mohammed, *Mastana Bahar and Indian Culture in Trinidad and Tobago*, 55. In 1998, *Mastana Bahar*, which for many years has also included a live "cultural pageant" (called by some a beauty contest), crowned as its queen the Afro-Trinidadian Christine Ramirez, who had been trained by the Shiv Shakti dance troupe, attracting praise from those who commended national integration and criticism from those who wondered how an "African" could represent "Indian culture."

41 Ryan, *The Jhandi and the Cross*, 200. His source is the *Sunday Mirror*, July 25, 1999.
42 *Sunday Express*, October 25, 1998, as cited ibid., 212.
43 *Express*, February 4, 1971, 9.
44 Raviji, personal communication, March 20, 2002. This method of advertisement was common until the 1970s on the outskirts of large Indian cities and remains popular in smaller towns and villages to this day.
45 Anita Samtani, India Overseas Limited, personal communication, April 19, 2002.
46 Basdeo, "Indian Cinema in Trinidad." See also Samtani, personal communication.
47 Parvati, interview, August 31, 1998.
48 A recent example of this kind of film is *Kabhi Khushi Kabhi Gham* (dir. Karan Johar, 2001).
49 "Non-European God-Soul," letter to the editor, *Daily Express*, June 7, 1975. But as a visit to any roti shop will testify, beef is one of the most common fillings for East Indian rotis. This is not to say that "God-Soul" is misleading the reader. It is to suggest that a particular definitional effect is sought to be achieved by the representation of "Indian" habits and tastes (including food) as different from those of other Caribbean people.
50 Rikki Jai, "Sumintra" (1989), on *Getting On* (Chalo's CP 004-89, 1989), also on *Chutney Soca Monarch* (Samraj Jaimungal, 1998).
51 Rikki Jai said that this phrase was selected by the producer-composer Kenny Phillips when Rikki played him samples of Lata Mangeshkar's music. Rikki had "not a clue" that it was a big song in India, and neither he nor Kenny knew what it meant. It proved to be an "intriguing" phrase for Trinidadians, who often ask Rikki what he was saying when he sang, "Bindiya chamkegi? Give me a chutney beat? Give me a chunky beat?" Some people "don't even know who Lata Mangeshkar is," he said. "They just like how it [the name] sounds. I wanted to convey the Trini-ness of my situation [by singing this]": filmed interview, May 4, 2004. Rikki sings "Bindiya chamkegi" on a lower note than in the original to match the refrain, "Give me soca."
52 These are references to two predominantly East Indian villages in southern Trinidad.
53 Rikki glossed "lavway" and "sesay" this way: "Lavway is a melodic phrase, the

way you create an expression, everybody have their own lavway. Sesay is a movement. These words are from French patois" (filmed interview, May 4, 2004).

54 Rikki Jai, "Sumintra."
55 Filmed interview, May 4, 2004.
56 Ramlakhan, "Hinduism Here to Stay Forever," *Daily Express*, December 6, 1999.
57 Ali, "A Social History of East Indian Women in Trinidad since 1870," 146.
58 Mohammed, "From Myth to Symbolism," 82.
59 An older East Indian woman whose family was closely associated with the Creole-dominated PNM said that, while many Africans came to her house when she was growing up and were treated in very friendly fashion, talk of intermarriage was avoided. As she put it, the message to the African was, "You can be my brother, but not my brother-in-law": Anisa, interview, May 4, 1997.
60 Drupatee Ramgoonai and Machel Montano, "Real Unity," on *Chutney/Soca* (JMCCD 1228, 2001).
61 John, "The Real Drupatee," 3.
62 Another version of this story is that Drupatee asked Machel what he wanted her to do, and he said: "There's an old song from the movie *Qurbani*." Drupatee knew the film's songs and started humming "Aap jaise koi." "When I hummed the piece, he said this is what he wanted" (filmed interview, May 10, 2004).
63 John, "The Real Drupatee."
64 Sheila Rampersad, personal communication, October 2001.
65 Famous Afro-Trinidadian female singers like Calypso Rose and Ella Andall have a long-standing connection to "Indian" music. In conversations in April 2004, Calypso Rose mentioned that she has sung with Sundar Popo in Surinam, Guyana, Trinidad and Tobago, and New York. She has also worked with Drupatee in some of these places. Ella Andall says that one of her favorite singers is Lata Mangeshkar. She knows verses from several Hindi film songs.
66 Denise Belfon, "Indian Man" (2004), on *Party Alliance 2004* (KMC Productions, 2004).

Afterword

1 I thank Steve Ouditt and Sat Sharma for introducing me to this brilliant concept.
2 The albums range from *Goan Crazy!* (Goana, 1984) and *Bombay City* (CBS, 1987) to *Politicians Don't Know How to Rock and Roll* (Magnasound, 1992) and *O Meri Munni* (Magnasound, 1998). His most recent albums include *India Beyond* (Face the Music, 2001), which marks a more trance-like turn in his music.
3 This is not to suggest that homogenization per se does not occur in Southern contexts, as, for example, in relation to pop music and film music in India vis-à-vis "folk" forms. However, these are different forms of homogenization that sometimes intersect with the ambitions of multinational music companies and

sometimes bypass them altogether in creating "national" or even "regional" circuits of production and consumption. What I am arguing for is a critical-creative intervention that can change the way music is produced by addressing the contexts of its production. I am grateful to Ritty Lukose for pressing me on this point and hope to address it more substantially in forthcoming research.

4 Unlike many other parts of India that experienced English rule, Goa, on the West Coast, was a Portuguese colony for over four hundred years, until the Indian Army "assisted" its incorporation into the Union of India in 1964.
5 Perhaps having more musicians would complicate the logistics of the process and actually make the project unmanageable.
6 His first recorded response is "Shambho Arambol," in which he added vocals, dholak, and flute to a "riddim" track put together by Mikie Bennett of Grafton Studios in Kingston.
7 "Coolie" in the Caribbean refers in a derogatory mode (which sometimes has been reclaimed and deployed positively by its referents) to people of Indian origin.
8 Remo is currently planning a Caribbean album with his own versions of the songs. The five recorded songs are "Shambho Arambol" (vocals by Remo, rhythm track by Mikie Bennett); "I'm Your Indian Man" (vocals by Remo and Denise Belfon, rhythm track by Kasey Phillips; produced by KMC and recorded at KMP Music Lab, Palmiste, Trinidad); "When Truth Keeps Silent" (vocals by Remo, rhythm track by Kasey Phillips; recorded at KMP Music Lab); "Where the Irie Breeze Blows" (vocals and flute by Remo, composed and mixed by Corey Wallace; recorded at Tunapuna, Trinidad); "Chutney-Soca" (vocals, lyrics, and melody by Remo and Rikki Jai; recorded and mixed at Gayatones Studio, Ste. Madeleine, Trinidad).
9 Two other fascinating sessions were (1) with Sheldon Holder's experimental band "12," a group of very young musicians in a garage, where Remo took the place of their absent drummer and Holder did most of the singing; and (2) with the faculty and students of the Department of Creative and Festival Arts at the University of the West Indies, where Remo was center stage, and a variety of instruments, including steel pan, trumpets, keyboards, guitars, and dholak, were brought in to give his compositions a Trinidadian flavor. "Ocean Queen," which had first led me to write to Remo, was performed here with a strong steel-band backing.
10 I had hoped that Drupatee Ramgoonai would collaborate with Remo. Although we met her several times, we could not schedule any jamming sessions.
11 Filmed interview, April 27, 2004.
12 KMP Music Lab is owned by Kenny Phillips, who has supported the careers of several major soca and chutney-soca stars, including Drupatee, Rikki Jai, and now Denise Belfon.

13 All quotes are from the filmed interview, May 12, 2004.
14 I cannot help wondering what Drupatee would have done if she had collaborated with Remo. Would she have played on her "Indianness"? Would she have been the winer woman or the demure dulahin? Would she have sung in Hindi or Bhojpuri or in Trinidadian English?

BIBLIOGRAPHY

Ali, Shameen. "A Social History of East Indian Women in Trinidad since 1870." M. Phil., University of the West Indies, St. Augustine, 1993.

Anderson, Benedict. "Exodus." *Critical Inquiry* 20 (Winter 1994): 314–27.

———. *The Spectre of Comparisons: Nationalism, Southeast Asia, and the World*. London: Verso, 1998.

Andrews, C. F., and W. W. Pearson. "Report on Indentured Labour in Fiji: An Independent Enquiry." Suva: National Archives of Fiji, 1916.

Angrosino, M. V. "Sexual Politics in the East Indian Family in Trinidad." *Caribbean Studies* 16, no. 1: 44–66.

Appiah, Kwame Anthony. *In My Father's House: Africa in the Philosophy of Culture*. London: Methuen, 1992.

———. "Ethnography and Its Critics." Pp. 85–106 in Appiah, *In My Father's House: Africa in the Philosophy of Culture*. London: Methuen, 1992.

Asad, Talal. "The Concept of Cultural Translation in British Social Anthropology." Pp. 141–64 in *Writing Culture: The Poetics and Politics of Ethnography*, ed. James Clifford and George Marcus. Berkeley: University of California Press, 1986.

Asad, Talal, ed. *Anthropology and the Colonial Encounter*. New York: Humanities Press, 1973.

Aziz, Alisa. "Indian Culture as Portrayed in Calypso." Caribbean studies thesis, University of the West Indies, St Augustine, 1992.

Baksh-Soodeen, Rawwida. "Why Do Our Hindu Women Break Out and Break Away—Inside the Chutney Chulha." *Sunday Express*, December 16, 1990, 24.

———. "Power, Gender and Chutney." *Trinidad and Tobago Review*, February 1991, 7.

Balkaransingh, Satnarine. "Chutney Crosses over into Chutney-Soca." Pp. 47–53 in *Identity, Ethnicity and Culture in the Caribbean*, ed. Ralph Premdas. St. Augustine: University of the West Indies, n.d.

Balliger, Robin. "Popular Music and the Cultural Politics of Globalisation among the Post-Oil Boom Generation in Trinidad." Pp. 54–79 in *Identity, Ethnicity and Culture in the Caribbean*, ed. Ralph Premdas. St. Augustine: University of the West Indies, n.d.

Balutansky, Kathleen M, and Marie-Agnes Sourieau, eds. *Caribbean Creolization*. Gainesville: University of Florida Press, 1998.

Banerjee, Sumanta. *The Parlour and the Streets: Elite and Popular Culture in Nineteenth Century Calcutta*. Calcutta: Seagull Books, 1989.

Baptiste, Fitzroy Andre. "The African Presence in India: A Preliminary Investigation." Unpublished ms., 1997. Paper in author's possession.

Barthes, Roland. "The Grain of the Voice." Pp. 179–89 in *Image–Music–Text*, ed. and trans. Stephen Heath. New York: Hill and Wang, 1977.

———. "From Work to Text." Pp. 155–64 in *Image–Music–Text*, ed. and trans. Stephen Heath. New York: Hill and Wang, 1977.

Basdeo, Amita. "Indian Cinema in Trinidad: Role and Impact." Caribbean studies thesis, University of the West Indies, St. Augustine, 1997.

Bassant, Reynold, and L. Siddhartha Orie. "Understanding the Chutney Phenomenon." *Trinidad Guardian*, July 26, 1991.

Bayly, Susan. *Caste, Society and Politics in India from the 18th Century to the Modern Age*. Cambridge: Cambridge University Press, 1999.

Beall, Jo. "Class, Race and Gender: The Political Economy of Women in Colonial Natal." Master's thesis, University of Natal, 1982.

Bhana, Surendra, ed. *Essays on Indentured Indians in Natal*. Leeds: Peepal Tree, 1990.

Bisnauth, Dale. *The Settlement of Indians in Guyana 1890–1930*. Leeds: Peepal Tree, 2000.

Braithwaite, Lloyd. *Social Stratification in Trinidad*. Kingston: Institute of Social and Economic Research, University of the West Indies, 1975.

Brereton, Bridget. *Race Relations in Colonial Trinidad, 1870–1900*. Cambridge: Cambridge University Press, 1979.

———. *A History of Modern Trinidad, 1783–1962*. Portsmouth, N.H.: Heinemann, 1981.

———. "The Experience of Indentureship, 1845–1917." Pp. 21–32 in *From Calcutta to Caroni*, ed. John La Guerre. St. Augustine: University of the West Indies, Extra-Mural Studies Unit, 1985.

Butler, Judith. *Bodies That Matter.* New York: Routledge, 1993.

Campbell, Carl C. "The East Indian Revolt against Missionary Education 1928–1939." Pp. 117–34 in *From Calcutta to Caroni: The East Indians of Trinidad*, ed. John La Guerre. St. Augustine: University of the West Indies, Extra Mural Studies Unit, 1985.

Campbell, Susan. "Carnival, Calypso, and Class Struggle in Nineteenth Century Trinidad." *History Workshop Journal*, no. 26 (1988): 1–27.

Chakrabarty, Bidyut. *Subhas Chandra Bose and Middle-Class Radicalism: A Study in Indian Nationalism 1928–1940.* Delhi: Oxford University Press, 1990.

Chatterjee, Partha. *Nationalist Thought and the Colonial World: A Derivative Discourse?* London: Zed Books, 1986.

———. *The Nation and Its Fragments: Colonial and Post-Colonial Histories.* Princeton, N.J.: Princeton University Press, 1993.

Chatterjee, Partha, and Pradeep Jeganathan, eds. *Community, Gender and Violence, Subaltern Studies 11.* Delhi: Permanent Black, 2000.

Chouthi, Sandra. "Take a Little Chutney, Add a Little Kaiso, and You Get Dougla Music." *Sunday Express*, January 8, 1995, 17.

Clarke, Colin. "Caste among Hindus in a Town in Trinidad: San Fernando." Pp. 165–99 in *Caste in Overseas Indian Communities*, ed. Barton Schwartz. San Francisco: Chandler, 1967.

———. *East Indians in a West Indian Town: San Fernando, Trinidad, 1930–1970.* London: Allen and Unwin, 1986.

Clifford, James. "On Ethnographic Authority." Pp. 21–54 in *The Predicament of Culture.* Cambridge, Mass.: Harvard University Press, 1983.

Constance, Zeno Obi. *Tassa, Chutney and Soca: The East Indian Contribution to the Calypso.* Duncan Village, San Fernando: self-published, 1991.

Cross, Malcolm. "Colonialism and Ethnicity: A Theory and Comparative Case Study." *Ethnic and Racial Studies* 1, no. 1 (1978): 37–59.

———. "East Indian-Creole Relations in Trinidad and Guiana in the Late Nineteenth Century." Pp. 14–38 in *Across the Dark Waters: Ethnicity and Indian Identity in the Caribbean*, ed. David Dabydeen and Brinsley Samaroo. London: Macmillan, 1996.

Cuffy, David. "Soca Song with a Little Chutney." *Savera* magazine, May 12, 1996, 7.

Dabydeen, David, and Brinsley Samaroo, eds. *India in the Caribbean.* London: Hansib/University of Warwick, 1987.

———. *Across the Dark Waters: Ethnicity and Indian Identity in the Caribbean.* London: Macmillan, 1996.

Danny, Phoolo. "No Culture Barrier for Drupatee." *Express*, February 7, 1988, 10.

———. "Chutney Chulha Still Hot, but Sandra Cool." *Sunday Express*, January 13, 1991, 13.

Das, Arvind N. "Long-Distance Nationalism." *Frontline*, November 4, 1994, 126–28.

Deosaran, Ramesh. "The 'Caribbean Man': A Study of the Psychology of Perception and the Media." Pp. 81–117 in *India in the Caribbean*, ed. David Dabydeen and Brinsley Samaroo. London: Hansib/University of Warwick, 1987.

Devonish, Hubert. "African and Indian Consciousness at Play: A Study in West Indies Cricket and Nationalism." Unpublished ms., 1993.

Eccles, Karen. "The Social and Demographic Revolution of Indo-Trinidadian Women." Caribbean studies thesis, University of the West Indies, St. Augustine, 1999.

Emmer, P. C. "The Meek Hindu: The Recruitment of Indian Indentured Labourers for Service Overseas, 1870–1916." In *Colonialism and Migration: Indentured Labour before and after Slavery*, ed. P. C. Emmer. Dordrecht: Martinus Nijhoff, 1986.

Eriksen, Thomas Hylland. "Liming in Trinidad: The Art of Doing Nothing." *Folk*, no. 32 (1990): 23–43.

Erikson, Erik. *Gandhi's Truth: On the Origins of Militant Non-Violence*. New York: Norton, 1969.

Espinet, Ramabai, ed. *Creation Fire: A Cafra Anthology of Caribbean Women's Poetry*. Toronto/Tunapuna: Sister Vision/ Caribbean Association for Feminist Research and Action (CAFRA), 1990.

———. "Representation and the Indo-Caribbean Woman in Trinidad and Tobago." Pp. 42–61 in *Indo-Caribbean Resistance*, ed. Frank Birbalsingh. Toronto: TSAR Publications, 1993.

Fabian, Johannes. *Language and Colonial Power: The Appropriation of Swahili in the Former Belgian Congo, 1880–1938*. New York: Cambridge University Press, 1986.

Fischer, Louis. *The Life of Mahatma Gandhi*. New York: Harper, 1950.

Foucault, Michel. *The History of Sexuality*, Vol. 1, trans. Robert Hurley. New York: Vintage, 1980.

Freund, Bill. *Insiders and Outsiders: The Indian Working Class of Durban 1910–1990*. Pietermaritzburg: University of Natal Press, 1995.

Gandhi, M. K. *The Collected Works of Mahatma Gandhi*, Vol. 13. Delhi: Publications Division, Ministry of Information and Broadcasting, Government of India, 1964.

———. "Indentured Labour." Pp. 247–50 in *The Collected Works of Mahatma Gandhi*, Vol. 13. Delhi: Publications Division, Ministry of Information and Broadcasting of India, 1964.

———. "Speech on Indentured Indian Labour." Pp. 132–34 in *The Collected Works of Mahatma Gandhi*, Vol. 13. Delhi: Publications Division, Ministry of Information and Broadcasting, Government of India, 1964.

———. *My Experiments with Truth: An Autobiography*, Vol. 1. Ahmedabad: Navjivan Publishing House, 1968.

———. *Satyagraha in South Africa: Volume 3, Selected Works*. Ahmedabad: Navjivan Publishing House, 1969.

Ghosh, Shohini. "The Troubled Existence of Sex and Sexuality: Feminists Engage with Censorship." Pp. 233–60 in *Image Journeys: Audio-Visual Media and Cultural Change in India*, ed. Christiane Brosius and Melissa Butcher. Delhi: Sage, 1999.

Gilroy, Paul. *There Ain't No Black in the Union Jack: The Cultural Politics of Race and Nation*. 1987. Chicago: University of Chicago Press, 1991.

———. *The Black Atlantic: Modernity and Double Consciousness.* London: Verso, 1993.

Ginwala, Frene. "Class, Consciousness and Control, Indian South Africans 1860–1946." Ph.D. thesis, Oxford University, 1974.

Gosine, Mahine. *East Indians and Black Power in the Caribbean: The Case of Trinidad.* New York: African Research Publications, 1986.

———. "East Indians in Trinidad and Their Inter-Ethnic Relations." Pp. 65–84 in *Global Migration of Indians*, ed. J. K. Motwani and J. Barot-Motwani. New York: First Global Convention of Peoples of Indian Origin, 1989.

Guha, Ranajit. "Dominance without Hegemony and Its Historiography." Pp. 210–309 in *Subaltern Studies* 6, ed. Ranajit Guha. Delhi: Oxford University Press, 1989.

Hansen, Miriam. "The Mass Production of the Senses: Classical Cinema as Vernacular Modernism." *Modernism/Modernity* 6, no. 2 (1999): 59–77.

Haraksingh, Kusha R. "Structure, Process and Indian Culture in Trinidad." *Immigrants and Minorities* 7, no. 1 (1988): 113–22.

Hofmeyr, J. H., and G. C. Oosthuizen. *Religion in a South African Indian Community.* Durban: Institute of Social and Economic Research, University of Durban-Westville, 1981.

Jain, R. K. "Overseas Indians in Malaysia and the Caribbean: Comparative Notes." *Immigrants and Minorities* 7, no. 1 (1988): 123–43.

James, C. L. R. *The Black Jacobins.* London: Allison and Busby, 1980 [1938].

Jha, J. C. "The Indian Heritage in Trinidad." Pp. 1–20 in *From Calcutta to Caroni: The East Indians of Trinidad*, ed. John La Guerre. St. Augustine: University of the West Indies, Extra Mural Studies Unit, 1985.

———. "Hinduism in Trinidad." Pp. 225–33 in *Indenture and Exile: The Indo-Caribbean Experience*, ed. Frank Birbalsingh. Toronto: TSAR Publications, 1989.

Jha, Prem Shankar. "The Platform of Hate." *Outlook*, September 23, 2002, 8.

John, Deborah. "Controversy Reigns." *The Express*, October 23, 1991.

———. "The Real Drupatee." *Sunday Express*, April 9, 2000, 3.

John, Mary E., and Janaki Nair, eds. *A Question of Silence? The Sexual Economies of Modern India.* Delhi: Kali for Women, 1998.

Johnson, Kim. "The Beat of a Different Drum: Unity of Dougla Music." *Express*, January 17, 1999.

Joseph, Terry. "The Dynamic Duet." *Sunday Express*, April 21, 1996, 3.

Kale, Madhavi. *Fragments of Empire: Capital, Slavery and Indian Indentured Labor Migration to the British Caribbean.* Philadelphia: University of Pennsylvania Press, 1998.

Kanhai, Rosanne, ed. *Matikor: The Politics of Identity for Indo-Caribbean Women.* St. Augustine: University of the West Indies, School of Continuing Studies, 1999.

Kapur, Geeta. "Mythic Material in Indian Cinema." *Journal of Arts and Ideas*, no. 14–15 (1987): 79–108.

Kassim, Halima Sa'adia. "Education, Community Organisation and Gender among Indo-Muslims of Trinidad, 1917–1962." Ph.D. thesis, University of the West Indies, St. Augustine, 1999.

Kaviraj, Sudipta. "Religion, Politics and Modernity." Pp. 295–316 in *Crisis and Change in Contemporary India*, ed. Upendra Baxi and Bhikhu Parekh. New Delhi: Sage, 1995.

Kelly, John D. *A Politics of Virtue: Hinduism, Sexuality, and Countercolonial Discourse in Fiji*. Chicago: University of Chicago Press, 1991.

Khan, Aisha. "Purity, Piety and Power: Culture and Identity among Hindus and Muslims in Trinidad." Ph.D. thesis, City University of New York, 1995.

Kingsley, Charles. *At Last, a Christmas in the West Indies*. London: Macmillan, 1910 [1871].

Klass, Morton. *East Indians in Trinidad: A Study of Cultural Persistence*. Prospect Heights, Ill.: Waveland Press, 1988 [1961].

———. *Singing with Sai Baba: The Politics of Revitalization in Trinidad*. Boulder: Westview Press, 1991.

Korom, Frank J. "Memory, Innovation, and Emergent Ethnicity: The Creolization of an Indo-Trinidadian Performance." *Diaspora* 3, no. 2 (1994): 135–55.

La Guerre, John, ed. *From Calcutta to Caroni: The East Indians of Trinidad*. St. Augustine: University of the West Indies, Extra-Mural Studies Unit, 1985 [1974].

———. *The Politics of Communalism: The Agony of the Left in Trinidad and Tobago, 1930–1955*, 2d ed. Port of Spain: Pan-Caribbean Publications, 1982.

Lamming, George. "The Indian Presence as a Caribbean Reality." Pp. 45–54 in *Indenture and Exile: The Indo-Caribbean Experience*, ed. Frank Birbalsingh, Toronto: TSAR Publications, 1989.

———. "The House of Reconciliation." Pp. 187–94 in *Conversations, Essays, Addresses and Interviews 1953–1990*, ed. Richard Drayton and Andaiye. London: Karia Press, 1992.

Laurence, K. O. *A Question of Labour: Indentured Immigration into Trinidad and British Guiana, 1875–1917*. Kingston: Ian Randle, 1994.

Liverpool, Hollis. *Rituals of Power and Rebellion: The Carnival Tradition in Trinidad and Tobago, 1763–1962*. Chicago: Research Associates School Times Publications, 2001.

Madhava Prasad, M. *The Ideology of the Hindi Film: A Historical Construction*. Delhi: Oxford University Press, 1998.

Mahabir, Anil. "Cro Cro and Ryan Dead Wrong." *Newsday*, March 4, 1996, 8.

Mahabir, Noor Kumar, ed. *The Still Cry: Personal Accounts of East Indians in Trinidad and Tobago during Indentureship, 1845–1917*. Tacarigua: Calaloux Publications, 1985.

Maharaj, Niala. "Some Aspects of Hindu Folk Songs in Trinidad." Caribbean studies thesis, University of the West Indies, St. Augustine, 1974.

Mahase, Anna Snr. *My Mother's Daughter: The Autobiography of Anna Mahase Snr, 1899–1978*. Union Village, Claxton Bay: Royards Publishing, 1992.

Malik, Yogendra. *East Indians in Trinidad*. New York: Oxford University Press, 1971.

Mangru, Basdeo. "The Sex Ratio Disparity and Its Consequences under the Indenture in British Guiana." Pp. 211–30 in *India in the Caribbean*, ed. David Dabydeen and Brinsley Samaroo. London: Hansib/University of Warwick, 1987.

Manuel, Peter. *Cassette Culture: Popular Music and Technology in North India*. Chicago: University of Chicago Press, 1993.

———. *Caribbean Currents: Caribbean Music from Rumba to Reggae*. Philadelphia: Temple University Press, 1995.

———. "Music, Identity, and Images of India in the Indo-Caribbean Diaspora." *Asian Music* 29, no. 1 (1997–98): 17–35.

———. "Chutney and Indo-Trinidadian Cultural Identity." *Popular Music* 17, no. 1 (1998): 21–43.

Marks, Shula, and Stanley Trapido, eds. *The Politics of Race, Class and Nationalism in Twentieth-Century South Africa*. London: Longman, 1987.

Mayers, Gennike. "Rajkumar Krishna Persad: A Pioneer of Indian Classical Dance in Trinidad and Tobago." Caribbean studies thesis, University of the West Indies, St. Augustine, 1999.

Mbembe, Achille. "Prosaics of Servitude and Authoritarian Civilities." *Public Culture* 5, no. 1 (1992): 123–45.

———. *On the Postcolony*. Berkeley: University of California Press, 2001.

McNeil, James, and Chimman Lal. *Report to the Government of India on the Conditions of Indian Immigrants in Four British Colonies and Surinam*. Simla: Government of India, 1914.

Meer, Y. S., et al., ed. *Documents of Indentured Labour: Natal 1851–1917*. Durban: Institute of Black Research, 1980.

Miller, Daniel. *Capitalism: An Ethnographic Approach*. Oxford: Berg, 1997.

Mohammed, Debra. "Women Who Sang Calypso: A Socio-Cultural Analysis, 1970–1990." Caribbean studies thesis, University of the West Indies, St. Augustine, 1992.

Mohammed, Patricia. "From Myth to Symbolism." Pp. 78–83 in *Matikor: The Politics of Identity for Indo-Caribbean Women*, ed. Rosanne Kanhai. St. Augustine: University of the West Indies, School of Continuing Studies, 1999.

———. "The Creolization of 'Indian' Women in Trinidad." Pp. 381–97 in *Trinidad and Tobago: The Independence Experience, 1962–1987*, ed. Selwyn Ryan. St. Augustine: University of the West Indies, Institute of Social and Economic Research, n.d.

Mohammed, Shamoon. *Mastana Bahar and Indian Culture in Trinidad and Tobago*. San Juan: Mastana Bahar Thesis Publication Committee, 1982.

Mohanty, Chandra Talpade. *Feminism without Borders*. Durham, N.C.: Duke University Press, 2003.

Mohapatra, Prabhu P. "Restoring the Family: Wife Murders and the Making of a Sexual Contract for Indian Immigrant Labour in the British Caribbean Colonies, 1860–1920." Unpublished ms. in author's possession.

———. "The Hosay Massacre of 1884: Class and Community among Indian Immigrant Labour in Trinidad." Unpublished ms. in author's possession.

———. "Longing and Belonging: Dilemma of Return among Indian Immigrants in the West Indies, 1880–1940." Paper presented at the Conference on Challenge and Change: The Indian Diaspora in Its Historical and Contemporary Context, St. Augustine, 1995.

Morton, Sarah E., ed. *John Morton of Trinidad, Pioneer Missionary of the Presbyterian Church in Canada to the East Indians in the British West Indies, Journals, Letters and Papers.* Toronto: Westminster Company, 1916.

Mukherjee, Meenakshi. "The Caribbean and Us." Paper presented at the Indian Association of Commonwealth Literature and Language Studies Annual Conference, Mysore, 1995.

Myers, Helen. *Music of Hindu Trinidad: Songs from the India Diaspora.* Chicago: University of Chicago Press, 1998.

Naipaul, V. S. *The Middle Passage.* Harmondsworth: Penguin Books, 1969 [1962].

———. *The Overcrowded Barracoon.* New York: Vintage Books, 1984 [1958].

Nanda, B. R. *Gokhale: The Indian Moderates and the British Raj.* Delhi: Oxford University Press, 1977.

Nevadomsky, Joseph. "Wedding Rituals and Changing Women's Rights among the East Indians in Rural Trinidad." *International Journal of Women's Studies* 4, no. 5: 484–96.

———. "Changing Conceptions of Family Regulation among the Hindu East Indians in Rural Trinidad." *Anthropological Quarterly* 55, no. 4 (1982): 189–96.

———. "Economic Organization, Social Mobility, and Changing Social Status among East Indians in Rural Trinidad." *Ethnology*, no. 22 (1983): 63–79.

Newton, Marva. "A Comparison of the Afro-Trinidadian Woman and the Indo-Trinidadian Woman as Portrayed in the Trinidad Calypso, 1980–1989." Caribbean studies thesis, University of the West Indies, St. Augustine, 1993.

Niehoff, Arthur. "The Function of Caste among the Indians of the Oropouche Lagoon, Trinidad." Pp. 149–63 in *Caste in Overseas Indian Communities,* ed. Barton Schwartz. San Francisco: Chandler, 1967.

Niranjana, Tejaswini. "'History, Really Beginning': Compulsions of Postcolonial Pedagogy." Pp. 246–59 in *The Lie of the Land: English Literary Studies in India,* ed. Rajeswari Sunder Rajan, Delhi: Oxford University Press, 1992.

———. *Siting Translation: History, Post-Structuralism and the Colonial Context.* Berkeley: University of California Press, 1992.

Niranjana, Tejaswini, P. Sudhir, and Vivek Dhareshwar, eds. *Interrogating Modernity: Culture and Colonialism in India.* Calcutta: Seagull Books, 1993.

Ottley, Rudolph. *Women in Calypso.* Arima, Trinidad: self-published, 1992.

Panday, Gyanendra. *The Construction of Communalism in Colonial North India.* Delhi: Oxford University Press, 1990.

Parekh, Bhikhu. "Some Reflections on the Indian Diaspora." *Journal of Contemporary Thought* (1993): 105–51.

Parmasad, Kenneth. "Ancestral Impulse, Community Formation and 1970: Bridging the Afro–Indian Divide." Pp. 309–18 in *The Black Power Revolution 1970: A Retrospective,* ed. Selwyn Ryan and Taimoon Stewart. St. Augustine: University of the West Indies, Institute of Social and Economic Research, 1995.

Patasar, Sharda. "The Evolution of Indian Musical Forms in Trinidad from 1845 to

the Present." Caribbean studies thesis, University of the West Indies, St. Augustine, 1998.
Persad, Kamal. "Viewpoint Column." *Sunday Express*, December 16, 1990, 43.
———. "The Hindu Agenda." *Sunday Express*, August 20, 2000, 16.
Phillips, Daphne. "Class Formation and Ethnicity in Trinidad." Master's thesis, University of the West Indies, St. Augustine, 1984.
Polak, H. S. L. *The Indians of South Africa: Helots within the Empire and How They Are Treated*. Madras: G. A. Natesan, 1909.
Premdas, Ralph, ed. *Identity, Ethnicity and Culture in the Caribbean*. St. Augustine: University of the West Indies, School of Continuing Studies, n.d.
Puri, Shalini. *The Caribbean Postcolonial: Social Equality, Post-Nationalism, and Cultural Hybridity*. New York: Palgrave, 2004.
Quevedo, Raymond. *Atilla's Kaiso: A Short History of Trinidad Calypso*. St. Augustine: University of the West Indies, 1983.
Rajadhyaksha, Ashish. "The Phalke Era: Conflict of Traditional Form and Modern Technology." Pp. 47–82 in *Interrogating Modernity: Culture and Colonialism in India*, ed. Tejaswini Niranjana, P. Sudhir, and Vivek Dhareshwar. Calcutta: Seagull Books, 1993.
Ramaya, Narsaloo. Hindi Film Songs—Impact and Contribution to the Culture of Trinidad and Tobago, Aagaman Commemoration Souvenir, Indian Arrival Day 1991. Port of Spain: Commemoration Committee on Indian Arrival and the High Commission of India, 1991.
———. "Evolution of Indian Music: From Field to Studio." *Trinidad and Tobago Review*, 1992, 22–23.
Ramdas, Sukhraj. "An Analysis of Indo-Trinidadian Songs." Caribbean studies thesis, University of the West Indies, St. Augustine, 1987.
Ramjas-Maharaj, D. L. "Indian Dance in Trinidad." Caribbean studies thesis, University of the West Indies, St. Augustine, 1978.
Ramlakhan, Rajnie. "Hinduism Here to Stay Forever." *Express*, December 6, 1999.
———. "Call to Close Ranks in Defence of Dharma." *Express*, August 21, 2000, 17.
Ramnarine, Tina. *Creating Their Own Space: The Development of an Indian-Caribbean Musical Tradition*. Kingston: University of the West Indies Press, 2001.
Ramnath, Marsha. "The Origin and Activities of the National Council of Indian Culture, 1971–1995." Caribbean studies thesis, University of the West Indies, St. Augustine, 1996.
Rampersad, Indrani. "The Hindu Voice in Chutney." *Trinidad Guardian*, December 25, 1990, 10.
Ramsingh, Hardeo. *The History of Felicity Village (1838–1996)*. N.p.: self-published, 1996.
Ray, Manas. "Bollywood Down Under: Fiji Indian Cultural History and Popular Assertion." Pp. 136–84 in *Floating Lives: The Media and Asian Diasporas*, ed. Stuart Cunningham and John Sinclair. Brisbane: University of Queensland Press, 2000.

Reddock, Rhoda. "Jahaji Bhai: The Emergence of a Dougla Poetics in Trinidad and Tobago." *Identities* 5, no. 4: 569–601.

———. "Social Mobility in Trinidad and Tobago 1960–1980." Pp. 210–33 in *Social and Occupational Stratification in Contemporary Trinidad and Tobago*, ed. Selwyn Ryan. St. Augustine: University of the West Indies, Institute of Social and Economic Research, 1991.

———. *Women, Labour and Politics in Trinidad and Tobago*. London: Zed Books, 1994.

Regis, Louis. *The Political Calypso: True Opposition in Trinidad and Tobago 1962–1987*. Kingston: University of the West Indies Press, 1999.

Ribeiro, Indra. "The Phenomenon of Chutney Singing in Trinidad and Tobago." Caribbean studies thesis, University of the West Indies, St. Augustine, 1992.

Richards, Peter. "A Racial Calypso, Ent?" *Sunday Guardian*, February 9, 1997, 9.

Rodney, Walter. *The Groundings with My Brothers*. London: Bogle-l'Ouverture, 1969.

———. *A History of the Guyanese Working People, 1881–1905*. Baltimore: Johns Hopkins University Press, 1981.

Rohlehr, Gordon. "Working Towards Then Beyond a Balance of Terror." Unpublished ms. in author's possession.

———. *Calypso and Society in Pre-Independence Trinidad*. Port of Spain: self-published, 1990.

———. *My Strangled City and Other Essays*. Port of Spain: Longman Trinidad, 1992.

———. *The Shape of That Hurt and Other Essays*. Port of Spain: Longman Trinidad, 1992.

Rolland, Romain. *Mahatma Gandhi*. Paris: Stock, 1924.

Rubin, Vera, and Marisa Zavalloni. *We Wish to Be Looked Upon*. New York: Teachers College Press, Columbia University, 1969.

Ryan, Selwyn. *Race and Nationalism in Trinidad and Tobago*. Toronto: University of Toronto Press, 1972.

Ryan, Selwyn, ed. *Social and Occupational Stratification in Contemporary Trinidad and Tobago*. St. Augustine: University of the West Indies, Institute of Social and Economic Research, 1991.

———. *The Jhandi and the Cross*. St. Augustine: University of the West Indies, Sir Arthur Lewis Institute of Social and Economic Studies, 1999.

Ryan, Selwyn, and Taimoon Stewart, eds. *The Black Power Revolution 1970: A Retrospective*. St. Augustine: University of the West Indies, Institute of Social and Economic Research, 1995.

Said, Edward. *Orientalism*. New York: Vintage, 1978.

Samaroo, Brinsley. "Politics and Afro–Indian Relations in Trinidad." Pp. 77–92 in *From Calcutta to Caroni: The East Indians of Trinidad*, ed. John La Guerre. St. Augustine: University of the West Indies, Extra Mural Studies Unit, 1985.

———. "The Indian Connection: The Influence of Indian Thought and Ideas on East Indians in the Caribbean." Pp. 43–59 in *India in the Caribbean*, ed. David Dabydeen and Brinsley Samaroo. London: Hansib/University of Warwick, 1987.

Sampath, Neils M. "An Evaluation of the 'Creolisation' of Trinidad East Indian Adolescent Masculinity." Pp. 235–53 in *Trinidad Ethnicity*, ed. Kevin Yelvington. London: Macmillan, 1993.

Sangari, Kumkum, and Sudesh Vaid, eds. *Recasting Women: Essays in Colonial History.* Delhi: Kali for Women, 1989.

Sanghvi, Vir. "Isle of Hope for Parivar Hawks." *Telegraph*, February 10, 1999, 1, 6.

Sankeralli, Burton. "Carnival, the Trinidadian Folk and the Indian Presence." Unpublished ms. in author's possession.

Sarkar, Tanika. *Hindu Wife, Hindu Nation: Community, Religion and Cultural Nationalism.* Delhi: Permanent Black, 2001.

Saywack, Rajendra. "From Caroni Gyal to Calcutta Woman: A History of East Indian Chutney Music in the Caribbean." Essay, Black & Puerto Rican Studies, Thomas Hunter College, New York, 1999. Available at http://www.saxakali.com/caribbean and at http://www.guyanaundersiege.com.

Schwartz, Barton, ed. *Caste in Overseas Indian Communities.* San Francisco: Chandler, 1967.

―――. "The Failure of Caste in Trinidad." Pp. 117–48 in *Caste in Overseas Indian Communities*, ed. Barton Schwartz. San Francisco: Chandler, 1967.

Scott, David. "Locating the Anthropological Subject: Postcolonial Anthropologists in Other Places." *Inscriptions* 5 (1989): 75–84.

―――. *Refashioning Futures: Criticism after Postcoloniality.* Princeton, N.J.: Princeton University Press, 1999.

Selvon, Samuel. "Three into One Can't Go—East Indian, Trinidadian, Westindian." Pp. 13–24 in *India in the Caribbean*, ed. David Dabydeen and Brinsley Samaroo. London: Hansib/University of Warwick, 1987.

Shah, Raffique. "Darkness Descends on India, Pakistan." *Express*, April 30, 2002.

Sheikh, Gulammohammed. "The Viewer's View: Looking at Pictures." Pp. 143–54 in *Interrogating Modernity: Culture and Colonialism in India*, ed. Tejaswini Niranjana, P. Sudhir, and Vivek Dhareshwar. Calcutta: Seagull Books, 1993.

Shepherd, Verene, Bridget Brereton, and Barbara Bailey, eds. *Engendering History: Caribbean Women in Historical Perspective.* New York: St. Martin's Press, 1995.

Singham, A. W., and Shirley Hune. *Non-Alignment in an Age of Alignments.* London: Zed Books, 1986.

Sinha, Mrinalini. "Gender in the Critiques of Colonialism and Nationalism: Locating the 'Indian Woman.' " Pp. 477–504 in *Feminism and History*, ed. Joan Wallach Scott. Oxford: Oxford University Press, 1996.

Small, Essiba. "Call It the Alla Padma If You Want to Know the Real Thing." *Sunday Express*, February 4, 1996, 1.

Smith, Faith. "Beautiful Indians, Troublesome Negroes, and Nice White Men: Caribbean Romances and the Invention of Trinidad." Pp. 163–82 in *Caribbean Romances: The Politics of Regional Representation*, ed. Belinda Edmondson. Charlottesville: University Press of Virginia, 1999.

Smith, Tricia. "Chutney Soca." Caribbean studies thesis, University of the West Indies, St. Augustine, 1998.

Sonpar, Shobna. "Caste and Affirmative Action in an Indian College." Center for the Study of Violence and Reconciliation, available at http://www.csvr.org.za/articles/artsonpr.htm (accessed January 21, 2005).

Sookram, Caldeo. "Evolution of Indian Music." *Express*, January 1, 2000.

Spivak, Gayatri C. *In Other Worlds: Essays in Cultural Politics*. New York: Routledge, 1987.

St. Bernard, Godfrey. "Ethnicity and Attitudes towards Interracial Marriages in a Multicultural Society: The Case of Trinidad and Tobago." Pp. 157–84 in *Identity, Ethnicity and Culture in the Caribbean*, ed. Ralph Premdas. St. Augustine: University of the West Indies, School of Continuing Studies, n.d.

Stuempfle, Stephen. *The Steelband Movement: The Forging of a National Art in Trinidad and Tobago*. Kingston: University of the West Indies Press, 1995.

Sunder Rajan, Rajeswari, ed. *The Lie of the Land: English Literary Studies in India*. Delhi: Oxford University Press, 1992.

Swan, Maureen. *Gandhi, the South African Experience*. Johannesburg: Ravan Press, 1985.

Syriac, Sharon. "The Chutney Phenomenon." Caribbean studies thesis, University of the West Indies, St. Augustine, 1993.

Tharu, Susie, and K. Lalita. "Empire, Nation and the Literary Text." Pp. 199–219 in *Interrogating Modernity: Culture and Colonialism in India*, ed. Tejaswini Niranjana, P. Sudhir, and Vivek Dhareshwar. Calcutta: Seagull Books, 1993.

Tharu, Susie, and K. Lalita, eds. *Women Writing in India, 600 B.C. to the Present: The Twentieth Century*, vol. 2. New York: Feminist Press, 1993.

Tharu, Susie, and Tejaswini Niranjana. "Problems for a Contemporary Theory of Gender." Pp. 232–60 in *Subaltern Studies 9*, ed. Shahid Amin and Dipesh Chakrabarty. Delhi: Oxford University Press, 1996.

Tikasingh, G. I. M. "The Establishment of the Indians in Trinidad, 1870–1900." Ph.D. thesis, University of the West Indies, St. Augustine, 1973.

Tinker, Hugh. *A New System of Slavery: The Export of Indian Labour Overseas 1830–1920*. London: Hansib, 1993 [1974].

Trotman, D. V. "The Image of Indians in Calypso: Trinidad 1946–1986." Pp. 385–98 in *Social and Occupational Stratification in Contemporary Trinidad and Tobago*, ed. Selwyn Ryan. St. Augustine: University of the West Indies, Institute of Social and Economic Research, 1991.

———. "Women and Crime in Late Nineteenth Century Trinidad." Pp. 251–59 in *Caribbean Freedom: Society and Economy from Emancipation to the Present*, ed. Hilary Beckles and Verene Shepherd. Kingston: Ian Randle, 1993.

Vertovec, Steven. "Religion and Ethnic Ideology: The Hindu Youth Movement in Trinidad." *Ethnic and Racial Studies* 13, no. 2 (1990): 225–49.

———. "Oil Boom and Recession in Trinidad Indian Villages." Pp. 89–111 in *South Asians Overseas*, ed. Colin Clarke, Ceri Peach, and Steven Vertovec. Cambridge: Cambridge University Press, 1990.

———. *Hindu Trinidad: Religion, Ethnicity and Socio-Economic Change*. London: Macmillan, 1992.

Waite, Gloria. "East Indians and National Politics in the Caribbean." *South Asia Bulletin* 2, no. 2 (1982): 16–28.

Walcott, Derek. "The Caribbean: Culture or Mimicry?" *Journal of Interamerican Studies and World Affairs* 16, no. 1 (1974): 3–13.

———. *The Antilles: Fragments of Epic Memory, The Nobel Lecture*. New York: Farrar, Straus and Giroux, 1993.

Warner-Lewis, Maureen. *Guinea's Other Suns: The African Dynamic in Trinidad Culture*. Dover, Mass.: Majority Press, 1991.

Webber, A. R. F. *Those That Be in Bondage: A Tale of Indian Indentures and Sunlit Western Waters*. Georgetown: Daily Chronicle Printing Press, 1917.

Weller, Judith Ann. *The East Indian Indenture in Trinidad*. Rio Pedras: University of Puerto Rico, Institute of Caribbean Studies, 1968.

Williams, Eric. *From Columbus to Castro: The History of the Caribbean 1492–1969*. New York: Vintage Books, 1984 [1970].

Working Women for Progress. "Why Race Calypsoes Flawed." *Express*, February 14, 1996, 9.

Yelvington, Kevin. "Vote Dem Out: The Demise of the PNM in Trinidad and Tobago." *Caribbean Review* 15, no. 4 (1987): 8–12, 29–33.

———. "Ethnicity 'Not Out': The Indian Cricket Tour of the West Indies and the 1976 Elections in Trinidad and Tobago." *Arena Review* 14, no. 1 (1990): 1–12.

———. "Ethnicity at Work in Trinidad." Pp. 99–122 in *The Enigma of Ethnicity: An Analysis of Race in the Caribbean and the World*, ed. Ralph Premdas. St. Augustine: University of the West Indies, School of Continuing Studies, 1993.

Yelvington, Kevin, ed. *Trinidad Ethnicity*. London: Macmillan, 1993.

INDEX

Andrews, C. F., 79–81, 233 n.75
Anti-Mandal agitation, 4, 9
Appiah, Kwame Anthony, 8, 11
Ataklan (Mark Jiminez), 206–8
Atilla the Hun (Raymond Quevedo), 132, 242 n.15

Baksh-Soodeen, Rawwida, 115
Balkaransingh, Satnarine, 107
Banerjee, Sumanta, 75–76
Baron (Timothy Watkins), 150
Barthes, Roland, 119–22, 241 n.114
Basdeo, Amita, 180
Belfon, Denise, 167, 189, 211–17
Best, Lloyd, 110
Bhaggan, Hulsie, 153–58
Bharatiya Janata Party, 4, 6
Black Power movement, 30
Black Stalin (calypsonian), 160, 246 n.86
Brereton, Bridget, 42, 245 n.71
Brother Marvin (calypsonian), 82, 107, 155, 157, 162–64
Brynner (calypsonian), 138

Calypso, 15, 84, 88; history of, 126–31
Campbell, Carl, 44
Caribbean, the: audience in, 3; population of, 19; society in, 22–23; structures of representation and, 12; teaching literary texts from, 5, 7–8
Caribbean Association for Feminist Research and Action, 86
Carnival, 86
Caste, 3, 4, 9, 38–41; recomposition of, 39
Chatterjee, Partha, 74–75, 247 n.17

Chutney, 84, 88–98, 104–7; commercialization of, 105–6; language of, 107; structure of, 104–5, 237 n.53. *See also* Chutney-soca; Popo, Sundar

Chutney-soca, 52, 88–89, 97, 99; female sexuality and, 110, 115, 117–20, 123; Indian modernity and, 54; musical context of, 94. *See also* Jai, Rikki; Ramgoonai, Drupatee

Clarke, Colin, 35, 40

Comparative studies, 5, 9–15, 18

Composer (calypsonian), 143

Constance, Zeno Obi, 97, 152, 235 n.21

Cozier, Christopher, 169, 171–73

Cro Cro (calypsonian), 151–52

Cultural authority, 3

Culture: East Indians and, 28, 36–37, 43, 51–52; invocation of, 6–7, 37; politics of, 15

Democratic Labor Party (DLP), 30, 46

Derivativeness, 36–38, 54

Destra (soca singer), 167; Shurwayne Winchester and, 167–68

Devonish, Hubert, 236 n.34

Diasporic communities, 7; India and, 21, 22; subalterns and, 18, 174

English studies, critique of, 4–5

Espinet, Ramabai, 234 n.14

Ethnographic authority, 3, 10

Fernandes, Remo, 189, 192; Ataklan and, 206–8; Denise Belfon and, 211–17; as "Indian," 200, 216–17; Indian pop and, 194; in Jamaica, 202–3; musical collaboration project and, 195–97, 220; Rikki Jai and, 208–11, 214

Gandhi, Mohandas Karamchand, 68; anti-indenture campaign and, 74, 78, 81; on indentured women, 55, 79, 80; South Africa and, 57–58, 73

Garcia, Chris, 161–62

Gilroy, Paul, 32–33, 170

Hansen, Miriam, 176

Haraksingh, Kusha, 23–24, 39, 105

Hindi film, 15, 52, 94, 169–89; broadcasting songs from, 171; exhibition of, 180–82; introduction of, into Trinidad, 171; modernity and, 172–74. *See also* Indianness

Hindu, 3, 42–43; in India and Trinidad, 43, 47–51

Hindutva (Hinduness), 32–33, 49, 51

Hindu wedding, 205–6

Hosay, 41–43, 80, 94

Indentureship, 15, 21; allegations of immorality and, 59, 60, 62, 68–70, 72–73; beginnings of, 23–24; campaign against, 26, 79–82, 73–74; composition of, 25; Creole middle class and, 80; disparate sex-ratio and, 24, 58–59; married women and, 59–60, 61; modernity and, 78; multiple relationships in, 67–68; nationalism and, 57; "wife murders" in, 69–71; women's labor under, 26, 63–64. *See also* Gandhi, Mohandas Karamchand; "Indian"; Women

"Indian," 4, 6, 18–19, 20, 41, 54, 56; colonial construction of, 31; in India and Trinidad, 30, 38, 50, 123, 220; representation in calypso, 125–68 *passim*

Indian National Congress, 57–58, 230 n.3

Indianness, 1, 3, 19, 31–33, 53; chutney-soca and, 52; Hindi film and, 51; models of, 29; Remo's claim to, 211;

women and, 54, 55. *See also* Hindi film

Jai, Rikki ("Sumintra"), 17, 182–84, 249 n.51; calypso and, 98, 105, 150; collaborates with Remo, 191, 209–11, 214–17; on performance style, 237–38 n.54; song of, with Black Stalin, 246 n.86; on structure of chutney and calypso, 237 n.53
Jain, R. K., 41
Jamaica, 19; dancehall music in, 85; estranging effect of, 204–5; perceptions of Indians in, 6
Jha, J. C., 42
Jha, Prem Shankar, 50
Johnson, Kim, 103, 242 n.14

Kanchan and Babla, 96, 235–36 n.29, 236 n.30
Kelly, John, 79–80
King Fighter (Shurland Wilson), 133, 138, 139–40, 146
Kingsley, Charles, 31, 67, 70, 82
Klass, Morton, 28, 39, 72–73, 235 n.19

La Guerre, John Gaffar, 28, 35
Laurence, K. O., 59, 68
Lord Executor (Philip Garcia), 132
Lord Kitchener (Aldwin Roberts), 138–39
Lord Melody (Fitzroy Alexander), 135–36, 146

Madhava Prasad, M., 176
Mahabir, Harry, 95, 177–78
Maharaj, Indira, 117–18
Maharaj, Niala, 91
Malik, Yogendra, 35
Mangru, Basdeo, 68
Manuel, Peter, 104–5, 108, 248 n.20

Maraj, Bhadase Sagan, 30, 45–46
Masculinity, 123, 211; calypso and, 131
Mastana Bahar, 95, 98, 116, 144, 178–79
Mbembe, Achille, 11, 225 n.21
Meighoo, Kirk, 238 n.70
Mighty Chalkdust, The (Hollis Liverpool), 43, 129, 144, 165–66, 178–79
Mighty Christo, The (Christopher Laidlow), 137
Mighty Dictator, The (Kenny St. Bernard), 134
Mighty Dougla, The (Cletus Ali), 2–3, 137
Mighty Killer, The (Cephas Alexander), 133, 134, 146
Mighty Sparrow, The (Slinger Francisco), 93, 146–49, 150
Mighty Striker, The (Percy Oblington), 136–37
Miller, Daniel, 107, 238 n.59
Modernity, 20; subaltern diaspora and, 22
Mohammed, Patricia, 185, 233 n.87, 236 n.34, 248 n.28
Mohapatra, Prabhu, 42, 228 n.71
Montano, Machel, 167, 185–89
Muslim, 3, 35, 38, 42–43, 153, 245 n.71
Myers, Helen, 93, 104, 176–77, 234–35 n.19, 235 n.20

Naipaul, V.S., 17, 36–37
National Alliance for Reconstruction (NAR), 47, 150
Nationalism, 3, 5; in the Caribbean, 30; feminism and, 83; in India, 37; Indian women and, 74–80, 82; long-distance, 21
National Joint Action Committee (NJAC), 143–44
Nevadomsky, Joseph, 27–29, 40, 46
Niehoff, Arthur, 29, 40

Panday, Basdeo, 47, 108, 158
Parekh, Bhikhu, 36
Patasar, Mungal, 89, 93, 246 n.81
Patasar, Sharda, 177
People's National Movement (PNM), 30, 35, 143, 158–60, 238 n.64
Persad, Kamal, 116–17, 229 n.86
Popo, Sundar, 89, 95–96, 160, 179
Presbyterians, 27, 64; on Indian women, 58–59, 65–67
Puri, Shalini, 237 n.42, 243 n.34

Rajadhyaksha, Ashish, 176
Ramaya, Narsaloo, 93
Ramgoonai, Drupatee, 84, 121–22, 150; career of, 98–103; criticism of, 112–13, 116; "Hotter than a Chulha," 97, 102–3, 112, 183; "Lick down mih Nani," 86–87, 100–101; Machel Montano and, 167, 185–89; "Mr.Bissessar," 101–2, 237 n.43
Ramlakhan, Rajnie, 49, 184–85, 229 n.85
Ramnarine, Tina, 234 n.8
Rampersad, Indrani, 114–15
Rampersad, Sheila, 118, 164
Ras Shorty I (Garfield Blackman), 88–89, 140–43, 145, 150, 165
Raviji, 115, 173–74
Ray, Manas, 175, 248 n.20
Reddock, Rhoda, 26, 59, 73, 74, 118, 161, 226 n.9, 226 n.12, 227 n.24, 231 n.20, 232 n.46
Ribeiro, Indra, 234 n.10
Rodney, Walter, 14, 26
Rohlehr, Gordon, 97, 112, 126, 241 n.1, 242–243 n.20, 245 n.74
Rudder, David, 104, 140, 152–53, 155, 166–67

Samaroo, Brinsley, 35, 45
Sampath, Neils, 172–73
Sanatan Dharma Mahasabha, 46, 145, 164, 184–85
Sanghvi, Vir, 50–51
Sankeralli, Burton, 242 n.12
Sarkar, Tanika, 77
Saywack, Rajendra, 235 n.23, 237 n.46, 238 n.65
Schwartz, Barton, 29, 39–40, 46
Scott, David, 225 n.22
Sexuality: chutney-soca and, 110–11; food and, 90, 93, 134, 148–49, 242–43 n.20; of indentured women, 15; representation of, 119–20; women and, 157
Shah, Raffique, 50
Sheikh, Gulammohammed, 176
Sinha, Mrinalini, 83
Sonny Mann, 108, 161, 238 n.63
Subaltern studies, 49
Sugar Aloes (calypsonian), 149
Syriac, Sharon, 106

Tharu, Susie, and K. Lalita, 76–77
Third World, 5, 7, 9–12, 223 n.1
Tikasingh, G. I. M., 60, 67, 71, 88, 130, 242 n.17, 243 n.22
Trinidad: compared to India, 19; indentureship and, 23; perceptions of Indians in, 6, 31, 84; population of, 31; slavery and, 23
Trotman, David V., 69, 137

United National Congress (UNC), 47, 108, 158–59, 166, 179, 238 n.64
Unity (calypsonian), 140

Valentino (calypsonian), 143
Vertovec, Steven, 29–30, 40–41, 45
Vishwa Hindu Parishad, 6, 48–49

Walcott, Derek, 8, 37–38
Warner-Lewis, Maureen, 129, 242 n.11

Weller, Judith, 64, 70
Williams, Eric, 30, 46
Women: comparisons between Indian and African, 82–83; in India, 20, 31, 56, 73, 82–83; in Trinidad, 20, 31, 73, 82–83; modernity and, 78
Working Women for Progress (WWP), 157–59

Tejaswini Niranjana is Senior Fellow at the Centre for the
Study of Culture and Society, Bangalore. Her publications
include (with P. Sudhir and Vivek Dhareshwar) *Interrogating
Modernity: Culture and Colonialism in India* (Seagull, 1993) and
*Siting Translation: History, Post-Structuralism, and the Colonial
Context* (California, 1992).

★

Library of Congress Cataloging-in-Publication Data
Niranjana, Tejaswini, 1958–
Mobilizing India : women, music, and migration
between India and Trinidad / Tejaswini Niranjana.
p. cm.
Includes bibliographical references and index.
ISBN-13: 978-0-8223-3828-4 (cloth : alk. paper)
ISBN-10: 0-8223-3828-9 (cloth : alk. paper)
ISBN-13: 978-0-8223-3842-0 (pbk. : alk. paper)
ISBN-10: 0-8223-3842-4 (pbk. : alk. paper)
1. Women, East Indian—Trinidad—Social conditions.
2. Women singers—Trinidad—Social conditions.
3. Gender identity—Trinidad. 4. Women, East Indian—
Trinidad—Ethnic identity. 5. Women, East Indian—
Race identity—Trinidad. I. Title.
HQ1525.7.N57 2006
305.48'891411072983—dc22   2006007730